CHURCH AND CHAPEL IN OXFORDSHIRE 1851

The Oxfordshire Record Society

CHURCH AND CHAPEL
IN OXFORDSHIRE
1851
The return of the census
of religious worship

Edited by Kate Tiller

Volume 55

1987

This Edition © Oxfordshire Record Society 1987
ISBN 0 902509 19 5

Printed in England by
PARCHMENT (Oxford) LIMITED, 60 Hurst Street, Oxford OX4 1HD.

TABLE OF CONTENTS

Page

FOREWORD

This, the first volume to be published since the resignation as General Editor of Dr. John Mason, is one of several that were commissioned under his editorship, and encouraged and guided by him in their early stages, but which will appear in print only after his departure from office. Much of the credit for this and future volumes rests with him.

The Society is deeply grateful to the Greening Lamborn Trust for its generous assistance towards the publication costs of this volume.

Oxford, June 1987   Christopher Day
                                                 Hon. Editor, O.R.S.

EDITOR'S PREFACE

The original Oxfordshire returns of the 1851 religious census have proved a rich source on which to spend the many hours entailed in the preparation of a volume such as this. My understanding of the returns has been greatly added to by the interest, advice, information and ideas generously provided by fellow Oxfordshire historians, amongst them, Dr. R. W. Ambler, Percy Beak, John Bell, Dr. David Eastwood, Sarah Gosling, Dr. Dennis Mills, Revd. Raymond Moody, Dr. Barrie Trinder and Brian Young. In particular I should like to thank Dr. Molly Barratt for her enthusiastic help and for reading the introduction in draft form. Any remaining errors are my own. I am grateful to Christopher Day, the Society's general editor, for his care and help in seeing the volume promptly through the press. It would never have seen the light of day but for the invaluable help of Shirley Hermon in typing successive drafts. My thanks are also due to Oxford University Department for External Studies for granting me a sabbatical term during 1986, which was largely devoted to work on this volume. Finally, as ever, my thanks to my husband, Liam, who not only tolerated the incursions of the religious census into our lives but actively helped with the figures, tables, and maps.

INTRODUCTION

CHURCH AND CHAPEL IN OXFORDSHIRE
1851

On Sunday 30 March 1851 everybody attending a place of worship in England and Wales was counted for the purposes of a national governmental census of accommodation and attendance at worship. This was the first and only exercise of its kind ever carried out, although some independent local surveys, mainly in urban areas, were to be attempted later in the century. Information for the 1851 religious census was collected on one of three standard forms. A blue form printed in black was sent to every clergyman in charge of a Church of England building asking where the church or chapel was situated, when and how it was consecrated, how it was endowed, how many sittings (free or appropriated) were available in it, how many people were estimated to have attended services in the morning, afternoon and evening on 30 March 1851, and how many on average had attended Sunday services during a stated number of recent months. If the church or chapel had been consecrated or licensed since 1 January 1800 information was sought on how, by whom and at what cost it had been erected. Finally a small space for remarks was provided. (This form and that for Nonconformist places of worship are reproduced at the end of this introduction). A second form, printed in red on blue paper, was distributed to people in charge of non-Anglican places of worship. This requested similar information but omitted questions about costs and endowments, whilst asking whether the building was separate and used exclusively for worship. A third form, in austere black and white, was drawn up specifically for the Society of Friends (Quakers); on accommodation it asked for the floor area of the meeting house and the number of persons capable of being seated, and on attendance simply for the numbers present at worship on 30 March 1851.

The religious census was conducted at the same time as the decennial population census and an attempted education census. The same organisational network was used for all three. With the thirty-one tons of population census forms dispatched by the Census Office in London went a further nineteen tons of religious and educational forms.[1] These were locally distributed and subsequently collected and initially checked, by enumerators and registrars, who then returned them to the Census Office in London. This volume presents the information returned on the

507 religious census forms discovered for the pre-1974 County of Oxfordshire and now in the Public Record Office at Kew (Class HO 129). How reliable and how revealing are these returns?

It is important to consider the often controversial background against which the religious census was taken. It was a new venture, carried out in a spirit of rigorous statistical and scientific enquiry highly characteristic of the time. The energetic organisation, headed by Horace Mann in London, which enabled the exercise to be undertaken was just one product of the growth of central government activity, particularly since the 1830's. Inquiries were undertaken into a wide range of issues, formerly considered spheres of local or private interest, including for example population size, education, public health, transport and poor relief. The 1851 religious census may be seen as part of these developments. As the state of the nation was quantified, problems identified and solutions mooted, many of those remedies were framed in terms of the need for moral, spiritual and social redemption through religious and educational institutions. Thus an exact measure of the number of sittings in places of worship as compared with the number of the local population was seen as important and relevant. In the event this concern with the fixed capital of religious provision in buildings and seats was to prove less interesting, both to contemporaries and later historians, than the second major area of enquiry, that is exactly how many people actually sat on the available seats on 30 March 1851. The detailed findings of the census are dealt with below but we may note that this additional census was yet another extension of governmental enquiry and as such necessary and up-to-date in some eyes, contentious in others.

The religious census took place at a time of great religious activity nationally, in Oxford and in Oxfordshire. For example, throughout the weeks surrounding the census local newspapers carried reports, often in fiercely partisan terms, of the passage through Parliament of the Prime Minister, Lord John Russell's, Ecclesiastical Titles Bill. This reflected the outcry against the Pope's restoration, in 1850, of a Roman Catholic hierarchy in England, headed by Cardinal Wiseman as Archbishop of Westminster. This so-called 'Papal Aggression' aroused not just the fiercely partisan militancy seen in the Orange Lodges and street disturbances of areas with large concentrations of Irish Catholics, like Lancashire, but also led to meetings, sermonising and pamphleteering throughout the country. This focussed on Russell's proposed legislation, which aimed at penalising the use of ecclesiastical titles adopted without acknowledgement of the royal supremacy. Although the death, 'produced by excitement', of a London house-painter agitated by hearing Russell's speech in support of the anti-Papal aggression measures read in a local pub, and reported in *Jackson's Oxford Journal* at the time[2], was an extreme example of popular involvement in religious issues, there was undoubtedly an atmosphere of controversy. This was not a period of tolerant inter-denominational balance but one where the non-Anglican churches were seeking to assert their emergent denominational statuses, and Anglicanism was aggressively defending its position as a national state church. For Nonconformists the taking of the 1851 religious census represented a welcome official recognition of the Dissenting presence. It was taken at a time when both the old Dissenting denominations of seventeenth-century origin, and the new Dissenters, principally Wesleyan and Primitive Methodist, had increased greatly in numbers. Their self confidence and influence, economically through association with leading industrial and manufacturing interests, and politically through links with Liberalism, was growing. The Dissenting influence was closely identified with a range of fiercely fought issues of freedom of conscience. Some of these battles had by 1851 been won in famous victories, others remained to be fought. Contentious issues had been or were the lack of rights of Nonconformists to be MPs and to hold local governmental office, to have access to universities, to print bibles, to provide separate, voluntarily funded schools and to be exempt from financial exactions associated with the Church of England, such as tithes and church rates. Nothing less than the Church of England's monopolist claim to be the national church was under debate, either on specific issues or, in some circles, through a call for disestablishment.

This was a time of combative proselytizing. For example, in March 1851 there was a meeting at Oxford Town Hall of the Oxford Auxiliary Branch of the London Society for Promoting Christianity among the Jews[3] which heard a report of the conversion of Baron Rothschild. This was recorded in *Jackson's Oxford Journal*, which in the same issue published an antagonistic report about Henry Wilberforce, brother of the Bishop of Oxford, who had recently been converted to Roman Catholicism. He was 'actively engaged in spreading in the cottages of the poor copies of his farewell address to his late parishioners, giving his reasons for the change. The latter embraces the usual arguments urged in support of the Papal claims, which are put in a very plausible manner. His attempts to make proselytes are being met with corresponding zeal [by the incumbent, which they hope will] have the effect of arming unstable minds against religious teachers and false doctrines.'

Many individuals and groups thus had an interest in the religious census, whether from the point of view of modern secular scientific enquiry, mistrust of government interventionism, protection of the Anglican position, or assertion of denominational identity and importance. Within this broad context, elements of which emerge from the Oxfordshire returns, Oxford, city, university, diocese and county, occupied a special position. In 1851 Samuel Wilberforce had been Bishop of Oxford for six years. Just as the Evangelical revival of the late eighteenth and early nineteenth century had generated growth in old and new Dissent so it had had a transforming effect upon an Established Church which was sluggish, often neglectful and sometimes corrupt. Samuel Wilberforce, as a son of William, the slavery reformer, was the product of one of the leading Anglican Evangelical families. A belief in practical action was their hallmark, and Samuel's Oxford episcopate (1845-69) is generally acknowledged[4] to provide an early model for the spiritual and organisational reforms which were to characterise mid- and late- Victorian Anglicanism. These included the restoration of existing churches and the building of new ones, the creation of new parishes (specific evidence for all of which is to be found in the census returns), and more generally the suppression of absenteeism and pluralism, the building of parsonage houses, an increase in the number of services, sermons, celebrations of holy communion and confirmations, the revival of organisational links within the diocese using rural deans and archdeacons, and the establishment of the ideal of a properly trained resident clergyman, preferably a family man, who would act as an influence and exemplar for all his flock.[5]

As his letter books[6] show Bishop Wilberforce had already, by 1851, made his presence felt both in initiating practical reforms and in establishing a remarkably close and detailed contact with the men who were the key to his reforms, the parochial clergy. His letters also show what a hornets' nest Oxford was at this time, with ecclesiastical and public opinion keenly engaged by the doctrinal and liturgical disputes between High Church and Low Church Anglicans and given particular point by the developing influence of the Tractarian or Oxford Movement. From its Evangelical beginnings, in liberal theological debates amongst dons and students (of whom Wilberforce had been one) at Oriel College in the 1820's, the influence of the Oxford Movement had grown to the point where clergyman trained in its Anglo-Catholic mould were at work in the parishes and some were teetering dangerously close to the Church of Rome. John Henry Newman had taken this course in 1845, as had Wilberforce's brother Henry and brother-in-law Henry (later Cardinal) Manning in 1850. E. B. Pusey of Christ Church, a leading Tractarian, stayed within the Church of England, but his views on issues such as the Real Presence or religious orders within Anglicanism made him a famous test of the borderline between Anglicanism and Roman Catholicism. In addition to these nationally known examples of threatened schism within the Church Wilberforce also had to contend with fiercely held opposing views amongst his clergy. In his diocesan dealings he always sought a *via media*, to accommodate all shades of opinion within a comprehensive national church. He argued this line in the House of Lords and elsewhere, and became a leading defender of the Established Church nationally.

In this defence he opposed the religious census of 1851 on the grounds that reliable and correct information could not be ensured, and that a distorted picture was likely to be drawn from any resulting figures and used to the detriment of the Church of England. On 18 March 1851 the Home Secretary told the Commons[7] that replying to the religious census questions would not be obligatory, as in the case of the population census, rather a circular to clergyman would urge them that 'it was very desirable to obtain the information'. In the Lords on 27 March Wilberforce returned to the attack. In presenting a petition from the Deanery of Newbury he argued that questions should either be made obligatory or dropped altogether. As it was, replies would not be made in many instances, those replies made would necessarily be vague and incorrect, 'the general result must be conducive to the propagation of error rather than truth', and incorrect information obtained 'would be made available to the prejudice of the great interests over which the ministers of the Church were bound to watch'. On this basis, 'if consulted by the clergy of his diocese as to the course they ought to pursue, he should be inclined to advise them not to answer the queries'. A government concession by Earl Granville that the question on Anglican endowments would be withdrawn was not enough to persuade the Bishop that he should 'do otherwise than sanction the objections to these returns likely to be offered by clergymen within his own diocese'. So, on Sunday 30 March 1851 the religious census went ahead. With what results?

The *Report* summarising the returns for England and Wales showed that Protestant Dissenters provided nearly half the church accommodation, that over 40 per cent of those worshipping in the morning and afternoon were Dissenters, that two-thirds of evening worshippers were Dissenters and that the number present at the best attended Dissenting services exceeded the number present at the best attended Anglican services. Further it was estimated that of 12,549,326 *potential* worshippers 5,288,294 stayed away.[8]

The results of the census were much discussed.[9] They must have fulfilled some of Bishop Wilberforce's worst fears. In a debate in the Lords on 11 July 1854[10] he declared the report unsound because its basic information was inaccurate. Since many clergy had refused to make returns, applications had been made to churchwardens and others, and the figures were consequently inaccurate. 'In his own diocese, in which not a very great number of clergymen refused to send the return, he desired that every clergyman should take the trouble, on several consecutive Sundays, to have the congregations numbered, and to send him the average of the congregations so numbered'. This, he declared, showed an Anglican attendance 19,011 higher (at 117,421) than that in the Registrar-General's return. But the greatest errors lay not in low figures for Anglicans but in the inflation of figures for Dissenters by 'nearly all denominations'. Errors were unsurprising as 'many of their minsters were not often in the same rank of life as the clergy of the Established Church', although the ministers of large town chapels did tend to be educated and dependable. The trouble was that 'inquiries were extended to very little places — to all the small licensed rooms in remote villages — to men who had not the advantages of education — and who were not the objects of general view and observation; and with regard to these he had no hesitation in saying there was continually a misrepresentation in point of fact as to the relative numbers of the Established Church and of the Dissenters'. Specifically Wilberforce alleged that support had been drummed up on census Sunday, that people attended a different chapel morning and evening to inflate numbers, that they crossed parish boundaries to attend chapel, that special sermons were billed, that some meeting houses could not have held the number claimed unless congregations included very small children, that bad weather kept Anglicans from distant parish churches, and that 'the Dissenters were wide awake on the occasion'. Earl Granville, refusing on behalf of the Government to make available the original returns, pointed out that the weather was equally bad for all worshippers.

How justified were Wilberforce's doubts in other ways? Horace Mann spoke to the Statistical Society about the accuracy of the returns in 1854. He felt that checks by the local enumerator and registrar on the returns safeguarded against blatant exaggeration. Where an Anglican clergyman refused to make a return a local officer, chosen without reference to religious adherence, collected the information. In only 10% of cases was this necessary. In all, information about 34,467 places of worship in England and Wales was received, often only — as the Oxfordshire returns frequently demonstrate — after stringent follow-ups from the Census Office in London, who sent supplementary return forms to the original respondent or invoked the local Registrar's help.

The Anglican Returns for Oxfordshire
    For detailed evidence on completeness and accuracy we must turn to
the original returns. Were Wilberforce's clergy more or less likely to fill
in their returns? Of returns for 258 Anglican places of worship in
Oxfordshire some 70 were made by someone other than the clergy
(registrar, or sometimes parish clerk, churchwarden or schoolmistress) or
show clerical failure to answer compulsory questions or carry statements
of clerical refusal. This represents 27.1% of Anglican returns[13], well over
double Mann's national figure of 10% non-respondent Anglican clergy.
In a few cases the incumbent merely happened to be away. In two
intriguing instances clerical absence was due to litigation; at Marsh
Baldon the Revd Frederick Reynoux, the curate, was unable to detail the
endowment because, 'The Rector is abroad and engaged in a lawsuit with
the Patron about tithes'; at Great Rollright local farmer and
churchwarden, Thomas Williams, explained that, 'The rector of this
church is absent (said to be on the Continent) in consequence of
pecuniary matters'. (He had begun to rebuild the rectory on a grand
scale, fallen into debt, and disappeared during 1851). The general
picture, however, is that the Anglican clergy in Oxfordshire in 1851 were
present in their livings; certainly very few gave other addresses.
    In some parishes resistance to completing a return is evident only
indirectly, in the form of an incomplete answer filled in by a registrar. In
others opposition is apparent in more direct ways. Instances of both
occur throughout the county, but there are interesting concentrations of
unresponsiveness, as around Cuxham, Pyrton, Chislehampton, Haseley,
South Weston, Little Milton, Albury, Stadhampton, Clifton Hampden,
Nuneham Courtenay, Sandford-on-Thames, Iffley, Dorchester,
Beckley, Stanton St. John, Forest Hill, Horspath, Garsington, and at
Cuddesdon, where Wilberforce's episcopal palace and new clerical
training college were situated. It is unlikely that this swathe of resistance
to the south and east of Oxford was coincidental. Here, and in other
areas of the county, collective clerical opposition, influenced by the
bishop's well-known stand, is strongly suggested. Other concentrations
of proxy returns or stated clerical resistance occur in the Cropredy area,
and in Middleton Stoney, Stratton Audley, Mixbury, Finmere,
Fringford, Stoke Lyne, Launton and Caversfield. At Stoke Lyne,
Launton and Stratton Audley the registrar wrote that, 'This account is as
correct as I possibly can get as the clergyman will not give any return'. At
Fringford the Revd H.D. Roundell politely declined to give more than
the name of his church and the number of sittings, 'Not knowing the law
which requires me to reply to all the above inquiries, neither the real
object of them, and suspecting no good to the Church of England to be

intended by them I humbly venture to decline to reply to them'. At Mixbury the Revd W.J. Palmer sharply remarked that, 'The Statues 13 & 14 Vict. c.53 [cited at the top of all the 1851 census forms] do not appear to relate to the subject of this form' and wrote no more. Puzzlingly he duly returned attendance figures for his other parish of Finmere.

Elsewhere there is articulate argument, as at Bletchingdon where answers were refused to questions (all except name and number of sittings) 'which appear to have been framed with a view of annoying me as a beneficed clergyman, as well as those which are calculated to excite religious dispute and animosities, and which, if answered would be likely to be mixed up or contrasted with exaggerated and incorrect statements'. Some clergy, like the Revd Jacob Lay, Vicar of St. Mary Magdalen, Oxford, complied only reluctantly: 'I have made a return, acting on my personal desire to promote the Census, but rather against my sense of the public good; for this sort of voluntary inquisition will some day be found to have been the too ready test of arbitary wills'. Others in a similar quandary, or merely wanting to avoid any issue, completed the forms in part. Sometimes this was done with an extreme reluctance which transcends the spaces of the printed government forms. At Charlbury, as late as 29 September 1851, a form drawn up in a clerkly hand and headed 'Protestant Church,' was minimally filled in by the Vicar, Thomas Silver, in a barely legible hand, with a spatting pen, seldom using the correct boxes.

A few seem to have relished the opportunity to offer information, and overflowed the space on the schedule to offer veritable essays, on the Church of England's rural ministry (Burford), the close links and blurred enumeration boundaries between Westcott and Steeple Barton, or on antiquarian details of the church (Waterperry). The Revd James Prosser, Vicar of Thame is, however, memorable amongst his Anglican brethren for his politely enthusiastic comment that, 'I have much pleasure in giving you the above information, as I shall have in replying to any further inquiries'.

The Oxfordshire returns show that the debate over whether the religious census should be taken was known and must have affected the response of the Anglican clergy locally. Although the name of Bishop Wilberforce nowhere appears, his influence may be deduced amongst the parochial clergy with whom he maintained such close links. The level of clerical resistance to the census was above average. Nevertheless the returns do not show any uniformity of response, rather considerable invituality in the degree, timing and expression of information and opinion. Certainly the annual meetings of rural deans, held at the Bishop's Palace at Cuddesdon to discuss current issues of concern to the

Church and clergy locally, did not concern themselves with the religious census at this time. Rather they were pre-occupied with baptismal doctrine, school inspection, marriage with a deceased wife's sister, administration of the sacrament, and the spread of Mormonites, to whom Christian burial was to be denied.[13] Eventually, despite opposition to the census only a handful of churches (Adwell, Brize Norton, Clanfield, Dorchester, South Weston, Wheatfield, Witney (parish church) and Wolvercote) yielded no return, as opposed to a proxy or grudging clerical return. A mass of information was successfully obtained.

The large majority of clergy who did make returns answered the questions on number of sittings and attendance with apparent care; questions dealing with endowment and average attendance received fewer replies. A few numbers may seem suspiciously round (eg. Banbury or Begbroke) but more are carefully explained in remarks, often because they are low. At Alvescot the incumbent feared he had 'underrated the average congregation'; at Bradwell 'colds and influenza prevented there being the average number'; at Sydenham 'in the afternoon several boys have to tend to their plough horses, and six or seven are bird minding'; whilst at Cowley 'in the afternoon a storm kept about 100 away'. These excuses vary little from those found in other areas, except that the traditional Midlent (or Mothering or Simnel) Sunday customs remarked on elsewhere seem absent in Oxfordshire. Overall the remarks on the returns may, as an earlier historian of the census concluded, 'be interpreted as a sign that worshippers were being enumerated conscientiously, and that when numbers seemed low the authors tended not to exaggerate but to explain.'[14]

The Non-Anglican Returns for Oxfordshire

Because non-Anglican places of worship were usually less long-established and well-recorded than the Anglican, it is not possible to establish in the same way whether they were all reached by the 1851 religious census. A cross-check of the chapels and meeting houses mentioned in the census returns with those recorded in a contemporary commerical directory of the county (Robert Gardner, *History, Gazetteer and Directory of the County of Oxford*, published in 1852) shows that the local census officials covered a very high proportion, indeed they reached some chapels not described in the directory. In all eight chapels mentioned in the directory do not seem to appear in the census returns. These were the Wesleyan Methodist at Thame, Steeple Aston, Westcott Barton, and Stonesfield, Stonesfield Primitive Methodist, Caversham

Rise Lady Huntingdon's Connexion, Iffley Baptist and Dorchester Presbyterian.

At the time of the census important elements in Oxfordshire Nonconformity, notably Primitive Methodism, were still emergent and had not yet attained permanent organisation or bricks-and-mortar meeting places in some areas. This does not mean that Dissenters were entirely absent from such places, although the Oxfordshire environment could be hostile, sometimes actively so. The returns may record no Dissenters in places where they are known to have existed. Bishop Wilberforce's visitation queries to his clergy in 1854 provide one useful check on this. In addition to questions about Anglican attendance incumbents were asked about Dissenting places of worship, number of Dissenters and the correctness of figures given in the religious census.[15] The Revd Thomas Dand of Bletchingdon, so unforthcoming in 1851, replied that 'there is a place where the Ranters [Primitive Methodists] come to preach occasionally but I believe there are no professed Dissenters except two Scotch Presbyterians and two Roman Catholics ... but many people here as elsewhere will attend both Church and meeting.' There were also semi-separatists, who conformed only sometimes to the Church of England and who made any assessment of Dissent difficult, then and now. The phenomenon of conforming schismatics was widely commented on at the visitation of 1854, and arises in the 1851 returns, for example at Westwell, where the Rector considered that, 'any calculation as to the proportion of dissent and church principles in this place ... taking into account the evening congregation at the meeting house *must* be fallacious, as it is attended in the evenings by many Church-People'. In interpreting the returns we must allow for the possibility that some attended more than one place of worship, perhaps in search of varied religious experience, perhaps because different observances fulfilled different functions, with the morning Church service 'the forum of respectability and deference' and chapel providing 'the arena for the saving souls'.[16] We must also remember that Dissent did not observe parish boundaries in the sense that chapels were sometimes located in settlements without a church, that those attending services or outdoor meetings could be gathered from a wide area, and that travelling preachers were the norm. Thus Dissent could have had an impact that remained uncrecorded in 1851. Stonesfield, for example, is recorded as having no meeting house. However, just as the report of the census was under debate in the House of Lords, 'the "Ranters" of this and some adjoining parishes met for an open air demonstration. After searching the place for some time in quest of a wagon or other agricultural vehicle, to serve as a rostrum, they succeeded in borrowing a

dung cart, which was accordingly taken to the meeting house, and loaded
with stools, benches etc., and from thence drawn to an open common, at
the outskirts of the village ... At about 9.00 a.m. parties, mostly
strangers were to be seen walking arm in arm about the village,
something after the manner of a recruiting party, only instead of the well
known "fife and drum", they had nothing but the organs of nature with
which to sound an alarm. Having paraded the principal parts of the
village, they marched to the Common before alluded to, where several
mounted the cart, and essayed to teach those who were present, (the
great majority of whom were drawn by curiosity), using the Bible as a
text book. We refrain from giving an abstract of the instruction so given;
suffice it to say that the Queen's English was, by some, rather roughly
handled'.[17] The account's lack of sympathy cannot gloss over a major
event in life of the village.

Given these necessary provisos the Nonconformist returns for
Oxfordshire were numerous,for some 240 chapels compared with 258
Church of England churches or chapels. There is little in the returns to
suggest ignorance, carelessness or mischief. Only one respondent,
William Butler, was illiterate, signing a return for the Wesleyan
Methodist chapel at Launton with his mark. Butler, described as
'occupier', was recording a meeting held in a dwelling house, which
could accommodate 50 worshippers but on 30 March attracted 16. His
remarks — 'The congregation has not been so large during the past
twelve months as formerly occasioned by gifts from other ministers
which have more influence' — is touchingly frank and far from self-
inflating. It is striking that two further returns for Launton Wesleyan
chapel were subsequently made; the census bureaucracy was checking
up. Generally the Nonconformist returns are less sophisticated than the
Anglican, in their handwriting (and thus often more legible), their
phrasing and overall painstaking care. The only Oxfordshire return to
quote Scripture is that completed by William Ray, Leader, Rose Hill, for
the New Jerusalem church meeting at Mr. Deben's in High Street,
Oxford St. Clements. He remarks that they 'Meet for the purpose of
worshipping Jehovah Jesus Christ. "In whom dwells *all* the fullness of
the Godhead bodily". Coll. 2-9.' The return for Thame New Jerusalem
Primitive Methodist Church was made by James Phillip, Leader and
Steward, Grocer, Thame, who remarked, 'Entirely poor that attend. It is
in the lowest part of the town. Not room sufficant for a school but it as
been a blessing to neighbourhood. Less fiting and quarling since the
room has beign open'.

The status of the respondents varied between Dissenting
denominations, as an analysis of the signatories reveals:

Denomination	Total	Status of Signatories		
		Minister	Unknown	Other
Wesleyan Methodist	76	13	35	28
Independent/Congregational	43	22	10	11
Primitive Methodist	39	11	17	11
Baptist	40	21	9	10
Particular Baptist	12	6	2	4
Society of Friends	12	–	4	8
Roman Catholic	8	6	–	2
Other[1]	8	2	1	5

1. This comprises New Jerusalem Chapel, Oxford St. Clements (respondent's status unknown); Jewish Synagogue, Oxford (tobacconist); Protestant Nonconformist chapel, Westwell (farmer); Plymouth Brethren, Burford (registrar); Presbyterian/Unitarian Church, Neithrop (minister); Lady Huntingdon's Connexion chapel, Goring, (minister); Wesleyan Reformed meeting, Oxford (confectioner); Mormonite Apostolic Baptist chapel, Aston Rowant (beer retailer).

The returns of those denominations with the most centralised organisation and clerical control were dominated by ministerial signatories, as is clear in the case of the Independents, Congregationalists and Baptists. The denominations with least clerical control were the Methodists, both Wesleyan and Primitive. Their lay signatories have by far the highest proportion of unknown status, indicating their local grass-roots character and the importance of local leadership, often of modest social status. These contrasts between 'old' and 'new' Dissent are striking. The composition of known lay signatories is also interesting for both differences and similarities. Of 28 such Wesleyan signatories no fewer than 11 were farmers and six shopkeepers, together with a land surveyor, a wheelwright, a carpenter, a shoemaker, a painter, a glover, a weaver, a carrier and a basket maker. Primitive Methodist signatories included only one farmer, three shopkeepers, two shoemakers, a land surveyor, a beer retailer, a carpenter and a chairmaker. The Independent and Congregationalist activists included one farmer, a maltster, two shoemakers, a blacksmith, a printer and bookseller, and a silversmith. The known Baptists were a farmer, a surgeon, a private resident, five shopkeepers, and a beer retailer; the Particular Baptists two grocers, a wheelwright and a schoolmaster. The returns for no less than six Quaker meeting houses were signed by drapers (three individuals), one of whom, Hannah Smith, was Oxfordshire's only woman signatory. Some signatures appear several times, thus revealing the denominational structures, the circuits of the Wesleyan and Primitive Methodists, the associations of the Baptists, and the Quaker hierarchy of Preparative, Monthly and Quarterly meetings. Those signing were frequently at pains to state their precise status in the congregation — from Absalom Wiblin, Prayer Leader of Kiddington Primitive Methodists to Stewards, Managers, Trustees, Local Preachers, or Class Leaders.

In this and other respects the Nonconformists' returns convey an impression of great care. Only seven are the work of registrars. As to allegations of exaggeration or distortion, Mann's system of local checking seems to have operated. Moreover the Dissenters clearly took the exercise seriously, and it was not in their interests to discredit it. Here too it seems that when numbers appeared too high or too low explanations were offered, rather than figures doctored. For example, the minister of Oxford Wesleyans remarked that, 'A special service was held in the afternoon, consequently the congregation was much larger, and the attendance at the evening service much smaller, than usual'. At Eynsham Particular Baptist Chapel we learn that, 'General sickness, and a temporary excitement in another religious denomination in the village, have produced a temporary depression in the numbers'. At Chinnor Primitive Methodist chapel claimed numbers seemed to exceed capacity by six. A lengthy explanation pointed to the smallness of the Sunday Scholars who were included. Perhaps local Dissenters did encourage the biggest possible congregations, for this was, as Bishop Wilberforce conceded, bound to be a trial of strength on both sides. Does this invalidate the results of the census as a reflection of religious observance and feeling? K.S. Inglis has concluded in general terms that, 'it may be presumed that any person who could be got to public worship on census day was zealous enough to be described legitimately as an active supporter of his denomination. As an index of sentiment attending worship on this particular Sunday is in a way comparable with registering a vote at an election'.[18] The Oxfordshire returns do not suggest otherwise.

The returns do, however, present the perennial problem for those studying levels of attendance of the people who may have been counted more than once because they attended more than one service, either at the same or different places of worship. Mann[19] suggested four possible formulae adjusting numbers for this factor. For the purposes of national figures of attendants he adopted that of counting the morning congregation plus half of that in the afternoon and one-third of that in the evening. This proved unfair to the Nonconformists since Anglican attendances were highest at the morning or occasionally afternoon services, whilst Dissenting congregations were universally largest in the evenings. This was clearly the case in Oxfordshire, where 89.4% of Anglican services were in the morning and/or afternoon. Only 9.8% of Anglican places of worship recorded in the 1851 returns had an evening service. Only 2.5% held three services on a Sunday. By contrast, 82% of Nonconformist places of worship included an evening service. Many more held three services (22.6%) than did the Anglicans, although 32.7% of Anglican and 32.6% of Nonconformist places of worship held only a single service. To count only one-third of evening attendances would clearly give a major underestimate of Nonconformist activity. Therefore in the following account of patterns of religious provision and attendance in Oxfordshire in 1851 total numbers of attendances in general congregations have been taken from the returns and expressed as a percentage of the population to give an index of attendance. Since Nonconformists were more inclined than others to attend two or three services in a day this may mean that the figures for Church of England and Roman Catholic services represent proportionately more individual attenders. Bearing that factor in mind this measure seems the most straightforward and consistent reflection of the evidence the returns offer of religious activity and enthusiasm within and between different denominations and places in the county.

The idea that different kinds of place are likely to produce distinctive patterns of religious allegiance and varying degrees of irreligion is well-established.[20] It is argued that the larger the place, the higher its population density and the more rapid its rate of growth before 1851 the greater the economic and social freedom, and the diversity of ideas, organisation and experience it will offer, and the weaker institutions of established authority, including the Church, are likely to be. On that basis it might seem that the results of the 1851 religious census would resolve themselves merely into a North-South, industrial-agrarian divide. Alan Everitt[21] points out that such broad generalisations are unsound: of 13 counties with over 100,000 non-Anglican sittings seven (eight if one counts Gloucestershire despite its woollen mills) were in the South and predominantly agrarian. In the North agrarian areas like the North and South Ridings were strong in Dissent, whilst Lancashire and Staffordshire had relatively low levels of Dissent yet were heavily industrial. Understanding these varying experiences requires detailed local study and the purpose of the following section is to sketch the geographical and social characteristics of Oxfordshire's religious patterns, using the religious census and other sources. It is hoped that this will provide both a data base and possible general explanations to help those studying individual entries or localities.

Distinctive local religious patterns may stem from the economic and the geographical basis of an area, with Dissent arising in woodlands, heathlands, moorlands or marshlands, areas often having larger Anglican parishes, scattered settlements (often with no church), weak manorial structures, and a greater variety of more specialist employments than fielden areas[22]. Dissent may occur outside main settlements, in boundary areas of large parishes, where worshippers would gather. Decaying market towns, with dispersed patterns of property ownership, could provide an encouraging base for Dissenters. Links between town and village may be close, with town meeting houses reflecting the religious colour of the surrounding countryside or acting as a basis for supporting and fostering Dissent in neighbouring, 'uncolonised' village centres. However, the main explanation of patterns of rural religion has been that the highest degree of Nonconformity arose in open as opposed to closed settlements.

The distinction between open and closed settlements was recognised and employed by 19th-century observers.[23] It has been further developed by 20th-century social historians, with inevitable refinements in search of definitions[24]. It is of interest here that high levels of religious observance, monopolised by the Church of England, have been taken to indicate a closed village, whilst the presence of Nonconformity or indifference to organised religion, are interpreted as signs of an open settlement. These patterns of behaviour, conforming or independent, appear only as descriptive characteristics, with the basic differences between settlements defined in terms of land ownership. Dennis Mills[25] provides a typical model in his four-fold spectrum of types of village:

A CLOSED   (i) *Squire's village*: resident landlord owning at least half the acreage.
(ii) *Absentee landlord's village*: at least half the acreage owned by absentee proprietor.

B OPEN   (iii) *Freehold village*: more than 40 proprietors, or 20-40 proprietors with an average of less than 40 acres each.
(iv) *Divided village*: fulfilling none of the above criteria.

Obelkevich and Ambler have each employed such an approach in studies of mid-19th century religion. Their work suggests that the open - closed model is useful in broad terms to account for local degrees and types of religious observance. However attempts to make more highly differentiated categorisations of places, for example in terms of proportionate levels of land ownership, produce less clear distinctions[26]. This framework also has the effect of focussing attention on landholding as the prime mover in open and closed communities, with closed settlements most readily defined, by landlord dominance, and open and divided settlements often only negatively determined. Sarah Banks[27] has pointed to the dangers of concentrating solely on this approach, not least through her case study of Castle Acre in Norfolk, notorious in 19th-century literature as an archetypal open village, large, uncontrolled, the nearest magistrate seven miles away, with high poor rates, shops, pubs and poor but plentiful housing. Castle Acre was certainly open, but was 97% owned by the Cokes of Holkham. The Cokes chose not to exercise a paternalist role in housing, education or charity. The active ingredient was rather, Banks argues, the 3% of small proprietors who owned a stock of cheap housing. Castle Acre, therefore, had a very positive pull on people from the surrounding area and, with its broader economic base, could support a growing population. Landowners in surrounding villages could draw on Castle Acre's labour surplus and had no need to build the estate housing of the classic closed estate village. Some large and impressive chapel buildings signal the presence of Nonconformity in Castle Acre. Open and closed settlements were, then, a reality; they could work in a symbiotic way, but their effect was not simply a product of a statistic of landholding. With these possible patterns in mind let us turn to Oxfordshire.

> The Squire's and clergyman's families had pews in the chancel, with backs to the wall on either side, and between them stood two long benches for the schoolchildren, well under the eyes of authority. Below the steps down into the nave stood the harmonium, played by the clergyman's daughter, and round it was ranged the choir of small schoolgirls. Then came the rank and file of the congregation, nicely graded, with the farmer's family in the front row, then the Squire's gardener and coachman, the schoolmistress, the maidservants, and the cottagers, with the Parish Clerk at the back to keep order.

This description of Sunday morning service in the Anglican parish church is drawn from that classic description of rural life in late 19th-century England, *Lark Rise to Candleford*.[28] Lark Rise is the hamlet of Juniper Hill in the north Oxfordshire parish of Cottisford, and it is Cottisford's modest parish church that is described. This seems a predictable pattern of religious experience for such a county: characteristically Anglican, conforming and hierarchical. What else would one expect of a relatively small county, containing a population in 1851 of 170,434 in 483,626 acres of fielden middle England, with no large towns and few industrial developments? Oxford had a population of some 24,000; Banbury was the next most important town with 8,000, whilst most Oxfordshire market towns had populations in the range of

3,000, with a number of decaying market centres nearer 1,500. Oxford was an administrative and service centre, with additional employment through the University and printing; Banbury had a declining plush trade and a barely emergent agricultural engineering industry; Witney had its blankets and Chipping Norton its tweed mill, and domestically based employments in gloving and lace were carried on in the west and southeast of the county respectively. However, this was overwhelmingly an agricultural county, given over to mixed farming. Major areas of woodland with dispersed settlement were to be found in Wychwood and the Chilterns, with marshland represented by Otmoor. In size, geography, and economy Oxfordshire was above all a traditional agricultural county in which one would expect Anglicanism to be dominant.

This is borne out by the number of sittings in 1851, of which 67.2% were Anglican and 32.8% Dissenting, putting Oxfordshire third only to Herefordshire and Rutland in degree of Anglican dominance of religious accommodation. Yet it is interesting to note that there was accommodation (whether Anglican or Dissenting) available for only 64.9% of Oxfordshire's population. When it came to attendance on census Sunday attendances (over three services) totalled 64.3% of the population, and of those attendances 62.7% were at Anglican places of worship. This does indeed seem a neat and tidy picture — accommodation for about ⅔ of the population, attendance by about ⅔ of the population, of whom about ⅔ were Anglican attendances and ⅓ Dissenting, which is in turn in keeping with the denominational division of available accommodation.

It is something of a relief on looking beyond this apparently unambiguous, uniform and predictable behaviour to find a much more varied, and sometimes ambiguous reality. To return to Cottisford as an example, Flora Thompson wrote of the people's attachment to the Established Church that,

> If the Lark Rise people had been asked their religion, the answer of nine out of ten would have been "Church of England", for practically all of them were christened, married, and buried as such, although, in adult life, few went to church between the baptisms of their offspring. The children were shepherded there after Sunday school and about a dozen of their elders attended regularly; the rest stayed at home, the women cooking and nursing, and the men, after an elaborate Sunday toilet, which included shaving and cutting each other's hair and much puffing and splashing with buckets of water, but stopped short before lacing up boots or putting on a collar and tie, spent the rest of the day eating, sleeping, reading the newspaper, and strolling round to see how their neighbours' pigs and gardens were looking.

Although 78.6% of those who attended worship in Cottisford in 1851 went to the parish church, only 52.3% of the population attended worship in the first place. Congregations do seem to have been heavily unbalanced by social class (higher social classes and their dependents), by age (the old and especially the young, upon whom so many resources were concentrated by organised religion and who seemed to have fulfilled a function of proxy observance for some parents), and by sex (with more female attenders). The *Christian Remembrancer*, reflecting on the levels of non-attendance revealed by the 1851 religious census, said 'The fact is, that those who do go to church, go with tolerable punctuality, are taken from certain classes and certain ages of life, ie. from the upper and middle classes, from servants, from a small portion of the old and infirm, and in large numbers from children; other classes and ages do not attend'.[29]

Another feature of Cottisford was that, despite many 'closed' characteristics, it had Dissent — in 1851 and in Flora Thompson's day. In 1851 30 Wesleyan Methodists met in an ordinary house every Sunday evening for worship, a pattern that seems to have changed little 40 years later when Flora Thompson describes how she and her brother, bored by the dull Sunday evening of a respectable working class family household, and having attended Anglican morning service, escaped to a very different, entertaining, and intriguing religious world. The meeting was held in the main living room of a local cottage, with whitewashed walls, lamp-lit, an open fire, cleared of everyday furniture except for the clock and a pair of red china dogs on the mantlepiece. The congregation were greeted by the householder with a handshake and a 'God bless you', sat down on scrubbed wooden benches, sang Sankey and Moody hymns unaccompanied, heard extempore and direct conversations with God — calling for rain or deliverance of a pig from disease. This direct, individual communication with the deity was at the heart of the religious experience. Flora, who thought God would know all these things already, found it unsophisticated, entertaining, and yet as a spectacle less impressive than the Anglican rituals of the morning. The high point was the arrival of the preacher, a layman, who had often walked miles. These men ranged from impressive sincerity and eloquence, to stumbling but also sincere inarticulacy. Some were self-seeking poseurs (where else perhaps could the shop assistant with a bunch of violets in his button hole get a hearing?). Yet Flora's final conclusion on Methodism in Cottisford is clear and revealing of the very different functions Dissent of this kind fulfilled as opposed to Anglicanism,

Methodism, as known and practised there, was a poor people's religion, simple and crude; but its adherents brought to it more fervour than was shown by the church congregation, and appeared to obtain more comfort and support from it than the church could give. Their lives were exemplary.

The Cottisford evidence also relates in an interesting way to general arguments about the incidence and location of Dissent. Although a small parish (1506 acres), Cottisford had a scattered settlement pattern. Juniper Hill, or Lark Rise, was an outlying hamlet with squatter origins, lying on heathland not enclosed until 1854. In short it had all the marks of an open settlement. Flora Thompson's father consciously chose to live there, despite having to pay house rent:

> The first charge on the labourers' ten shillings was house rent. Most of the cottages belonged to small tradesmen in the market town, and the weekly rents ranged from one shilling to half a crown. Some labourers in other villages worked on farms or estates where they had their cottages rent free; but the hamlet people did not envy them, for "Stands to reason", they said, "they've allus got to do just what they be told, or out they goes, neck and crop, bag and baggage". A shilling, or even two shillings a week, they felt was not too much to pay for the freedom to live and vote as they liked and go to church or chapel or neither as they preferred.

In the light of this contrast between Juniper Hill and Cottisford or other nearby villages it is perhaps unsurprising that the 1851 Cottisford Methodist return was made by Thomas Lavine, who described himself as 'Tenant, Juniper'. Elsewhere in the Oxfordshire returns one can point to similar 'pairs' of settlements, with the main village of an ancient ecclesiastical parish containing only the Anglican church and other, often growing, settlements in the parish containing Dissenting places of worship. Examples include Broughton and North Newington, Swalcliffe with its 'satellites' of Epwell, Shutford, and the Sibfords, Church Hanborough and Long Hanborough, and Shipton and Milton under Wychwood.

Another characteristic of Cottisford was its proximity to a market town, Brackley, where Flora's father worked and thus placed himself outside the usual direct chain of rural dependence and employment, and from whence the circuit minister and local preachers came.

Our picture of this parish also illustrates another pattern already observed, the practice of going to one denomination in the morning and to another in the evening. A clerical commentator on the census, drawing on his urban experiences, concluded that, 'The morning service may be said to be the service of *necessity*, the afternoon service that of *convenience*, and the evening one that of *devotion*.[30] The evidence of the 1851 returns, the 1854 visitation enquiries, and Flora Thompson all suggests similar elements in the Oxfordshire pattern.

Cottisford in Flora's day also had its family of Roman Catholics, who kept the inn. They were perceived as devout, respected individually (not least, perhaps, because of their occupation), but suspected collectively at the level of fierce, folk prejudice. Anglo-Catholicism also made its appearance, in the shape of an elderly curate whose preaching and obvious conviction were much appreciated, but with whose theology few engaged. The curate did, however, cause the Methodists to leave off going to Church. It is striking that they still had no chapel of their own and met in a cottage. Despite the general advance of Dissent, as it passed from earlier sectarian struggles to more prosperous and accepted denominationalism, in some environments that transition was not achieved. Without a well-off sponsor or protector it was difficult to aspire to a chapel building. It could happen, as for example at Moreton, in Thame parish[31], where 'a respectable farmer', Mr. Joseph Way and his wife befriended Primitive Methodist missionaries, giving them the use of a barn, and in 1839 donating a site and help for building a chapel and Sabbath school. Such progress was not always possible. Flora Thompson could still write of the Methodists in the 1880s, that, 'Provided they did not attempt to convert others, religion in them was tolerated'. Rural depression and depopulation from the later 1870's cannot have helped rural Dissent to develop.

And then there were the 48% of Cottisford people who did not go to church or meeting in 1851. Here and elsewhere the indifferents were hardly ever conscious secularists.

> Many in the hamlet who attended neither church nor chapel and said they had no use for religion, guided their lives by the light of a few homely precepts, such as "Pay your way and fear nobody"; "Right's right and wrong's no man's right"; "Tell the truth and shame the devil", and "Honesty is the best policy".

Honesty, telling the truth, mutual help in adversity, and a degree of sharpness and criticism of anyone getting above, or breaking with, the common experience — these were the features of a strong moral code. This 'popular religion'[32] was a loose combination of unofficial Christianity and large elements of superstition and custom, selectively validated by institutional religion. This occasional and instrumental use of formal religion accompanied by a distinct, independent and stern morality of their own has also been observed in urban, working class communities.[33] It generally proved impervious to well-intentioned attempts to woo the mass of the working class to conventional religious observance, as the graphic descriptions in *Lark Rise* of the pastoral visits of the Rector and his daughter to the villagers show. At least the Rector had the saving grace of never mentioning religion.

If the Cottisford picture indicates a characteristic spectrum of religious experience in 19th-century Oxfordshire, what do the 1851 returns taken as a whole reveal? In summary, they show that a person was more likely to live in a place with some Dissent than one totally Anglican.[34] 132 places had Dissent (in the form of place(s) of worship), and will hereafter be called 'mixed places', whilst 103 were wholly Anglican. The term place rather than parish has been chosen because it seems inappropriate to judge Dissent wholly in terms of Anglican parochial structures when the returns frequently identify places of worship at sub-settlements within larger parishes. Also, by 1851 the presence of Anglican district churches, additional churches, and divided parishes shows that the Church of England was itself thinking in terms of distinct settlements, and of the souls they contained, rather than of ancient parish churches as the only focus of activity.

What were the general levels of religious observance in mixed and Anglican places?

In Anglican places 48% of the population attended worship.
In mixed places 62% of the population attended worship.
In mixed places 33% of the population attended Anglican worship.

One assumption about likely patterns of observance in a traditional, agrarian society is that Christian religion and the status quo were little challenged and levels of conformity, usually to the Established Church, were high. Secondly, not least because of the combative atmosphere in which the 1851 religious census was carried out and discussed, and because of the denominational spirit in which much religious history has been approached, there is likely to be an assumption that we are dealing simply with shares of an already observant population. These Oxfordshire figures suggest otherwise in terms of the percentage of the population *not* attending worship. Further the difference between overall levels of attendance in mixed (62%) and Anglican (48%) places is almost 15%, whereas the Anglican share in mixed places (33%) leaves nearly 30% of attendances there to be accounted for. This indicates not merely a winning by the Dissenters of worshippers from established Anglican congregations but that Dissent attracted additional levels of observance not present in a purely Anglican setting.

Oxfordshire Dissent was found in larger places:
Ave. acreage of Anglican places = 1617.14
Ave. acreage of mixed places   = 2333.41
This pattern is consistent with Dissent occurring in places with open characteristics.
Similarly Dissent was found in places with higher population densities, the average being over twice that for Anglican places:
Ave. population density (people per acre) in Anglican places = 0.19
Ave. population density (people per acre) in mixed places = 0.59
Mixed places had lower average farm sizes than Anglican places;
Ave. farm size (acres per farmer) in Anglican places = 430
Ave. farm size (acres per farmer) in mixed places = 290
This factor provides support for Dissent occurring in open villages with more dispersed landholding, but also indicates that Oxfordshire was not a county of peasant open villages with 40-acre freeholder farmers. It was a county predominantly of closed, absentee landlord or divided villages.[35] The average acreages per farmer may appear surprisingly high to those with knowledge based on research into individual Oxfordshire parishes. For example Gardner, on whose 1852 county directory these figures are based, lists 20 farmers for North Leigh, giving an average acreage of 125. Census enumerators' books for North Leigh in 1851 list 25 farmers, ten of whom (farming 657 acres) do not appear in Gardner. The average farm size according to the census was 108 acres. Such cases suggest the value of considering additional detailed sources to check the directory for under-recording, in particular of small farmers. Despite this shortcoming the distinction between average acreages in mixed and Anglican places made above is clear.

Levels of attendance were highest in smaller places. Small rural villages are considered more likely to be closed, and thus more Anglican, but the Oxfordshire figures suggest that small places were more observant generally, as the following table shows:

Population	Average Attendance (as percentage of total population)		
	In Settlements with C. of England only	In Mixed Settlements	
		Total Attendance	Dissenting Attendance
0-299	54.8	76.7	36.3
300-499	40.5	71.8	40.2
500-749	47.4	60.7	25.5
750-999	30.7	41.7	17.6
1,000+	13	56.3	25.6

Larger places, both towns and villages, had the greatest number of Dissenting places of worship, but not necessarily the greatest proportion of Dissenting attendances, reflecting the greater choice in, and diversity of, the communities.

No. of Dissenting Places of Worship	No. of Places	Average Population	Ave. % of Popn. Attending Dissenting Places of Worship
1	80	568	23.6
2	33	834	42.0
3	11	1535	27.5
4 or more	8	6127	30.8

Oxfordshire Dissent was more likely to be found in places with more craft- and tradesmen, i.e. more open places, and this was not just a function of population size as the table below shows:

Population	Ave no. of Craft- and tradesmen	
	Anglican Places	Mixed Places
0-300	2.04	4.74
301-600	8.18	11.67
601 +	15.08	23.52

(Excluding 14 towns (all 'mixed' places), i.e. Bampton, Burford, Banbury, Bicester, Chipping Norton, Charlbury, Deddington, Eynsham, Henley, Oxford, Thame, Watlington, Witney and Woodstock).

We now turn to the geographical spread of Dissent. Map 1 shows meeting houses all over the county. Some concentration occurs in the north in Banburyshire, to a lesser extent in the west, and in a band focussing on Thame. Some clustering in and around major towns is apparent. The topographically distinct regions of Wychwood, Otmoor, and the Chilterns show no concentrations of meeting houses, rather the reverse. Map 2 shows that around the county average of 31.34% Dissenting sittings considerable variations occurred. The strongholds of Nonconformity were in the registration districts of Banbury followed by Thame, Witney, and Henley. Its weakest areas were in the centre of the county, in the registration districts of Chipping Norton, Woodstock, Bicester, Headington and Oxford.

A more detailed anatomy of Dissent by denomination shows

differences in distribution between 'old' and 'new' Dissent, which accounted for 41.93% and 54.57% respectively of Oxfordshire Dissenting attendances. It also suggests historical factors underlying the incidence of meeting houses. Amongst the old Dissenters the Quakers (Map 3) were markedly concentrated in Banburyshire, with other meetings in the west, in Oxford and Henley. Their attendances were small, usually 10-20, and the distribution follows closely that in the 17th century. The much more numerous Independents or Congregationalists (Map 4), show a wider geographical spread but with very clear areas of concentration, again in Banburyshire, and in the west around Witney, and the south around Henley, with the addition of a band across to Thame and a positive cluster of meeting houses around Bicester. The last seems to reflect an old-established Independent congregation in Bicester, where a chapel had been erected in 1729, around which the energetic prozelytising of the early 19th-century religious revival had resulted in the building of new village chapels during the ten years preceding the census, as at Blackthorn, Ambrosden, and Launton. This was the fastest growing old Dissenting denomination in 19th-century Oxfordshire. The chronology of meeting house building recorded by the returns is shown in the following table.

OXFORDSHIRE MEETING HOUSES, 1851 — DATE OF ERECTION

	Date not Specified	Dwelling House, Room Barn etc.	Before 1800	1800/25	1826/51
Wesleyan Methodist	5	5	8	24	34
Independent/Congregational	3	5	8	7	20
Primitive Methodist	2	12	2	2	24
Baptist	4	5	8	7	14
Particular Baptist	1	1	—	4	8
Quaker	—	—	11	1	—
Roman Catholic	1	—	2	—	5
Other	—	4	1	—	2

The Baptists (Map 5), both General and Particular, had a group of chapels around Oxford but otherwise showed a pattern of distribution again concentrating on the north and west, and on the Thame band. These marked contrasts between strong and weak areas for 'old' Dissent clearly mirror those found in late 17th- and early 18-century Oxfordshire.[36] Nineteenth-century Dissenters maintained these bases, and, in the more energetic cases, expanded out from them. Some of the factors that may have determined earlier location, such as Anglican dominance in Oxford and the more efficient servicing of surrounding areas by clergy who could travel out from the city, and the number of large, landlord-controlled estates in the central area of the county, would still have some effect. Others, like the development of Nonconformist activity near county boundaries during the penal period before 1689, in order to cross jurisdictional divides and avoid prosecution, are merely echoed in the 1851 returns.

'New' Dissent in the form of Wesleyan Methodism (Map 6) filled in some of the gaps in Nonconformist provision in the centre and north-east of the county. For example, a comparison of the location of Baptist and Wesleyan meeting houses shows relatively few overlaps, although one may still detect that Banburyshire and the Thame band were susceptible to Dissent generally and that the area around Oxford was inhospitable ground. The distribution of Primitive Methodism (Map 7), only relatively recently organised — with circuits established at Witney (1826), at Banbury (after 1836), at Faringdon (1836), at Wallingford (1837), and at Oxford (1845) — reverts to the historical pattern and again shows that some areas were not favourable to Nonconformity. A contemporary history of Primitive Methodism describes how missionary preachers repeatedly met with physical and verbal abuse in Oxfordshire,[37] and whilst they found poor inhabitants of villages like those around Witney living in 'darkness, sin and misery', ripe for salvation and ready to join in worship and mutual help, they also found popular ridicule, and alleged that it was fomented by upper class inhabitants, as at Dorchester in 1839, where

> the missionaries had to encounter the most formidable and determined opposition, and to endure violent and brutal persecution. For some time they were stoned both as they entered and left the village on Sabbath mornings. On one occasion Mrs. Wheeldon was hit on the eye with a stone, a pious aged female had her head cut open, and another member of society had two of his teeth knocked out with a stone. A number of young persons of the baser sort were encouraged in their savage treatment of preachers by some in the higher classes; and the lives of the missionaries were often exposed to imminent peril. A pious and humane gentleman wished to persuade them to discontinue their visits, saying the ruffians would no more mind killing one of them than killing a dog. But the heroic missionaries were not to be easily persuaded to do this; the thought of relinquishing the place was intolerable, and they resolved to persevere in their efforts, even should they have to suffer death in consequence. And deliverance came at length. Several of the gentlemen who had been the abettors in the persecution were suddenly arrested by affliction, and in a few days were called into the presence of their Maker. This event produced

a deep and solemn impression among the inhabitants, and the persecutors soon afterwards ceased to stone the preachers. When the dreadful storm of persecution was passed over the good seed which had been sown sprang up, and the society flourished. Several of the persecutors were subdued by the power of divine grace, and were made new creatures in Christ Jesus among others the constable, who had frequently been employed by the gentlemen to drive the preachers from the village, and who had been a great drunkard, was converted to the Lord and became a new man. A cottage was obtained for preaching during the winter, and this becoming too small, efforts were made to secure a new chapel. A site was obtained for the purpose, many of the former opponents rendered cheerful assistance, and the humble sanctuary was opened for worship on the 18th September, 1839.[38]

This passage makes an interesting contrast with the description of a Ranter meeting from the 'opposition' viewpoint already quoted above. From both it appears that if the early emergence of Nonconformity had been difficult in 17th-century Oxfordshire, and particularly so in some areas of the county, so it was for a new Dissenting movement in the mid 19th century, and especially so in the same geographical areas.

The meeting houses of other Protestant Nonconformist groups represent interesting but isolated instances, often associated with particular individuals or small groups in the community, as, for example, at Westwell, where the Plymouth Brethren meeting was held in a room attached to a local farmhouse, with the farmer himself as preacher. A Jewish synagogue was found only in Oxford.

Roman Catholicism in Oxfordshire in 1851 was localised and far-flung, with only eight places of worship (Map 8). They were chiefly dependent on the presence of leading Roman Catholic families, as at Radford, Chipping Norton, and Heythrop, which was the seat of the Talbots, earls of Shrewsbury. As the Anglican Rector of Heythrop remarked, 'We have no school. We can get no accommodation, the church and the whole parish belonging to the Earl of Shrewsbury'. Similar focuses of Catholicism occurred at Hethe and Hardwick ('Several Roman Catholics ... (about 15 adults and 10 children) attend service in a chapel in the parish of Hethe'), and in Pyrton parish, which contained Stonor Park.

Historians of particular places and areas within the county will wish to explore some of these possible explanations of patterns of religious provision and allegiance. They may look at individuals, congregations, and meeting houses in more detail and employ other evidence, such as surviving records of individual chapels, circuits, and associations, more fully than has been possible here. What more, for example, can be discovered about events at Dorchester on Thames in 1839? Why does no return at all appear for Dorchester parish church? Why does the priest at St. Birinus Roman Catholic Church in Dorchester clearly state that his church was erected in 1828-9 when other sources suggest that this happened twenty years later?[39] These are just some of the questions generated by a detailed examination of church, chapel and religious indifference in the light of the Oxfordshire returns of 1851.

REFERENCES

1. *Jackson's Oxford Journal*, 15 March 1851.
2. *Ibid.*
3. *Ibid.* 22 March 1851.
4. R.K. Pugh, 'The Episcopate of Samuel Wilberforce, Bishop of Oxford 1845-69 and of Winchester 1869-73', (University of Oxford D.Phil. thesis, 1957); Standish Meecham, *Lord Bishop. The Life of Samuel Wilberforce 1805-1873* (Harvard, 1970).
5. See Diana McClatchey, *Oxfordshire Clergy 1777-1869* (Oxford 1960).
6. Ed. R.K. Pugh, *The Letter-books of Samuel Wilberforce 1843-68*, (O.R.S. vol. xlviii, 1969).
7. *Parliamentary Debates*, 3rd series, vol. cxv, cols. 113-4 (House of Commons).
8. *Parliamentary Papers* (1852-3), lxxxix. In respect of non-worshippers Mann, the author of the report, omitted 'valid' absentees — such as the very young and very old, invalids, and transport workers — from his calculation.
9. 21,000 copies of the report were sold according to Earl Granville, *Parliamentary Debates*, 3rd series, vol. cxxxv, col. 32.
10. *Ibid.*, cols. 23-33.
11. K.S. Inglis, 'Patterns of Religious Worship in 1851', *Journal of Ecclesiastical History*, vol. 11 (1960), 74-86; D.M. Thompson, 'The Religious Census of 1851', ed. R. Lawton, *The Census and Social Structure* (1978), 241-286.
12. H. Mann, 'On the statistical position of the religious bodies in England and Wales', *Journal of the Statistical Society*, vol. XVIII (1855).
13. Minutes of Annual Meetings of Rural Deans 1850-56 (Oxfordshire Record Office, MS. Deanery Papers Islip e 1).
14. Inglis, *op. cit.* 77.
15. Printed in ed. E.P. Baker, *Bishop Wilberforce's Visitation Returns for the Archdeaconry of Oxford in the year 1854*, (O.R.S. vol. xxxv, 1954).
16. James Obelkevich, *Religion and Rural Society: South Lindsey 1825-1875* (1976). The best and most suggestive discussion of religious behaviour in rural areas at this period. The functions of church and chapel-going are extensively dealt with, e.g. 145, 157, 214-5, 315 et seq.
17. *Jackson's Oxford Journal*, 8 July 1854. Gardner's *Directory* describes both Wesleyan and Primitive Methodist chapels at Stonesfield.
18. Inglis, *op. cit.* 77.
19. H. Mann, *op. cit.*, 151-2. This point is fully discussed in Thompson, *op. cit.* 251-3.
20. Eg. A.D. Gilbert, *Religion and Society in Industrial England: Church, Chapel and Social Change 1740-1914* (1976); Hugh McLeod, *Religion and the Working Class in Nineteenth-century Britain* (1984).

21. Alan Everitt, 'Nonconformity in Country Parishes', ed. J. Thirsk, *Land, Church and People* (1970), 178-99.
22. See Alan Everitt, *op. cit.*, and *The Pattern of Rural Dissent: The Nineteenth Century* (1972).
23. B.A. Holderness, ' 'Open' and 'close' parishes in England in the Eighteenth and Nineteenth centuries', *Agricultural History Review*, vol. 20 (1972), 126-39.
24. Everitt, *op. cit.* (1970 and 1972); D. Mills, *Lord and Peasant in Nineteenth-century Britain* (1980); Obelkevich, *op. cit.*; ed. R.A. Ambler, *Lincolnshire Returns of the Census of Religious Worship 1851*, (Lincoln Rec. Soc. vol. lxxii (1979)), Introduction.
25. Mills, *op cit.*, chaps. 4, 6.
26. The land tax assessments of 1831, the latest in a series available in many counties, have been widely used to establish a definition of open and closed on a county-wide basis. However the time gap of twenty years to 1851 led to their being discounted for present purposes.
27. Sarah J. Banks, *'Open and Close Parishes in Nineteenth-century England'* (University of Reading Ph.D. thesis 1982).
28. Flora Thompson, *Lark Rise to Candelford* (1945), chap. 14.
29. *Christian Remembrancer*, vol. 27 (April 1854), 405-6.
30. A Hume, *Remarks on the Census of Religious Worship for England and Wales* (1860), 17.
31. John Petty, *History of the Primitive Methodist Connexion* (1864), 329.
32. See Obelkevich, *op. cit.*, chap. 6.
33. Eg. Elizabeth Roberts, *A Woman's Place: An Oral History of Working Class Women 1890-1940* (1984).
34. The following figures are based on the 1851 Religious Census returns, taken together with population totals from the 1851 population census, acreages from the Ordnance Survey (quoted in *V.C.H. Oxon.* vol. 2, 214-24), and listings of occupations in R. Gardner, *History, Gazetteer, and Directory of the County of Oxford* (1852).
35. See p. xxv above.
36. Ed. Mary Clapinson, *Bishop Fell and Nonconformity.* (O.R.S. vol. lii, 1980).
37. J. Petty, *op. cit.*, 229-32, 319-20, 324-331, 445-9, 454-5.
38. *Ibid.*, 330.
39. I owe this information to Mr. Percy Beak of Dorchester on Thames.

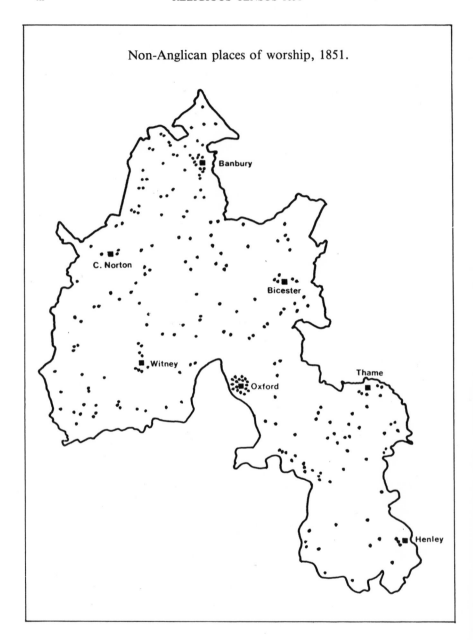

Non-Anglican places of worship, 1851.

Map 1

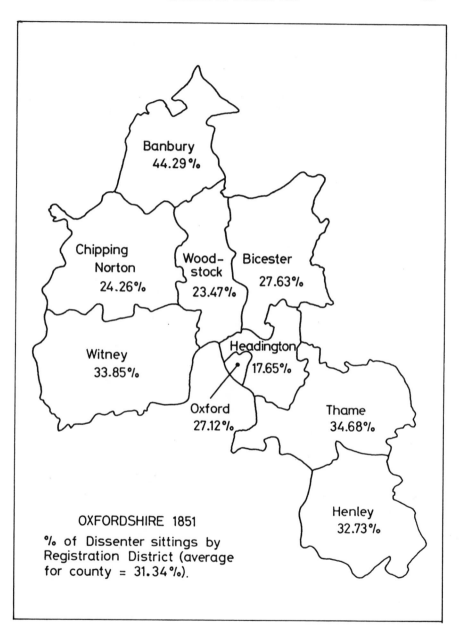

Banbury
44.29%

Chipping
Norton
24.26%

Wood-
stock
23.47%

Bicester
27.63%

Witney
33.85%

Headington
17.65%

Oxford
27.12%

Thame
34.68%

Henley
32.73%

OXFORDSHIRE 1851

% of Dissenter sittings by
Registration District (average
for county = 31.34%).

Map 2

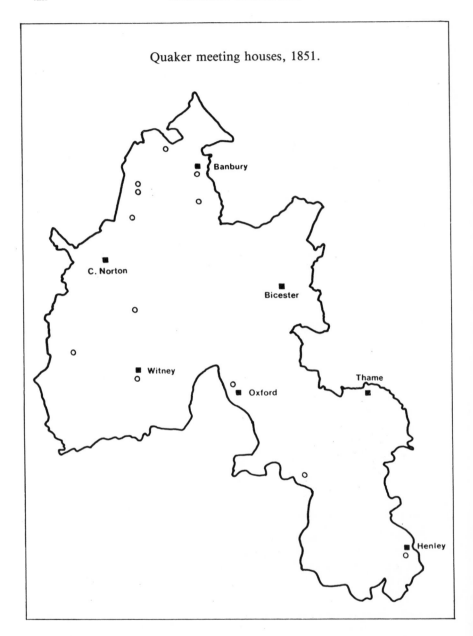

Quaker meeting houses, 1851.

Map 3

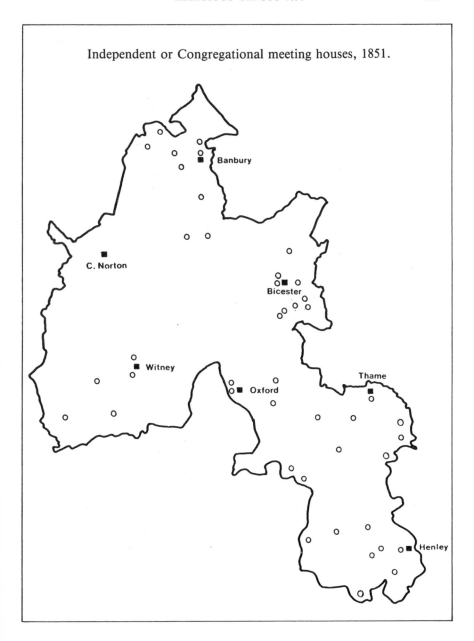

Independent or Congregational meeting houses, 1851.

Map 4

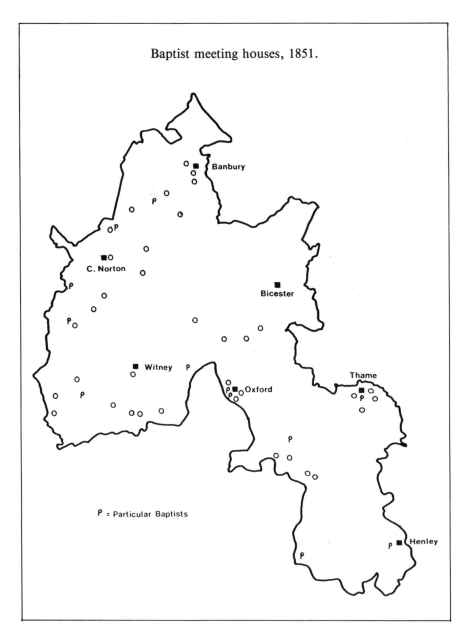

Baptist meeting houses, 1851.

P = Particular Baptists

Map 5

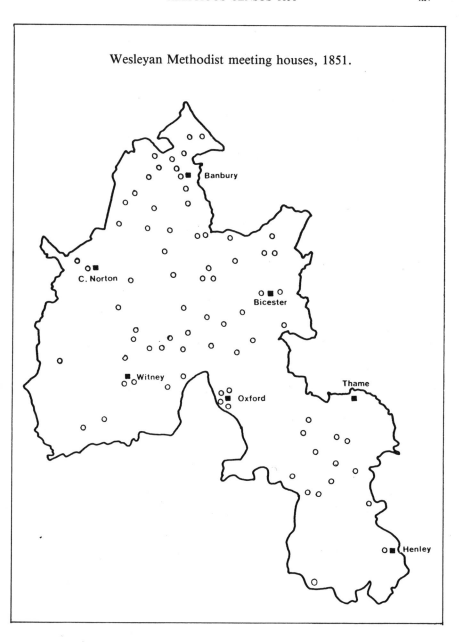

Wesleyan Methodist meeting houses, 1851.

Map 6

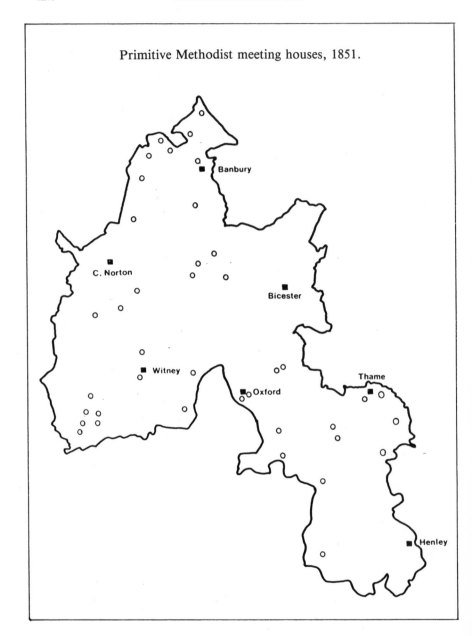

Primitive Methodist meeting houses, 1851.

Map 7

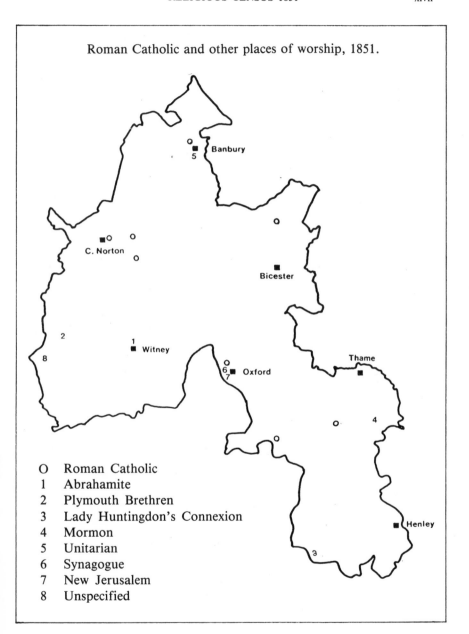

Roman Catholic and other places of worship, 1851.

O   Roman Catholic
1   Abrahamite
2   Plymouth Brethren
3   Lady Huntingdon's Connexion
4   Mormon
5   Unitarian
6   Synagogue
7   New Jerusalem
8   Unspecified

Map 8

A RETURN of the several Particulars to be inquired into respecting the under-mentioned Church or
     Chapel in England, belonging to the United Church of England and Ireland.

A similar Return (*mutatis mutandis*) will be obtained with respect to Churches belonging to the Established
Church in Scotland, and the Episcopal Church there, and also from Roman Catholic Priests, and from the
Ministers of every other Religious Denomination throughout Great Britain, with respect to their Places of
Worship.]

	NAME AND DESCRIPTION OF CHURCH OR CHAPEL.			
I.				

		Parish, Ecclesiastical Division or District, Township, or Place.	Superintendent Registrar's District.	County and Diocese.
II.	WHERE SITUATED.			

	WHEN CONSECRATED OR LICENSED.	UNDER WHAT CIRCUMSTANCES CONSECRATED OR LICENSED.
III.		

IN THE CASE OF A CHURCH OR CHAPEL CONSECRATED OR LICENSED SINCE THE 1st JANUARY 1800; STATE

	HOW OR BY WHOM ERECTED.	COST, HOW DEFRAYED.
IV.		By Parliamentary Grant - - - Parochial Rate - - - Private Benefaction or Subscription, or from other Sources - } Total Cost - - £

V.	VI.
HOW ENDOWED.	SPACE AVAILABLE FOR PUBLIC WORSHIP.
£	£
Land - - - Pew Rents - - - Tithe - - - Fees - - - - Glebe - - - Dues - - - Other Permanent Endowment - } Easter Offerings - - Other Sources - -	Free Sittings - - - Other Sittings - - - Total Sittings -

	ESTIMATED NUMBER OF PERSONS ATTENDING DIVINE SERVICE ON SUNDAY, MARCH 30, 1851.				AVERAGE NUMBER OF ATTENDANTS during Months next preceding March 30, 1851. (See Instruction VII.)			
VII.		Morning.	Afternoon.	Evening.		Morning.	Afternoon.	Evening.
	General Congregation - -} Sunday Scholars -				General Congregation - -} Sunday Scholars -			
	Total -				Total -			

VIII.	REMARKS.

I certify the foregoing to be a true and correct Return to the best of my belief.
Witness my hand this_____day of_____1851.
    IX. (*Signature*) _____
        (*Official Character*) _____ *of the above-named.*
        (*Address by Post*) _____

A return for Anglican places of worship.
(Bodl. Libr. Parl. Papers, H.C., 1852-3, LXXXIX, p. clxxii).

FORM B.

CENSUS OF GREAT BRITAIN, 1851.

(13 & 14 Victoria, Cap. 53.)

A RETURN of the several Particulars to be inquired into respecting the under-mentioned Place of Public Religious Worship.

[N.B.—A similar Return will be obtained from the Clergy of the Church of England, and also from the Ministers of every other Religious Denomination throughout Great Britain.]

I.	II.	III.	IV.	V.	VI.	VII.	VIII.	IX.
Name or Title of Place of Worship.	Where situate: specifying the Parish or Place. District. County. (1) (2) (3)	Religious Denomination.	When erected.	Whether a separate and entire Building.	Whether used exclusively as a Place of Worship (except for a Sunday School).	Space available for Public Worship. Number of Sittings already provided. Free Sittings. Other Sittings. (4) (5) Free Space or Standing Room for	Estimated Number of Persons attending Divine Service on Sunday March 30, 1851. Morning. Afternoon. Evening. General Congregation. Sunday Scholars. TOTAL. Average Number of Attendants during Months. (See Instruction VIII.) General Congregation. Sunday Scholars. TOTAL.	REMARKS.

I certify the foregoing to be a true and correct Return to the best of my belief. Witness my hand this _____ day of _____ 1851.

X. (Signature) _____ of the above-named Place of Worship.

(Official Character) _____

(Address by Post) _____

The Particulars to be inserted in Divisions I. to VI. inclusive, and in IX., may be written either along or across the Columns, as may be more convenient.

A return for non-Anglican places of worship.
(Bodl. Libr. Parl. Papers, H.C., 1852-3, LXXXIX, p. clxxiv).

The form of entries

The original returns in the Public Record Office are bound by census registration district. For the purposes of this text they have been rearranged alphabetically for ease of reference. The original location of each return may be traced from the reference given at the beginning of each entry and which consists of the group letters, the class number and the piece number (eg. HO 129/125/41).

Information is given in the order that it appears on the original forms, omitting sections which were left blank.

Section III of the Anglican returns ('When consecrated or licensed') has been rendered as 'erected', as this is the sense in which the question was commonly taken.

Where a total sum for endowment, in addition to the amounts of the constituent parts of the endowment, is given on Anglican returns, it is not usually stated unless e.g. the total shows some discrepancy.

The remarks have been given with modern spelling and punctuation unless specifically indicated thus — [sic]. Capital letters have been retained. Extended contractions are indicated by [ ].

The addresses of Anglican clergy are omitted unless they are other than the local parish. The addresses of Nonconformist respondents are included.

The dates of returns are noted only if of particular interest, e.g. by their lateness.

The population figure from the 1851 census is added at the top of the first entry for each place as essential background to the interpretation of the returns. Whenever sub-settlements within a parish can be identified as the locations of places of worship they are separately entered, with cross reference to the parish in which they lie and a distinct population figure wherever they are separately enumerated. Cross references to sub-settlements also appear in the main parish entry. All place-names not the subject of principal entries or additionally referred to in entries for other places may be traced through the index of places.

Wherever non-clerical signatories have been identified from a contemporary commercial directory (Robert Gardner, *History, Gazetteer, and Directory of the County of Oxford*, 1852) this information appears as a footnote to the entry.

1. ADDERBURY EAST[1]   Population 978   HO 129/163/24
Average attendance 240.[2]
1. A township in Adderbury parish.
2. An unsigned and extremely scant Anglican return, apparently referring to the parish church of St. Mary the Virgin, Adderbury.

2. ADDERBURY EAST   HO 129/163/25
WESLEYAN METHODIST CHAPEL. *Erected* 1810. A separate and entire building. Used exclusively for worship. *Free sittings* 40; *other sittings* 80. *On 30 March* In morning Sunday Scholars 12; in afternoon General Congregation 23, Sunday Scholars 13; in evening General Congregation 36. *Signed* James Claridge, Local Preacher, Blenheim Place, Banbury.

3. ADDERBURY WEST[1]   Population 370   HO 129/163/23
INDEPENDENT CHAPEL. *Erected* 1829. A separate and entire building. Used exclusively for worship. *Free sittings* 112; *other sittings* 60. *On 30 March* In morning General Congregation 51, Sunday Scholars 20; in afternoon Sunday Scholars 19; in evening General Congregation 120. *Average attendance* during previous 12 months, in morning General Congregation 60, Sunday Scholars 20; in afternoon Sunday Scholars 20; in evening General Congregation 100. *Remarks* In reference to the Sunday School, as soon as the children are old enough to be admitted to the National School (there being no other Public School in the place) they are obliged to attend the Church Sunday School or be excluded from the day school in consequence of which many children who would continue are prevented. *Signed* James Crockett, Minister, Adderbury West.
1. A township in Adderbury parish. The parish of Adderbury consisted of the townships of Adderbury East and Adderbury West, the chapelries of Barford St. John (*q.v.*) and Bodicote (*q.v.*), and Milton (*q.v.*) hamlet. The total population of the parish was 2,310.

4. ADDERBURY WEST   HO 129/163/28
FRIENDS' MEETING HOUSE. *Erected* 1675. A separate and entire building. Used exclusively for worship. *Admeasurement* in superficial feet floor area 561; in galleries 402. *Estimated Number of Persons capable of being seated* 102 and in galleries 60. *On 30 March* In morning 16 attendants; in afternoon no meeting held this afternoon; in evening not held in the six winter months. *Remarks* A meeting is held at 3 o'clock p.m. during the six winter months, and one at 5 o'clock p.m. during the six summer months, but both are omitted one week in four. The average attendance at these for the last 12 months is 12 persons. *Signed* Henry Beesley, Adderbury West.

5. ALBURY   Population 234   HO 129/156/58
ESTABLISHED CHURCH. *On 30 March* In morning General
Congregation 100; in afternoon General Congregation 150. *Average
attendance* in morning General Congregation 100; in afternoon General
Congregation 150. *Signed* John Jonas Shrimpton[1], Relieving Officer,
Long Crendon, Bucks.
1. Sections on erection, endowment and sittings in the church are blank except for various
annotations, 'cannot find out' or 'cannot get the information'.

6. ALKERTON   Population 190   HO 129/163/43
ST. MICHAEL'S PARISH CHURCH. *Erected* before 1800. *Endowed*
with land 91 acres or thereabouts. *Free sittings* about 96; *other sittings*
42. *On 30 March* In afternoon General Congregation about 90. *Remarks*
Children of this parish attend the Sunday School of the parish of
Shenington, which adjoins. *Signed* Robert E. Hughes, Rector.

7. ALVESCOT   Population 375   HO 129/161/30
PARISH CHURCH. *Erected* more than 7[?] 00 years since. *Free sittings*
about 170;*other sittings* about 80, rough guess. *On 30 March* In morning
General Congregation 110, Sunday Scholars 40; in afternoon ditto.
Average attendance in morning General Congregation 110, Sunday
Scholars 40; in afternoon ditto. *Remarks* I think I may have underrated
the average congregation. *Signed* Arthur Neate, Rector.

8. ALVESCOT   HO 129/161/31
PARTICULAR BAPTIST CHAPEL. *Erected* 1833. A separate and
entire building. Used exclusively for worship. *Free sittings* 160. *On 30
March* In morning Prayer Meeting General Congregation 45. *Average
attendance* during previous 12 months, in morning General
Congregation 120; in afternoon General Congregation 60. *Signed* James
Knapp, Deacon, Grocer, Clanfield.

9. ALVESCOT   HO 129/161/32
PRIMITIVE METHODIST CHAPEL. *Erected* 1851. A separate and
entire building. Used exclusively for worship. *Sittings* 100. *On 30 March*
In morning Prayer Meeting; in afternoon General Congregation 60; in
evening General Congregation 150. *Average attendance* 100. *Signed*
Henry James[1], Primitive Methodist Lay Preacher, Alvescot.
1. *Gardner* describes Henry James, Alvescot, as a farmer.

10. AMBROSDEN[1]   Population 172   HO 129/159/40
PARISH CHURCH. Built in the reign of Edward I and dedicated to St.

Mary. *Endowed* with tithe £97, glebe £153, fees annual average £2. *Sittings* 300. *On 30 March* In morning General Congregation 87, Sunday Scholars 25; in afternoon General Congregation 45, Sunday Scholars 25. *Signed* L. G. Dryden, Vicar, Ambrosden.
1. The parish of Ambrosden also included the chapelries of Arncot (*q.v.*) and Blackthorn (*q.v.*). The total population of the parish was 937.

11. AMBROSDEN   HO 129/159/42
INDEPENDENT CHAPEL. *Erected* August 1846. Not a separate and entire building. Not used exclusively for worship. *Free sittings* 30. *On 30 March* In evening General Congregation 25, Sunday Scholars 15. *Average attendance* in evening General Congregation 20, Sunday Scholars 12. *Signed* Thomas Young, Local Preacher, Wretchwick, nr. Bicester.

12. ARDLEY   Population 152   HO 129/159/12
PARISH CHURCH. *Endowed* with great and small tithes commuted, glebe 60 acres, fees very trifling. *Free sittings* chiefly. The church will contain about 100 persons. *On 30 March* In morning General Congregation from 50-60 including children; in afternoon General Congregation from 60-90 including children. *Average attendance* in morning 40; in afternoon 60. *Signed* John Lowe, Rector.

13. ARNCOT¹   Population 348   HO 129/159/43
WESLEYAN METHODIST CHAPEL. *Erected* 1834. A separate and entire building. Used exclusively for worship and Sunday School. *Free sittings* 140; *other sittings* 84. *On 30 March* In morning Sunday Scholars 59; in afternoon General Congregation 200, Sunday Scholars 59; in evening General Congregation 200. *Average attendance* during previous 12 months, in morning Sunday Scholars 60; in afternoon General Congregation 200, Sunday Scholars 60; in evening General Congregation 200. *Signed* Joseph Barnes, Steward, Upper Arncot.
1. A chapelry in Ambrosden parish.

14. ASCOTT UNDER WYCHWOOD
                        Population 456   HO 129/162/21
PARISH CHURCH. *Erected* before 1800. *Endowed* with land £21, tithe £19 6s 8d, glebe £23, other permanent endowment £39, fees £1, total £103 6s 8d less income tax. *Free sittings* 100; *other sittings* 200. *On 30 March* In morning General Congregation 130, Sunday Scholars 24. *Remarks* At Ascott church there is one service on Sunday. It is alternate in the morning and afternoon. The congregation in the afternoon on

Sundays is about 250. *Signed* Frederick E. Lott, Incumbent.[1]
1. The name of George Gomm, Churchwarden, is written under this signature in the same hand. *Gardner* describes George Gomm, Ascott under Wychwood, as a farmer.

15. ASCOTT UNDER WYCHWOOD HO 129/162/22
BAPTIST CHAPEL. *Erected* 1812. A separate and entire building. Used exclusively for worship. *Free sittings* 100. *On 30 March* In afternoon General Congregation 23. *Average attendance* during previous 12 months, in afternoon General Congregation 25. *Signed* Edward Spiers, Manager, Leafield.

16. ASTHALL Population 383 HO 129.161/58
ST. NICHOLAS' CHURCH. *Endowed* with land £57, other permanent endowment £26 13s, other sources £4. *Free sittings* about 150; *other sittings* 35, exclusive of benches for children 40. *On 30 March* In morning General Congregation 50, Sunday Scholars 12. *Remarks* The service is alternate. The morning congregation always is small compared with that in the afternoon when in favourable weather the pews and free sittings are fully occupied. *Signed* Henry Gregory, Vicar.

17. ASTON HO 129/161/23
ST. JAMES' CHAPEL OF EASE. *Erected* 1839 as an additional church by subscription. No separate endowment. *Free sittings* 450; *other sittings* 70. *On 30 March* In afternoon General Congregation 160, Sunday Scholars 34. *Remarks* The parish of Bampton has three portions and vicars, who between them are responsible for the duty of the several chapels in the parish. There are therefore no separate endowments for each. *Signed* Dacre Adams, Vicar of Bampton 2nd Portion.

18. ASTON AND COTE[1] Population 734 HO 129/161/18
BAPTIST BRITISH SCHOOL. *Erected* 1845. A separate and entire building. Not used exclusively for worship. *Free sittings* 160. *On 30 March* In evening General Congregation 80. *Average attendance* during previous 36 months, in morning General Congregation 130. *Remarks* The Sunday Scholars attend Divine Worship at Coat Chapel (ie. such as are old enough to walk thiter [sic]) on Lord's Day morning. *Signed* John Jackson, Minister of Coate, Aston House, nr Bampton.
1. Hamlets in Bampton parish, which were enumerated together for census purposes.

19. ASTON ROWANT[1] Population 901 HO 129/156/17
PARISH CHURCH. *Erected* before 1800. *Endowed* with land £24, tithe £95, glebe £72, surplus [sic] fees £5, other sources £1 10s. *Free sittings* 95;

other sittings 135 independent of gallery. *On 30 March* In morning
General Congregation 110, Sunday Scholars 58; in afternoon General
Congregation 205, Sunday Scholars 72. *Average attendance* in morning
General Congregation 112, Sunday Scholars 58; in afternoon General
Congregation 210, Sunday Scholars 50. *Signed* Robert Williams, Vicar.
1. The parish included the township of Kingston Blount (*q.v.*).

20. ASTON ROWANT   HO 129/156/19

APOSTOLIC BAPTIST CHURCH (Mormonites). *Erected* 1833.
Dwelling house and not entire. Used exclusively for dwelling house and
public worship. No School. *Free seats* already provided number 6. *On 30
March* In afternoon General Congregation 18; in evening General
Congregation 26. *Average attendance* during previous 12 months, nil not
having been open 12 calendar months. *Signed* Thomas Hailey, Kingston,
Aston Rowant.[1]
1. *Gardner* describes Thomas Hailey, Kingston Stirt, as a beer retailer.

21. BALSCOTT[1]   HO 129/163/61

ST. MARY MAGDALENE CHAPEL. *Erected* before 1800. *Free
sittings* 70; *other sittings* 90. *On 30 March* In afternoon General
Congregation 64, Sunday Scholars 21. *Signed* Michael Harrison, Curate,
Wroxton.
1. A chapelry in Wroxton parish.

22. BALSCOTT   HO 129/163/64

WESLEYAN METHODIST CHAPEL. *Erected* 1850. A separate and
entire building. Used exclusively for worship. *Free sittings* 48; *other
sittings* 36. *On 30 March* in afternoon General Congregation 51; in
evening General Congregation 95. *Signed* Issac Wrench, Steward,
Balscott.

23. BAMPTON[1]   Population 851   HO 129/161/22

ST. MARY'S PARISH CHURCH. *Erected* before 1800. *Free sittings*
about 200; *other sittings* 900. *On 30 March* In morning General
Congregation 280, Sunday Scholars 120; in afternoon General
Congregation 500, Sunday Scholars 130. *Signed* Dacre Adams, Vicar of
2nd Portion, Bampton.
1. The parish of Bampton also included the hamlets of Lew (*q.v.*), Brighthampton, Aston
and Cote (*q.v.*), Chimney, and Weald (*q.v.*) together with the chapelry of Shifford (*q.v.*).
The total population of the parish was 2,780.

24. BAMPTON   HO 129/161/25
BAPTIST CHAPEL. *Erected* before 1800. A separate and entire
building. Used exclusively for worship. *Free sittings* 100 [?]. *On 30
March* In evening General Congregation 70. *Average attendance* during
previous 36 months, in morning General Congregation 80. *Remarks* This
is one of four other small chapels connected with Coate chapel, the
minister of which officiates here in connection with other members of
Coate congregation on Lord's day evenings. *Signed* John Jackson,
Minister of Coate chapel, Aston House, Near Bampton.

25. BANBURY[1]   Population 4026   HO 129/163/103
ST. MARY'S PARISH CHURCH *Endowed* with land £170, tithe £15,
glebe £20, other permanent endowment £5 17s, fees £90, Easter
Offerings £6. *Free sittings* including children 506; *other sittings* all of
which are freehold by add pat.[2] 1205. *On 30 March* In morning General
Congregation 1000, Sunday Scholars 300; in afternoon General
Congregation 400, Sunday Scholars 300; in evening General
Congregation 1300. *Remarks* There is an additional early celebration of
the Holy Communion every Sunday. The children of the Sunday School
in the afternoon are separated from the General Congregation and have
a separate service to themselves. *Signed* William Wilson Jun., Vicar.
1. The parish of Banbury also included Neithrop (*q.v.*) township. The total population of
the parish was 8206.
2. i.e. additional payment?

26 BANBURY   HO 129/163/102
FRIENDS' MEETING HOUSE. *Erected* 1750. A separate and entire
building. Used exclusively for worship. *Admeasurement* in superficial
feet floor area 900; in galleries 400. *Estimated Number of Persons
capable of being seated* 250 and in galleries 100. *On 30 March* In morning
60 attendants; in afternoon 39 attendants. *Signed* John Harlock,[1]
Banbury.
1. *Gardner* describes John Harlock, Parsons Street, Banbury, as a draper.

27. BANBURY   HO 129/163/104
WEST STREET CHAPEL.[1] *Erected* 1829. A separate and entire
building. Used exclusively for worship. *Free sittings* 90. *On 30 March* In
morning General Congregation 70; in evening General Congregation 50.
1. This unsigned return refers to no specific denomination but describes the Strict Baptist
chapel founded in 1829 by Joseph Gardner, a local tradesman and member of Middleton
Cheney Baptist chapel (see *VCH Oxon*, Vol. X, p.116).

28. BANBURY HO 129/163/105
INDEPENDENT CHAPEL. *Erected* before 1800. A separate and entire building. Used exclusively for worship. *Free sittings* 50; *other sittings* 370. *On 30 March* In morning General Congregation 100; in evening General Congregation 120. *Average attendance* in morning Sunday Scholars 87. *Signed* J.B. Luckett, Deacon, Banbury.

29. BANBURY HO 129/163/106
WESLEYAN METHODIST CHAPEL. *Erected* 1811. A separate and entire building. Used exclusively for worship. *Free sittings* 173; *other sittings* 427. *On 30 March* In morning General Congregation 361, Sunday Scholars 197; in afternoon General Congregation 118; in evening General Congregation 470.[1] *Signed* John Fisher, Chapel Steward, Revd R. Hornabrook, Banbury.

1. An arrow is drawn from the figure 470 into the afternoon column, possibly intended to indicate that the afternoon attendance by General Congregation was 470, and that by Sunday Scholars 118.

30. BANBURY HO 129/163/107
PRIMITIVE METHODIST CHAPEL, Broad Street. *Erected* 1839. A separate and entire building. Used exclusively for worship. *Free sittings* 88; *other sittings* 133. *On 30 March* In morning General Congregation 72, Sunday Scholars 87; in afternoon General Congregation 123, Sunday Scholars 89; in evening General Congregation 144. *Average attendance* during previous 12 months, in morning General Congregation 200, Sunday Scholars 100. *Signed* James Blencowe, Chapel Steward, Bridge Street, Banbury.

31. BANBURY HO 129/163/108
BRIDGE STREET BAPTIST CHAPEL. *Erected* 1841. A separate and entire building. Used exclusively for worship. *Free sittings* 125; *other sittings* 375. *On 30 March* In morning General Congregation 150, Sunday Scholars 50; in evening General Congregation 200. *Signed* William Thomas Henderson, Minister, Banbury.

32. BANBURY HO 129/163/109
ST. JOHN'S ROMAN CATHOLIC CHURCH. *Erected* 1838. A separate and entire building. Used exclusively for worship. *Sittings* 350 in all, more than half free. *On 30 March* In morning General Congregation 250; in evening General Congregation 230. *Signed* W. Tandy, Catholic Priest, St. John's, Banbury.

33.   BARFORD ST. JOHN[1]   Population 125   HO 129/163/21
ST. JOHN'S CHURCH. *Average attendance* 15 to 20.
1. A chapelry in Adderbury parish.

34.   BARFORD ST. MICHAEL   Population 392   HO 129/163/17
ST. MICHAEL'S CHURCH. *Average attendance* 80.

35.   BARFORD ST. MICHAEL   HO 129/163/18
BAPTIST CHAPEL. A separate and entire building. Used exclusively
for worship. *Average attendance* 20.

36.   BARFORD ST. MICHAEL   HO 129/163/19
WESLEYAN METHODIST CHAPEL. *Erected* 1840. A separate and
entire building. Used exclusively for worship. *Free sittings* 50; *other
sittings* 100. *On 30 March* In morning General Congregation 40, Sunday
Scholars 20; in evening General Congregation 92, Sunday Scholars 30.
Signed John Pearce, Minister, Brackley, Northamptonshire.

37.   BARTON[1]   HO 129/160/15
WESLEYAN METHODIST CHAPEL. *Erected* about 1814. A separate
and entire building. Used exclusively for worship. *Free sittings* 100; *other
sittings* 120. *On 30 March* In morning General Congregation 180,
Sunday Scholars 40; in evening General Congregation 220. *Signed*
Samuel Cooke, Minister, Chipping Norton.
1. This entry refers to Westcott Barton: see *VCH Oxon*, Vol. XI, p.74.

38.   BECKLEY[1]   Population 352   HO 129/157/14
PARISH   CHURCH.   *Average   attendance*   in   morning   General
Congregation 60. *Remarks* As near as I could ascertain. *Signed* Richard
Wood, Registrar.
1. The parish of Beckley also included Horton-cum-Studley hamlet and Studley hamlet.
The total population of the parish was 778.

39.   BEGBROKE   Population 98   HO 129/160/38
ST. MICHAEL'S PARISH CHURCH. *Erected* before 1800. *Endowed*
with glebe 30 acres, dues, clerk collects 4d from each house for himself.
Free sittings 90; *other sittings* 30. *On 30 March* In morning General
Congregation between 50 and 60. Sunday Scholars 15 included above; in
afternoon General Congregation between 60 and 70, Sunday Scholars
included. *Average attendance* it does not vary, in mornings 50 to 60; in
afternoons 60 to 70. *Signed* J.E. Coulson, Minister and Curate.

40. BENSINGTON   Population 1231   HO 129/125/43
BENSINGTON PARISH CHURCH. *Erected* before 1800. *Endowed* with tithe £156, glebe £46, other permanent endowment from Christ Church Oxford £13, and fees £5. *Signed* Samuel Hay Cooke, Perpetual Curate.

41. BENSON[1]   HO 129/125/44
BAPTIST CHAPEL. Opened for Public Service about 5 years. Part of a dwelling house. Used exclusively for worship. *Free sittings* 100. *On 30 March* In afternoon General Congregation 35. *Remarks* Place only open for one service on Sundays only. *Signed* George Painter, Chalgrove.[2]
1. Otherwise Bensington.
2. *Gardner* describes George Painter, Chalgrove, as a baker and grocer.

42. BENSON   HO 129/125/45
INDEPENDENT CHAPEL. *Erected* before 1800. A separate and entire building. Used exclusively for worship. *Free sittings* 150. *On 30 March* In afternoon General Congregation 77, Sunday Scholars 10; in evening General Congregation 69, Sunday Scholars 12. *Average attendance* during previous 12 months, in afternoon General Congregation about 80, Sunday Scholars 15; in evening General Congregation 70, Sunday Scholars 12. *Remarks* Sunday School held in the morning but no other service. *Signed* James Burgis, Deacon, Benson.[1]
1. *Gardner* describes James Burgis, Benson, as a maltster and corn dealer.

43. BENSON   HO 129/125/47
WESLEYAN METHODIST CHAPEL. Not used as a place of worship till 1843. A separate building. Used exclusively for worship. *Free sittings* 50; *other sittings* 42. *On 30 March* In morning General Congregation 35; in evening General Congregation 27. *Average attendance* in morning General Congregation 40, in evening General Congregation 48. *Signed* H.S. Green,[1] Chapel Steward, Bensington.
1. *Gardner* describes Henry S. Green, Benson, as a land surveyor.

44. BERRICK SALOME   Population 152   HO 129/125/42
PARISH CHURCH of Berrick Salome otherwise Lower Berrick. *Erected* before 1800. *Endowed* with tithe[+] £200, glebe[#] £4 10s, fees given to Clerk, total £204 10s.[*] *Free sittings* 137. *Average attendance* during previous 12 months, in morning General Congregation from 20-30; in afternoon General Congregation from 40-60. *Remarks* + gross amount mentioned as Tithe Commutation Apportionment, variable with the price of corn. # inclusive of rent of churchyard.* Deduct about £34 for

Rates etc. and 5 per cent for collection. This Church is held with Chalgrove (as one benefice) for which a separate return has been made. *Signed* Robert French Laurence, Rector.

45. BICESTER   Population 3054   HO 129/159/50
PARISH CHURCH. *Endowed* with glebe £226, fees £30, Easter Offerings £25. *Free sittings* 312; *other sittings* 1200. *On 30 March* In morning General Congregation 502, Sunday Scholars 171; in afternoon General Congregation 810, Sunday Scholars 171; in evening General Congregation 313. *Average attendance* during previous 6 months, in morning General Congregation 500, Sunday Scholars 171; in afternoon General Congregation 1000, Sunday Scholars 171; in evening General Congregation 450. *Signed* John William Watts, Vicar.

46. BICESTER   HO 129/159/49
INDEPENDENT CHAPEL, Water Lane, Market End. *Erected* 1729. A separate and entire building. Used exclusively for worship. *Free sittings* 94; *other sittings* 206. *On 30 March* In morning General Congregation 102, Sunday Scholars 85; in afternoon Sunday Scholars 105; in evening General Congregation 138. *Signed* James Smith, Deacon, Printer and Bookseller, Bicester.

47. BICESTER   HO 129/159/51
WESLEYAN METHODIST CHAPEL. *Erected* 1841. A separate and entire building. Used exclusively for worship. *Free sittings* 72; *other sittings* 144. *On 30 March* In morning General Congregation 55, Sunday Scholars 43; in evening General Congregation 52, Sunday Scholars 18. *Average attendance* in morning General Congregation 70, Sunday Scholars 43; in evening General Congregation 70, Sunday Scholars 18. *Signed* George Bowerman,[1] Assistant Chapel Steward, Church Street, Bicester.
1. *Gardner* describes George Bowerman, Church Street, Bicester, as a baker.

48. BICESTER   HO 129/159/52
WORKHOUSE CHAPEL, Market End. Licensed 1836. *Erected* by parochial rate 52. *Sittings* 150. *On 30 March* In afternoon General Congregation 85. *Average attendance* during previous 12 months, in morning General Congregation 80. *Remarks* The above return is for the Bicester Union Workhouse Chapel situate at Bicester Market End. *Signed* Joseph Henry Mansell, Governor, Union Workhouse, Bicester.

49. BICESTER HO 129/159/53
INDEPENDENT CHAPEL, Crockwell, Market End. Began to be used as a preaching room 1846. Not a separate and entire building. Not used exclusively for worship. *Free sittings* 40. *On 30 March* In afternoon General Congregation 34. *Average attendance* during previous 3 months, in afternoon General Congregation 30. *Signed* John Baker, Local Preacher, Market Hill, Bicester.

50. BINSEY Population 77 HO 129/123/29
PARISH CHURCH. *Erected* before 1800. *Free sittings* 24; *other sittings* 1. *On 30 March* In morning General Congregation 20, Sunday Scholars 8; in afternoon General Congregation 20; Sunday Scholars 8. *Average attendance* In Morning General Congregation 20, Sunday Scholars 8, in afternoon General Congregation 20, Sunday Scholars 8. *Signed* William Hutt, Registrar, Cumnor.

51. BIX Population 367 HO 129/155/31
PARISH CHURCH. *Erected* centuries ago. *Endowed* with tithe commuted at £625 2s 6d, glebe about 50 acres, fees about £2. *Free sittings* about 105; *other sittings* about 60, school children about 20. *On 30 March* In morning General Congregation 80, Sunday Scholars 12, total 80 including scholars. *Average attendance* in morning General Congregation between 70-85, Sunday Scholars from 10-20 according to the weather or other circumstances. *Signed* H.R. Pechell, Rector.

52. BLACK BOURTON Population 278 HO 129/161/26
PARISH CHURCH. An ancient church consecrated it is presumed before the Reformation. Its legal and proper designation is the church of Burton Abbots, not Blackbourton as it is vulgarly called. *Endowed* with land £166, tithe £26, other permanent endowment £25, £38. *Sittings* sufficient. *On 30 March* In morning General Congregation 91; in afternoon General Congregation 70. *Remarks* Of those who attended in the afternoon there were about twenty who were not present in the morning. The day's attendance represents the average. The church attendance therefore will be about 110 every Sunday. *Signed* James Lupton, Vicar, Burton Abbots.

53. BLACK BOURTON HO 129/161/27
PRIMITIVE METHODIST MEETING HOUSE. *Erected* 1826. A separate and entire building. Not used exclusively for worship. *Free sittings* 60. *On 30 March* In morning Sunday Scholars 22; in afternoon General Congregation 100. *Average attendance* in afternoon General

Congregation 80. *Remarks* The reason of the increase of numbers to 100 is owing to more room being made in the place, it being used for other purposes as well as for religious worship. *Signed* John Maisey, Local Preacher, Black Bourton.

54. BLACKTHORN[1]   Population 417   HO 129/159/41
INDEPENDENT OR CONGREGATIONALIST CHAPEL. *Erected* 1841. A separate and entire building. Used exclusively for worship. *Free sittings* all.[2] *On 30 March* In afternoon General Congregation 150; in evening General Congregation 120. *Signed* Robert Ann, Minister, Marsh Gibbon, Bucks.
1. A chapelry in Ambrosden parish.
2. HO 129/159/40A is a supplementary return stating that there were 100 free sittings and 50 appropriated sittings. It is endorsed, 'This return is as correct as I can give there may be room to accommodate more in five [?] sittings. R. Ann'.

55. BLADON   Population 720   HO 129/160/36
ST. MARTIN'S PARISH CHURCH. *Erected* before 1800. *Endowed* with tithe £237, glebe £170. *Sittings* 330. *Average attendance* in morning General Congregation 100; in afternoon General Congregation 200. *Remarks* There are no Sunday or other Schools in this parish under the care of the Church. There is a School supported and managed entirely by the Duke of Marlborough. *Signed* G.W. St. John, Rector of Bladon with Woodstock.

56. BLADON   HO 129/160/37
WESLEYAN METHODIST CHAPEL. *Erected* 1843. A separate and entire building. Used exclusively for worship. *Free sittings* 40; *other sittings* 94. *On 30 March* In morning General Congregation 42, Sunday Scholars 50; in afternoon Sunday Scholars 50; in evening General Congregation 94, Sunday Scholars 30. *Average attendance* in morning General Congregation 35, Sunday Scholars 50; in afternoon Sunday Scholars 50; in evening General Congregation 100. *Signed* Thomas Jones, Local Preacher, Islip.

57. BLETCHINGDON   Population 673   HO 129/159/24
ST. GILES' PARISH CHURCH. *Erected* before 1800. *Free sittings* for adults 121, for children 70; *other sittings* 90. *Remarks* The questions which appear to have been framed with a view of annoying me as a beneficed clergyman, as well as those which are calculated to excite religious dispute and animosities, and which, if answered would be likely to be mixed up or contrasted with exaggerated and incorrect statements, I have declined to answer. *Signed* Thomas Dand, Rector.

58. BLOXHAM[1]   Population 1336   HO 129/163/12
BLOXHAM MOTHER CHURCH. *Erected* above 600 years. *Endowed* with land vicarial allotment, tithe enclosures 1794, rent about £200, other permanent endowment, exclusive of Milcomb £60 more, Provost and Fellows of Eton College Great Tithes. *Free sittings* about 150; *other sittings* about 450. *On 30 March* In morning General Congregation 250, Sunday Scholars 100; in afternoon General Congregation 250, Sunday Scholars 100. *Signed* George Bell,[2] Vicar of Bloxham cum Milcomb capella adjoining.

1. The parish of Bloxham included Milcombe chapelry (*q.v.*). The total population of the parish was 1577.
2. The following disjointed comments were added by Bell on the outside of the return. 'I have no Sunday School which is not also also [sic] a Day School both of boys or girls — and under the same roof the girls school as Roomy and convenient as the boys in the churchyard or Court House — G. Bell, Vicar. The Sunday School schedule is *in our* case superfluous. The probable amount of the whole number of scholars will be little above 1/8 of the population and quite enough. GB. I wish their *morals* were as satisfactory as their education, young or old, rich or poor, parents or chilen. Since we have had an endowed school the Sunday School forms an inseperable portion of the same — by the endowment also mensuration and planning form part of the Education therein, forgotten and omitted in the school schedule. G. Bell, Vicar. Twenty years ago we had no other than a parvetion [?] Sunday School supplied by voluntary subscription.'

59. BLOXHAM   HO 129/163/15
BAPTIST CHAPEL. *Erected* 1812. A separate and entire building. Used exclusively for worship and Sabbath School. *Free sittings* 160. *On 30 March* In afternoon General Congregation 75, Sunday Scholars 25; in evening General Congregation 100. *Signed* David Nunnick, Minister, Bloxham.

60. BLOXHAM   HO 129/163/16
WESLEYAN METHODIST CHAPEL. Registered for worship 1821. A separate and entire building. Used exclusively for worship. *Free sittings* 100; *other sittings* 34. *On 30 March* In afternoon General Congregation 126, Sunday Scholars 27; in evening General Congregation 120. *Signed* William Allen, Steward and Lay Preacher, Bloxham.

61. BODICOTE[1]   Population 673   HO 129/163/22
CHAPEL OF ST. JOHN THE BAPTIST. Consecrated May 1st 1844. An ancient chapel in part rebuilt and enlarged by private subscription aided by a donation from New College, and a grant from Church Building Society, at a total cost of £1500 or thereabouts of which £90 was raised by parochial rate, £1410 by private subscription and other sources. *Endowed* with land £90 paid by Vicar of Adderbury from land belonging

to the Vicarage of Adderbury in the gift of New College, Oxford. *Free sittings* 218, of these 54 for children; *other sittings* 172, allowing 20 in. for adults and 16 in. for children. *On 30 March* In morning General Congregation 156; in afternoon General Congregation 190. *Average attendance* not ascertained. *Remarks* The church is usually well attended particularly in the afternoon. On Sunday 30th only three pews were vacant. If there were more pew accommodation it would be filled as it is some cannot obtain seats. *Signed* George Warriner, Curate, Bloxham Grove.

1. A chapelry in Adderbury parish.

62. BODICOTE   HO 129/163/26
BAPTIST AND INDEPENDENT CHAPEL. *Erected* 1817-18. A separate and entire building. Used exclusively for worship. *Free sittings* 150; *other sittings* 150. *On 30 March* In afternoon General Congregation 50. *Average attendance* no Sunday School. *Signed* John Wilson,[1] Deacon, Bodicote.

1. *Gardner* lists Mr. John Wilson amongst the private residents of Bodicote.

63. BODICOTE   HO 129/163/27
WESLEYAN METHODIST CHAPEL. *Erected* 1846. A separate and entire building. Used exclusively for worship. *Free sittings* 100. *On 30 March* In morning Sunday Scholars 54; in evening General Congregation 60. *Signed* George Blake[1], Steward, Bodicote.

1. *Gardner* describes George Blake, Bodicote, as a butcher.

64. BOURTON[1]   Population 573   HO 129/163/83
CHAPEL built about time it is supposed of Henry VII and used as such till the Reformation. The curate of Cropredy preaches a lecture in the school room on Sunday evenings. *Free sittings* from 80 to 90. *On 30 March* In evening General Congregation 80. *Remarks* As there has been no Sunday evening service in Great Bourton, the curate of Cropredy preaches an evening lecture on Sunday in the school room. *Signed* James Copeland, School Master, Great Bourton.

1. Great and Little Bourton together formed a township in Cropredy parish.

65. BRADWELL[1]   Population 211   HO 129/161/62
PARISH CHURCH of St. Peter and St. Paul or St. John (uncertain). *Erected* before 1800. *Endowed* with land £118, glebe £12, fees average about £4 10s, Easter Offerings £14. Gross not net income £135 4s, net income about £105. *Free sittings* 117; *other sittings* 132. *On 30 March* In morning General Congregation 81, Sunday Scholars 79; in afternoon

General Congregation 63, Sunday Scholars 56. *Average attendance* during previous 12 months, in morning General Congregation 96, Sunday Scholars 81; in evening General Congregation 80, Sunday Scholars 60. *Remarks* Colds and influenza prevented there being the average number. Three fourths of the population live in the hamlet of Filkins a mile and a mile and half from the Church. Church and endowment sadly wanted there. An average of 18 attend the small church of Broughton, a village adjoining Filkins. Robbed of the great tithes. *Signed* T.W. Goodlake, Vicar and Parish Priest.

1. Sometimes called Broadwell. The parish of Bradwell also included Filkins (*q.v.*) hamlet, and the chapelries of Holwell (*q.v.*) and Kelmscott (*q.v.*). The total population of the parish was 1107.

66. BRIGHTWELL BALDWIN Population 294   HO 129/155/40
CHURCH. *On 30 March* In morning General Congregation 100; in afternoon General Congregation 110. *Remarks* Information given by the Clerk of Brightwell Baldwin.

67. BRITWELL PRIOR[1]   Population 46   HO 129/155/35
CASTLE CHAPEL. A chapel originally private to the Castle now destroyed and not a parish Church or Chapel of Ease. *Endowed* with rent charge and glebe. *Free sittings* 40; *other sittings* 30. *On 30 March* In evening General Congregation 65. *Average attendance* in evening General Congregation 60-70. *Remarks* There is only one service in a fortnight in the above mentioned Chapel, the last service was on 23 March. It is only about a hundred yards from Britwell Salome Church in which there are two full services every Sunday. *Signed* Edward H. Boardman, Curate.

1. A hamlet in Newington parish.

68. BRITWELL SALOME Population 248   HO 129/155/36
PARISH CHURCH. *Endowed* with rent charge and glebe. *Free sittings* 70; *other sittings* 45. *On 30 March* In morning General Congregation 75, Sunday Scholars 35; in afternoon General Congregation 65, Sunday Scholars 28. *Average attendance* during previous 12 months, in morning General Congregation 90, Sunday Scholars 30, total 120*; in afternoon General Congregation 85, Sunday Scholars 30. *Remarks** A moveable bench is used to sit upon when the fixed seats are all occupied. *Signed* Edward H. Boardman, Curate.

69. BRITWELL SALOME   HO 129/155/37
WESLEYAN METHODIST CHAPEL. *Erected* 1832. A separate and entire building. Used exclusively for worship. *Free sittings* 42; *other*

sittings 30. *On 30 March* In afternoon General Congregation 39; in evening General Congregation 52. *Signed* Josiah Russell, Steward, Britwell.

70. BRIZE NORTON   Population 720   HO 129/161/33
CONGREGATIONAL CHAPEL. A barn used for worship from 1840. A separate and entire building. Used exclusively for worship. *Free sittings* 30. *On 30 March* In evening General Congregation 140. *Remarks* Supplied by lay agency. *Signed* Robert Maitland Tozer[1], Manager, Curbridge.
1. *Gardner* describes Robert M. Tozer, Curbridge, as a farmer.

71. BROUGHTON [POGGS] Population 122   HO 129/161/66
PARISH CHURCH *Free sittings* 38; *other sittings* 50. *On 30 March* In morning General Congregation 30, Sunday Scholars 24; in afternoon General Congregation 18, Sunday Scholars 24. *Signed* John Jos. Goodenough, Rector.

72. BROUGHTON[1]   Population 180   HO 129/163/29
BROUGHTON CHURCH. *Erected* before 1800. *Endowed* with land 317 acres, tithe between £2 and £3, fees about £15, Easter offerings about £8. *Free sittings* 200; *other sittings* 150. *On 30 March* in morning General Congregation 140, Sunday Scholars 51; in afternoon General Congregation 102, Sunday Scholars 56. *Average attendance* during previous 12 months, in morning General Congregation 160, Sunday Scholars 60; in afternoon General Congregation 120, Sunday Scholars 60. *Signed* C.F. Wyatt, Rector.
1. The parish of Broughton also included North Newington (*q.v.*) hamlet. The total population of the parish was 616.

73. BUCKNELL   Population 343   HO 129/159/14
THE CHURCH. *Erected* before 1800.[1] *Endowed* with land 340 acres, tithes £1 16s, fees trifling. *On 30 March* In morning General Congregation 110, Sunday Scholars 30; in afternoon General Congregation 108, Sunday Scholars 30. *Remarks* The afternoon congregation is generally much larger. The Sunday Scholars at each time usually more numerous. *Signed* William Master, Rector.
1. HO 129/159/13 is a supplementary return stating that there were free sittings 115, appropriated sittings 90, 'besides about 40 children in the Sunday School who are provided with forms in the Chancel which is large'.

74. BURFORD [1]   Population 1819   HO 129/161/72
PARISH CHURCH OF ST. JOHN BAPTIST. *Erected* probably anterior to Norman dynasty, carcass of Rectory of that date. *Free sittings* about 600; *other sittings* about 400. *On 30 March* In morning General Congregation 330, Sunday Scholars 194; in evening General Congregation 400, Sunday Scholars 100. *Remarks* The above attendance is slightly below an average, there being a collection under the Queen's Letter. *Signed* James Gerald Joyce, Vicar, Burford.

1. HO 129/161/619 and 71 are returns for the chapels of Boraston, Shropshire and Nash, Shropshire respectively. These were Chapels of Ease to Burford served by the Rector of Burford, 1st Portion, the Revd Hubert McLaughlin, who was resident at Boraston Rectory. Details of these returns have been omitted because they do not refer to Oxfordshire. However, McLaughlin, as Rural Dean accompanied them with a general report (HO 129/161/70) as follows:

'In obedience to the wishes of Government I have made the required return, but I beg to add this note, not only for myself, but for the surrounding district for which I am Rural Dean. The number of those who attend public worship in this neighbourhood on any particular Sunday, or on any average number of Sundays, gives but an inadequate idea of the number of persons to whom the ministrations of the Clergy extend. The state of almost all the parishes in this agricultural district is very similar to my own. Let us take it as an example. The population assigned to my charge as Rector of the 1st Portion of Burford is about 430. Of these there are not more than five persons who habitually decline attendance at church, and upon one of them (although I could never influence him to attend Divine Service during the 13 years I have been Rector) I have been in constant attendance for the last three months. He is very ill, and is now glad to have the private ministrations of his Clergyman, though he has hitherto neglected the public ones. Nor is this an isolated case. Some time ago, I constantly visited a man for more than twelve months, until he died, whom I could not induce during his days of health, to go to Church. It is but fair therefore to consider my ministrations as extending to those 430 persons, and not merely to the average number of attendants at the two chapels, in which I serve. It may also be fairly said respecting all my brother Clergyman in this Deanery, and perhaps in the country districts generally, that their ministrations extend to everyone in their parishes, not professed dissenters: and the thought that the Church's usefulness in this matter receives no recognition in these returns, nay, is entirely passed over, is the reason that makes them so unpopular among the Clergy. Indeed in this neighbourhood, where the population is so scattered, and the roads so bad, the weekly duty of visitation is far more laborious than the Sunday duty. It should also be remarked that the weather has a great effect on our congregations. When there has been much rain, the path becomes saturated with water, and the women and children, whose shoes are frequently thin and torn, can scarcely be expected to come to church on such Sundays. They must remain with their feet extremely wet during Divine Service, and their health suffer in consequence. I have also made the required return of the gross income of my benefice, but about £50 which I pay for rates and other necessary outgoings, and £41 10s 10d which I have paid this year to Queen Ann's [sic] Bounty for this house ought fairly to be deducted in order to ascertain the real value.

Hubert McLaughlin, Rural Dean and Rector of Burford,
1st Portion,
County of Salop, Diocese of Hereford.
Address Rectory, Boraston, Tenbury   March 31 1851

75. BURFORD HO 129/161/73
WESLEYAN METHODIST CHAPEL. Altered from a mansion in the year 1849. A separate and entire building. Used exclusively for worship. *Free sittings* 18; *other sittings* 150. *On 30 March* In afternoon General Congregation 100, Sunday Scholars 90, total 270 [sic]; in evening General Congregation 250. *Average attendance* during previous 12 months, in morning General Congregation 300, Sunday Scholars 90. *Signed* John Dowty, Minister, Witney.

76. BURFORD HO 129/161/74[1]
PLYMOUTH BRETHREN CHAPEL, College Yard. An old soap and candle loft. Not a separate and entire building. *Free sittings* 650. *On 30 March* General Congregation about 20. *Remarks* The best information I could obtain. *Signed* Thomas Cheatle, Registrar.
1. See also Burford Baptist Chapel. Cheatle used one form for two entries.

77. BURFORD HO 129/161/74[1]
BAPTIST CHAPEL. *Erected* about the year 1800. A separate and entire building. Used exclusively for worship. *On 30 March* General Congregation about 100, Sunday Scholars about 30. *Remarks* The best information I could obtain. *Signed* Thomas Cheatle, Registrar.
1. See also Burford Plymouth Brethren Chapel.

78. BURFORD HO 129/161/75
FRIENDS' MEETING HOUSE. *Erected* before 1800. A separate and entire building. Used exclusively for worship. *Admeasurement* in superficial feet floor area 618; in galleries 165. *Estimated Number of Persons capable of being seated* 176 and in galleries 48. *On 30 March* In morning 5 attendants; in afternoon 5 attendants. *Signed* Robert Sessions,[1] Charlbury.
1. *Gardner* describes R. Sessions, Charlbury, as a draper and grocer.

79. CASSINGTON Population 454 HO 129/160/49
PARISH CHURCH. *Erected* in the twelfth century by Geoffrey de Clinton, according to published records. *Endowed* with land in lieu of tithe under an Enclosure Act, permanent endowment Parliamentary Grant Fund, Queen Anne's Bounty, fees inconsiderable. *Free sittings* about 200; *other sittings* about 100. *On 30 March* In morning General Congregation 73, Sunday Scholars 40; in afternoon General Congregation 49, Sunday Scholars 40. *Signed* Thomas Forster, Vicar, 3 St. John's Terrace, Oxford.

80. CAULCOTT[1]   HO 129/159/9
WESLEYAN METHODIST CHAPEL. A separate and entire building.
Used exclusively for worship. *On 30 March* In afternoon General
Congregation 80; in evening General Congregation 88. *Average
attendance* in morning General Congregation 50. *Remarks* A return was
sent from the Superintendent of the Circuit from the Brackley district.
Signed George Cooper, Overseer, Lower Heyford.
1. Caulcott was a hamlet in Lower Heyford parish. Other returns for this chapel were made
under Lower Heyford (see below).

81. CAVERSFIELD[1]   HO 129/159/54
Free sittings 40, *other sittings* 60. *On 30 March* In afternoon General
Congregation 41, Sunday Scholars 16. *Average attendance* in afternoon
General Congregation 41, Sunday Scholars 16.
1. Transferred from Buckinghamshire in 1844. Caversfield does not appear to be separately
enumerated in printed figures drawn from subsequent population censuses for Oxfordshire
(*VCH Oxon.* Vol. 2, pp. 214-24). This return presumably refers to the Anglican Church of
St. Lawrence, the fabric of which dates in part from late Saxon times.

82. CAVERSHAM   Population 1752   HO 129/155/23
CHURCH. *On 30 March* In morning General Congregation 260; in
afternoon General Congregation 2[?]10. *Remarks* The Parish Clerk
informs me the above numbers are a fair estimate. *Signed* Robert Coates,
Registrar.

83. CAVERSHAM   HO 129/155/24
INDEPENDENT CHAPEL. A separate and entire building. Used
exclusively for worship. *Free sittings* 200. *On 30 March* In morning
Sunday Scholars 14, in afternoon Sunday Scholars 40; in evening
General Congregation 60. *Average attendance* during previous 9 months,
in morning Sunday Scholars 35; in afternoon Sunday Scholars 50; in
evening General Congregation 60. *Remarks* I have services held by
myself in this place, 3 sabbaths each month and rest are supplied by lay
preachers from Reading. There are besides week services. *Signed* John
Davies, Minister, 33 Broad Street, Reading.   ·

84. CHADLINGTON   Population 709[1]   HO 129/162/15
ANCIENT CHAPEL. *Sittings* 205. *Average attendance* in morning
General Congregation 85, Sunday Scholars 70; in evening General
Congregation 110, Sunday Scholars 40. *Remarks* The sittings are all free,
but most of them appropriated by the churchwardens. *Signed* Thomas
Andrew Walker, Curate, Chadlington.
1. A chapelry in Charlbury parish.

85. CHADLINGTON   HO 129/162/16
BAPTIST CHAPEL. *Erected* 1840. A separate and entire building. Used exclusively for worship. *Free sittings* 230. *On 30 March* In afternoon General Congregation 60, Sunday Scholars 60; in evening General Congregation 95. *Average attendance* in afternoon General Congregation 140; in evening ditto.[1] *Remarks* Our congregation on morning affected by the weather. *Signed* Thomas Eden, Baptist Minister, Chadlington.

1. Unclear whether ditto refers to the evening attendance figure of 95 on 30 March, which appears above, or to that of 140, the average afternoon attendance, which appears alongside.

86. CHADLINGTON   HO 129/162/17
BAPTIST CHAPEL. Not a separate and entire building. Not used exclusively for worship. *Free sittings* 40. *On 30 March* In morning General Congregation 12; in evening General Congregation 12. *Average attendance* during previous 12 months, in evening General Congregation 30. *Remarks* This place is occupied as a dwelling house and was opened for public worship in 1846. *Signed* William Willis, Manager, Chadlington.

87. CHALGROVE   Population 616   HO 129/156/2
PARISH CHURCH. *Erected* before 1800. *Endowed* with land £1 5s[+], tithe £152 7s 6d,[#] glebe £2 10s-, other permanent endowments £10 10s, total £176 12s 6d.* *Free sittings* 109; *other sittings* 228, Sunday Scholars 50. *On 30 March* In afternoon General Congregation 103, Sunday Scholars 33; in evening General Congregation 20. *Average attendance* during previous 12 months, in morning General Congregation from 80-113, Sunday Scholars from 30-40; in afternoon General Congregation from 130-150, Sunday Scholars from 30-40; in evening General Congregation from 20-70. *Remarks* + is rent of churchyard; # mentioned in apportionment of rent charge but variable; - is exclusive of House Garden and Orchard; * this is the gross amount. Deduct about £37 for rates and about 5 per cent for collection. This church is held with Berrick Salome, a return for which is made separately. *Signed* Robert French Laurence, Vicar.

88. CHALGROVE   HO 129/156/3
WESLEYAN METHODIST CHAPEL. *Erected* about 1821. A separate and entire building. Used exclusively for worship. *Free sittings* 70; *other sittings* 50. *On 30 March* In morning General Congregation 82; in evening General Congregation 100. *Average attendance* during previous

12 months, in morning General Congregation 50; in afternoon General Congregation 70; in evening General Congregation 50. *Remarks* Alternately the service is held morning and afternoon. *Signed* John Auger, Steward, Wheelwright, Chalgrove.

89. CHARLBURY[1]   Population 1477   HO 129/162/9
PROTESTANT CHURCH.[2] *Erected* So old nobody knows when. *Free sittings* All open except the Lord of the Manor, the Rector and Vicar.*Average attendance* General Congregation from 4 to 500, Sunday Scholars and weekdays about 159. *Signed* Thomas Silver, Vicar.
1. The parish of Charlbury included Fawler, Finstock (*q.v.*), and Walcot hamlets, and the chapelries of Chadlington East (*q.v.*), and Shorthampton (*q.v.*).
2. This title, the date (29 September 1851), and the address are written in a clerk's hand. The remaining incomplete information is scrawled in and signed by Thomas Silver, Vicar.

90. CHARLBURY   HO 129/162/10
FRIENDS' MEETING HOUSE, Thames Street. *Erected* before 1800. A separate and entire building. Used exclusively for worship and occasionally for meetings of the Bible and Peace Societies etc. *Admeasurement* in superficial feet floor area 897. *Estimated Number of Persons capable of being seated* about 250. *On 30 March* In morning 39 attendants; in afternoon 27 attendants. *Signed* Robert Sessions[1], Charlbury.
1. *Gardner* describes R. Sessions, Charlbury, as a draper and grocer.

91. CHARLBURY   HO 129/162/11
WESLEYAN METHODIST CHAPEL. *Erected* 1823. A separate and entire building. Used exclusively for worship. *Free sittings* 86; *other sittings* 150. *On 30 March* In afternoon General Congregation 200, Sunday Scholars 30; in evening General Congregation 220. *Signed* W.S. Allen, Steward, Tailor and Draper, Charlbury.

92. CHARLTON ON OTMOOR[1]
                          Population 368   HO 129/159/5
PARISH CHURCH. *Erected* before 1800. *Free sittings* 300. *On 30 March* In morning General Congregation 80, Sunday Scholars 30; in afternoon General Congregation 80, Sunday Scholars 30. *Average attendance* in morning General Congregation 80, Sunday Scholars 30; in afternoon General Congregation 80, Sunday Scholars 30.
1. The parish of Charlton on Otmoor also included Fencot and Murcott (*q.v.*) hamlets. The total population of the parish was 657.

93. CHARLTON ON OTMOOR   HO 129/159/17
BAPTIST CHAPEL. *Erected* about 1836. A seperate and entire building. Used exclusively for worship. *Free sittings* 180. *On 30 March* In morning General Congregation 40, Sunday Scholars 20; in evening General Congregation 61, about 70 [sic], Sunday Scholars 14.

94. CHARLTON ON OTMOOR   HO 129/159/18
WESLEYAN METHODIST CHAPEL. *Erected* 1840. A separate and entire building. Used exclusively for worship. *Free sittings* all.[1] *On 30 March* In afternoon General Congregation 25, in evening General Congregation 29. *Signed* Frederick Clements, Wesleyan local preacher, Kirtlington.[2]

1. There is an unreferenced supplementary return for this chapel stating that all sittings were free, appropriated sittings 20, total sittings 100. This was also signed by Frederick Clements.
2. *Gardner* describes Frederick Clements, Kirtlington, as a shoemaker.

95. CHASTLETON   Population 236   HO 129/162/32
PARISH CHURCH OF ST. MARY THE VIRGIN. *Erected* before 1800. *Endowed* with land i.e. tithe £518. *Free sittings* 80; *other sittings* 80. *On 30 March* In morning General Congregation 103, Sunday Scholars 27; in afternoon General Congregation 75, Sunday Scholars 27. *Average attendance* during previous 12 months, in morning General Congregation 70, Sunday Scholars 27; in afternoon General Congregation 70, Sunday Scholars 27. *Signed* Horatio Westmacott, Rector.

96. CHECKENDON   Population 410   HO 129/155/25
ST. PETER AND ST. PAUL'S PARISH CHURCH. Very ancient, partly built before the Norman Conquest. *Endowed* with tithe £560 but each £100 rapidly decreasing now to £70, glebe £94, rectory house, garden and 3 small meadows. *Free sittings* 200. *On 30 March* In morning General Congregation 66, Sunday Scholars 46; in afternoon General Congregation 53, Sunday Scholars 46. *Average attendance* during previous 12 months, in morning General Congregation 115, Sunday Scholars 46; in afternoon General Congregation 70, Sunday Scholars 46. *Remarks* The Rent-charge proportioned was £560 but each £100 now had decreased to £96 11s 5d and rapidly decreasing to about £70. *Signed* William Crabtree, Rector.

97. CHESTERTON   Population 435   HO 129/159/15
PARISH CHURCH. *Erected* before 1800. *Endowed* with land gross rent £200, glebe say £15, fees say £2. *Free sittings* 95; *other sittings* 105

besides children's benches. *On 30 March* In morning General Congregation 85, Sunday Scholars 46; in afternoon General Congregation 108, Sunday Scholars 47. *Average attendance* in morning probably General Congregation 100, Sunday Scholars 50; in afternoon General Congregation 120, Sunday Scholars 54. *Signed* William F. Fortescue, Vicar.

98. CHILSON[1]   HO 129/162/14
PRIMITIVE METHODIST CHAPEL. *Erected* in 1844. Not a separate and entire building. It is also a dwelling house. *Free sittings* 80. *On 30 March* In morning General Congregation 70; in evening General Congregation 75. *Signed* Henry Heys, Minister, Witney, and Joseph Robinson, Leader.

1. A hamlet in the Shorthampton chapelry of Charlbury parish. *Gardner* describes it as consisting of two farm houses, several cottages, and 400 rateable acres. Joshua Robinson, Chilson, is listed as beer retailer.

99. CHINNOR   Population 1257   HO 129/150/8
ST. ANDREW'S PARISH CHURCH. *Erected* before 1800. *Endowed* with tithe £330, glebe £20. *Free sittings* 350; *other sittings* 100. *On 30 March* In afternoon 216. *Average attendance* during previous 6 months, in morning General Congregation 40, Sunday Scholars 80; in afternoon General Congregation 180, Sunday Scholars 80. *Remarks* The above return of income is the net not the gross rental. *Signed* W.A. Musgrave, Rector.

100. CHINNOR   HO 129/150/16
PRIMITIVE METHODIST CHAPEL, Chapel Row. *Erected* July 20 1847. A separate and entire building. Used excusively for worship. *Free sittings* 100; *other sittings* 70. *On 30 March* In morning General Congregation 60, Sunday Scholars 30; in afternoon General Congregation 140, Sunday Scholars 36; in evening General Congregation 170. *Average attendance* during previous 12 months, in morning General Congregation 60, Sunday Scholars 30; in afternoon General Congregation 140, Sunday Scholars 36; in evening General Congregation 170. *Remarks* By the filling up you will see the figures do not exactly correspond in the M[orning] 60 attend, besides 30 children. Total 90. A[fternoon] 140 and 36 children Total 176 because the children are smaller and as the chapel is full A[fternoon] and Ev[ening] it will just correspond to the lower one for A[fternoon] (viz.) 176. *Signed* Henry J.Allen, P.M. Minister, Chinnor (Chapel House).

101. CHINNOR HO 129/150/18
INDEPENDENT CHAPEL. *Erected* A.D. 1805. A separate and entire building. Used exclusively for worship. *Free sittings* 272; *other sittings* 205. *On 30 March* In morning General Congregation 190, Sunday Scholars 116; in afternoon Sunday Scholars 127; in evening General Congregation 170. *Average attendance* during previous 12 months, in morning General Congregation 225, Sunday Scholars 116; in afternoon Sunday Scholars 127; in evening General Congregation 200. *Remarks* Divine Service in this place every Sunday morning and evening which the Minister performs, the afternoon being devoted to the scriptural instruction of the children in the Sunday School. There are also two services in every week, and to which the Minister attends. *Signed* Joseph Mason, Minister, Chinnor.

102. CHIPPING NORTON[1] Population 2932 HO 129/162/47
ST. MARY'S PARISH CHURCH. *Erected* before 1800. *Endowed* with land £118, other permanent endowment £27, fees £20, other sources £20. *Free sittings* 455; *other sittings* 730. *On 30 March* In morning General Congregation 373, Sunday Scholars 154; in afternoon General Congregation 453, Sunday Scholars 160. *Average attendance* during previous 9 months in morning General Congregation 400; in afternoon General Congregation 500; Sunday Scholars about the same as on the 31 March. *Remarks* The congregation varies very much, the average is the lowest, it rises often to 7 and 800 in the evening. *Signed* Alexander Whishaw, Vicar.
1. The parish of Chipping Norton included Over Norton hamlet. The total population of the parish was 3,368.

103. CHIPPING NORTON HO 129/162/48
TRINITY ROMAN CATHOLIC CHURCH. *Erected* 1837. A separate and entire building. Used exclusively for worship. *Free sittings* 80; *other sittings* 80. *On 30 March* In morning General Congregation 127; in evening General Congregation 100. *Signed* John Mitchell, Roman Catholic Clergyman, Chipping Norton.

104. CHIPPING NORTON HO 129/162/49
WESLEYAN METHODIST CHAPEL. *Erected* 1798. A separate and entire building. Used exclusively for worship. *Free sittings* 120; *other sittings* 200. *On 30 March* In morning General Congregation 150, Sunday Scholars 120; in afternoon General Congregation 40; in evening General Congregation 280. *Remarks* The afternoon service has been but recently commenced. *Signed* Samuel Cooke, Minister, Chipping Norton.

105. CHIPPING NORTON   HO   129/162/50
BAPTIST CHAPEL, New Street. *Erected* before 1800. A separate and
entire building. Used exclusively for worship. *Free sittings 83; other
sittings* 215, and gallery for 120 Sunday School children. *On 30 March* in
morning General Congregation 198, Sunday Scholars 105; in evening
General Congregation 295. *Signed* Thomas Bliss, Minister, Church
Street, Chipping Norton.

106. CHIPPING NORTON   HO   129/162/51
PARTICULAR BAPTIST ROOM. Not a separate and entire building.
Used exclusively for worship. *Free sittings* 80. *On 30 March* In morning
General Congregation 5; in afternoon General Congregation 80. *Signed*
Robert Roff, Minister, Stow on the Wold, Gloucestershire.

107. CHIPPING NORTON   HO   129/162/52
FRIENDS' MEETING HOUSE, New Street. *Erected* 1804. A separate
and entire building. Used exclusively for worship and occasionally for
meetings of the Bible and Peace Societies etc. *Admeasurement* in
superficial feet floor area 1225. *Estimated Number of Persons capable of
being seated* about 550. *On 30 March* In morning 15 attendants; in
afternoon 13 attendants. *Signed* Robert Sessions,[1] Charlbury.
1. *Gardner* describes R. Sessions, Charlbury, as a grocer and draper.

108. CHISLEHAMPTON   Population 152   HO 129/123/47
ST. KATHERINE'S CHAPEL. *Free sittings* 120. *On 30 March* In
morning General Congregation 60, Sunday Scholars 50. *Signed* John
Polley, Registrar of Births and Deaths.

109. CHRISTMAS COMMON[1]   HO 129/155/43
WESLEYAN METHODIST CHAPEL. *Erected* 1824. A separate and
entire building. Used exclusively for worship. *Free sittings* 110; *other
sittings* 35. *On 30 March* In afternoon General Congregation 50, Sunday
Scholars 22; in evening General Congregation 47. *Average attendance*
during previous 12 months, in afternoon General Congregation 60,
Sunday Scholars 20; in evening General Congregation 55. *Signed*
Benjamin Seymour, Chapel Steward, Christmas Common.
1. Hamlet in Watlington parish.

110. CHURCHILL   Population 645   HO 129/162/29
ALL SAINTS' PARISH CHURCH. Consecrated October 20 1827 in
lieu of an old church too much dilapidated to admit of repair. *Erected*, at
a cost of £10,000, at the sole expense of James Haughton Langston Esq.

Endowed with land commutation at the time of enclosure £127, other permament endowment charged upon estate at Merriscourt. *Free sittings* 500. *On 30 March* In morning General Congregation 96, Sunday Scholars 100; in afternoon General Congregation 328, Sunday Scholars 114. *Average attendance* in morning General Congregation 100, Sunday Scholars 110; in afternoon General Congregation 350, Sunday Scholars 120. *Signed* Charles Barter, Vicar.

111. CLANFIELD   Population 591   HO 129/161/28
WESLEYAN METHODIST CHAPEL. *Erected* 1823. A separate and entire building. Used exclusively for worship. *Free sittings* 80. *On 30 March* In afternoon General Congregation 82; in evening General Congregation 84. *Signed* James Clack, Manager, Clanfield.

112. CLANFIELD   HO 129/161/29
PRIMITIVE METHODIST CHAPEL. *Erected* 1844. A separate and entire building. Used exclusively for worship. *Free sittings* 60; *other sittings* 16. *On 30 March* In morning General Congregation 45, Sunday Scholars 24; in afternoon Sunday Scholars 24; in evening General Congregation 102. *Average attendance* during previous 12 months, in evening General Congregation 90. *Remarks* There have not been either morning service or Sabbath school of 12 months. *Signed* Thomas Merrick, Steward, Clanfield.

113. CLAYDON[1]   Population 330   HO 129/163/86
CHURCH. *On 30 March* In morning General Congregation 150. *Remarks* Revd Mr. Sheldon refused to make any return. *Signed* Thomas Pearce, Registrar, Bourton, nr. Banbury.
1. A chapelry in Cropredy parish.

114. CLAYDON   HO 129/163/79
PRIMITIVE METHODIST CHAPEL. *Erected* 1837. A separate and entire building. Used exclusively for worship. *Free sittings* 45; *other sittings* 45. *On 30 March* In afternoon General Congregation 46, Sunday Scholars 5; in evening General Congregation 50, Sunday Scholars 3. *Signed* John Tarvey, Leader of the Society, Carpenter, Claydon.

115. CLEVELEY[1]   HO 129/162/59
BAPTIST MEETING HOUSE. Not a separate and entire building. A dwelling house not used exclusively for worship. *Free sittings* 95. *On 30 March* In afternoon General Congregation 91, no school. *Average attendance* during previous 15 months in afternoon generally the same.

Remarks There has been a cause in the hamlet of Cleveley for near 40 years. We have no School for want of room. *Signed* Thomas Eden, Minister, Chadlington.
1. A hamlet in Enstone parish.

116. CLIFTON HAMPDEN Population 369　　HO 129/123/51
ST. MICHAEL'S EPISCOPAL CHAPEL. *On 30 March* In morning General Congregation 140, Sunday Scholars 60. *Signed* John Polley, District Registrar.

117. CLIFTON[1]　　　　　　　　　HO 129/160/5
WESLEYAN METHODIST CHAPEL. *Erected* about 1815. A separate and entire building. Used Exclusively for worship. *Free sittings* 24; *other sittings* 55. *On 30 March* In morning General Congregation 50; in afternoon General Congregation 40. *Signed* Cornelius Davis,[2] Chapel Steward, Deddington.
1. A hamlet and township in the parish of Deddington. Its population in 1841 was 277.
2. *Gardner* describes Cornelius Davis, Deddington, as a painter etc.

118. CLIFTON　　　　　　　　　　HO 129/160/6
CLIFTON CHURCH. At present a barn is fitted up and used for Divine Service called 'Clifton Church'. A site is given and stone being dug for a church to be named 'St. James'. Probably it will at present be a Chapel of Ease. The barn is used with the consent of the Bishop. The barn is rented by Revd W. Wilson of Over Worton House. The church will be erected by subscription, but *principally* by the Revd W. Cotton Risley. Cost unknown but perhaps £500 with the worth of site etc. *Free sittings* 230, the church about to be erected. The barn all free sittings 200. *On 30 March* In evening General Congregation 182. *Average attendance* during previous 5 months, in evening General Congregation 140 and slowly increasing. *Remarks* The information is somewhat vague but the circumstances will explain the cause of this. As many of the Sunday Scholars as can do so go to the Parish Church in the morning and afternoon. Any who attend in the evening do not come as Sunday Scholars. *Signed* George Venables, Curate, Officiating Minister, Deddington.

119. COGGES　　　Population 814　　HO 129/161/50
ST. MARY'S CHURCH. Permanent endowment believed about £70. *Free sittings* about 300; *other sittings* 100. *On 30 March* In afternoon General Congregation about 120; Sunday Scholars 20. *Signed* Henry Gregory, Acting Curate, Cogges.

120. COGGES   HO 129/161/52
NEWLAND WESLEYAN METHODIST CHAPEL. *Erected* 1824. A
separate and entire building. Used exclusively for worship. *Free sittings*
All.[1] *On 30 March* In afternoon General Congregation 60. *Signed* Joseph
Harris, Manager, Cogges.

1. HO 129/161/51 is a supplementary return, signed Joseph Harris, Chapel Keeper, stating
that the chapel contained 100 free sittings.

121. CORNWELL   Population 110   HO 129/162/31
PARISH CHURCH. *Erected* before 1800. *Endowed* with glebe 100 acres
vide remarks. *Free sittings* 43; *other sittings* 36, children's sittings 8. *On
30 March* In morning General Congregation 39, Sunday Scholars 26.
Average attendance in morning General Congregation 40, Sunday
Scholars 25. *Remarks* Tithes commuted for 100 acres of land. I sh[ou]ld
say that the attendance on the 30th was the average attendance
throughout the year. *Signed* James Beck, Curate.

122. COTE[1]   HO 129/161/19
BAPTIST CHAPEL. *Erected* more than 100 years ago. A separate and
entire building. Used exclusively for worship. *Free sittings* 250. *On 30
March* In morning General Congregation 200, Sunday Scholars 40.
Average attendance during previous 36 months, in morning General
Congregation 200, Sunday Scholars 50. *Remarks* Coate Chapel has
connected with it four other small chapels situate at Bampton, Aston,
and Standlake, Oxon., and Buckland, Berks., at each of which the
minister of Coate and other members of the congregation officiate in
succession. *Signed* John Jackson, Minister, Aston House, nr Bampton.

1. see also Aston and Cote.

123. COTTISFORD   Population 263   HO 129/159/62
PARISH CHURCH situated about the centre of a scattered parish. *Free
sittings* 70; *other sittings* 40. *Average attendance* in morning General
Congregation 30, Sunday Scholars 40; in afternoon General
Congregation 80, Sunday Scholars 20. *Remarks* The gross annual value
and the net annual value of the living of Cottisford are equal; that is £338
3s. The glebe land and the tithe being let and compounded for at the
above sum. The tenants paying all parochial rates and other out goings
except land tax and income tax. The above is exclusive of the value of the
rectory house, garden and orchard, but includes one acre of land lately
added to the curacy adjoining to the rectory house. *Signed* W. Talman,
Curate. Mr. Talman quits Cottisford April 3rd and is succeeded as curate
by Mr. Dewar.

124. COTTISFORD   HO 129/159/63
WESLEYAN METHODIST CHAPEL. *Erected* 1844. Not a separate
and entire building. Not used exclusively for worship. *Free sittings* 50.
On 30 March In evening General Congregation 30. *Remarks* Services
constantly held in a dwelling house. *Signed* Thomas Lavine, Tenant,
Juniper, Cottisford.

125. COWLEY   Population 775   HO 129/157/24
ST. JAMES' PARISH CHURCH. *Erected* before 1800. *Endowed* with
land £50, fees £3, other sources £36 10s. *Free sittings* 300. *On 30 March*
In morning General Congregation 219, Sunday Scholars 58; in afternoon
General Congregation 135, Sunday Scholars 48. *Remarks* In the
afternoon a storm kept about 100 away. *Signed* R.M. Benson, Perpetual
Curate.

126. CRAWLEY[1]   Population 245   HO 129/161/40
ST. PETER'S CHAPEL. A Chapel of Ease to Witney. Crawley is a
hamlet with separate parochial rates, but is part of the tithing of Witney.
Consecrated August 13th 1847 as an additional church. *Erected*
principally by the private benefaction of the Rector of Witney at a cost of
about £300. No endowment. *Free sittings* 144; *other sittings* 6. *On 30
March* In afternoon General Congregation 91, Sunday Scholars 24.
Average attendance during previous 12 months, in morning General
Congregation 50; in evening General Congregation 60. *Remarks* The
service is more frequently in the evening. *Signed* George Crabb Rolfe,
Officiating Minister, Hailey Parsonage.
1. A hamlet and chapelry in Witney parish.

127. CRAWLEY   HO 129/161/41
INDEPENDENT CHAPEL. *Erected* before 1800. A separate and entire
building. Used exclusively for worship. *Free sittings* 60. *Average
attendance* in afternoon General Congregation 20. *Remarks* The chapel
is sold to the Society of Quakers by the Independents paying a sum yearly
they are allow[d] to preach therein. *Signed* Thomas East, Deputy
Registrar, Witney.

128. CROPREDY[1]   Population 596   HO 129/163/78
PARISH CHURCH *On 30 March* In morning General Congregation
200; in afternoon General Congregation 300. *Average attendance* in
morning Sunday Scholars 40; in afternoon Sunday Scholars 40. *Remarks*
The Revd Mr. Burdett[2], refused to make any return. I should say that the
return of attendants at morning and evening is rather under than over the

number. *Signed* Thomas Pearce, Registrar, Bourton, nr. Banbury.
1. The parish of Cropredy also included the township of Great and Little Bourton, (*q.v.*) the chapelries of Claydon (*q.v.*) and Wardington (*q.v.*), and part of the chapelry of Mollington (*q.v.*). The total population of the parish was 2,602.
2. Revd H.R. Burdett.

129. CROPREDY   HO 129/163/80
WELSLEYAN METHODIST CHAPEL. *Erected* about 1820. A separate and entire building. Used exclusively for worship. *Free sittings* 60, *other sittings* 100. *On 30 March* In morning Sunday Scholars 45; in afternoon General Congregation 73, Sunday Scholars 56; in evening General Congregation 90, Sunday Scholars 10. *Signed* James Wise,[1] Manager, Cropredy.
1. *Gardner* describes James Wise, Cropredy, as a basket maker.

130. CROWELL   Population 157   HO 129/156/18
PARISH CHURCH. *Erected* before 1800. *Endowed* with tithe commuted at £243 10s, glebe £6 10s, gross annual amount. *Free sittings* 36; *other sittings* 106. *On 30 March* In afternoon General Congregation 53, Sunday Scholars 26. *Average attendance* during previous 12 months, in morning General Congregation 40, Sunday Scholars 20; in afternoon General Congregation 70, Sunday Scholars 20. *Signed* James Beauchamp, Rector.

131. CROWMARSH GIFFORD   Population 373   HO 129/125/51
ST. MARY MAGDALEN'S PARISH CHURCH. *Erected* before 1800. *Endowed* with tithe £247, fees £1 10s. *Free sittings* 80; *other sittings* 120. *Average attendance* during previous 12 months, in morning General Congregation 50, Sunday Scholars 20; in afternoon General Congregation 130, Sunday Scholars 18. *Signed* John Trollope, Rector.

132. CUDDESDON[1]   Population 337   HO 129/157/3
PARISH CHURCH.[2] *Average attendance* in morning General Congregation 250.
1. The parish of Cuddesdon also included Chippinghurst hamlet, Denton Chapelry and Wheatley (*q.v.*) Chapelry. The total population of the parish was 1542.
2. See Garsington. In 1854 the incumbent was Revd Alfred Pott, who reported in response to Bishop Wilberforce's visitation queries that the average Sunday congregation was constant at '200 adults about'. There were no Dissenting places of worship or Dissenters.

133. CULHAM   Population 417   HO 129/123/52
PARISH CHURCH. *Endowed* with glebe about £100, fees £1. *Free sittings* about 150; *other sittings* 25 exclusive of children. *On 30 March*

Good congregation. *Average attendance* in morning good, in afternoon good. *Remarks* I have no exact account of the number of sittings and I do no enumerate my congregation. *Signed* Robert Walker, Vicar.

134. CURBRIDGE[1]   Population 767   HO 129/161/42
PARISH CHURCH. *Erected* before 1 January 1800. *Free sittings* 358; *other sittings* 600. *Average attendance* during previous 12 months, in morning General Congregation 276, Sunday Scholars 124; in afternoon General Congregation 270, Sunday Scholars 20. *Remarks* The gross income of the Rectory is about £2000. *Signed* Thomas East, Deputy Registrar.
1. A hamlet in Witney parish.

135. CUXHAM   Population 172   HO 129/155/38
CHURCH. *On 30 March* In morning General Congregation 40; in afternoon General Congregation 45. *Remarks* Information given by the Clerk of Cuxham.

136. DEDDINGTON[1]   Population 2178   HO 129/160/2
ST. PETER AND ST. PAUL'S PARISH CHURCH. *Erected* before 1800. *Endowed* with land £65, glebe £9, other permanent endowment £80, fees £6, Easter Offerings £5. *Free sittings* 320, *other sittings* 580, besides forms for the school children. *On 30 March* In morning General Congregation 314, Sunday Scholars 210; in afternoon General Congregation 410, Sunday Scholars 180. *Average attendance* during previous 12 months, in morning General Congregation 229, Sunday Scholars 140; in afternoon General Congregation 287, Sunday Scholars 120. *Remarks* The congregation has been gradually increasing since February 1850. *Signed* George Venables, Curate, Deddington.
1. The parish of Deddington also included Clifton (*q.v.*) and Hempton (*q.v.*) hamlets.

137. DEDDINGTON   HO 129/160/3
INDEPENDENT OR CONGREGATIONAL CHAPEL. First used as a chapel about 1820. Reopened 1846. A separate and entire building. Used exclusively for worship. *Free sittings* 50; *other sittings* 150. *On 30 March* In morning General Congregation 103, Sunday Scholars 20; in evening General Congregation 123, Sunday Scholars 10. *Average attendance* during previous 15 months, in morning General Congregation 110, Sunday Scholars 30; in evening General Congregation 130, Sunday Scholars 20. *Signed* Obed Parker, Minister, Deddington.

138. DEDDINGTON   HO 129/60/4
WESLEYAN METHODIST CHAPEL. *Erected* before 1800. A separate and entire building. Used exclusively for worship. *Free sittings* 40; *other sittings* 130. *On 30 March* In afternoon General Congregation 160; in evening General Congregation 147. *Signed* John Calcutt,[1] Steward, Deddington.

1. *Gardner* describes one John Calcutt, Deddington, as a bookseller, stationer and printer, and another as a farmer.

139. DORCHESTER   Population 1061   HO 129/125/24
ST. BIRINUS' ROMAN CATHOLIC CHURCH. *Erected* in 1828-9. A separate and entire building. Used exclusively for worship. *Free sittings* 50; *other sittings* 15. *On 30 March* In morning General Congregation 60; in afternoon General Congregation 60. *Average attendance* in morning General Congregation 60. *Signed* Robert Newsham, Catholic Priest, Dorchester.

140. DORCHESTER   HO 129/125/25
BAPTIST CHAPEL. *Erected* about 1837. A separate and entire building. Used exclusively for worship. *Free sittings* 26. *On 30 March* In afternoon General Congregation 76; in evening General Congregation 100. *Average attendance* in afternoon General Congregation; in evening General Congregation 120. *Remarks* The sittings are all free. Dorchester is a Village 4 miles distance from the town of Wallingford. *Signed* John Oldham, Minister, Wallingford, Berkshire.

141. DORCHESTER   HO 129/125/26
PRIMITIVE METHODIST CHAPEL. *Erected* 1839. A separate and entire building. Used exclusively for worship. *Free sittings* 132; *other sittings* 18. *On 30 March* In evening General Congregation 80. *Signed* G. Wallis, Minister, Wallingford, Berkshire.

142. DRAYTON[1]   Population 327   HO 129/123/49
ST. LEONARD'S PARISH CHURCH. *Erected* before 1800. *Endowed* with land £35, other permanent endowment £75, fees £1. *Free sittings* 100, *other sittings* 80. *On 30 March* In morning General Congregation 60, Sunday Scholars 30; in afternoon General Congregation 48, Sunday Scholars 10. *Average attendance* The above is about the average number of Attendants at this Church. *Signed* Joseph Coley, Perpetual Curate.

1. In Dorchester Hundred.

143. DRAYTON   HO 129/123/50
WESLEYAN METHODIST CHAPEL. *Erected* 1814. A separate and
entire building. Used exclusively for worship. *Free sittings* 46; *other
sittings* 58. *On 30 March* In morning Sunday Scholars 41; in afternoon
General Congregation 58, Sunday Scholars 35; in evening General
Congregation 91. *Signed* James Horn, Steward, Drayton.[1]
1. *Gardner* describes James Horn, Drayton, as a shopkeeper.

144. DRAYTON[1]   Population 224   HO 129/163/65
ST. PETER'S CHURCH. *Erected* in 14th century or before. *Endowed*
by land and corn rents, fees p.a. £1. *Free sittings* 200; *other sittings* 60.
On 30 March In morning General Congregation 50; in afternoon General
Congregation 80. *Signed* William Lloyd, Rector.
1. In Bloxham Hundred.

145. DUCKLINGTON[1]   Population 443   HO 129/161/48
ST. BARTHOLOMEW'S PARISH CHURCH. *Erected* before 1800.
Free sittings 100; *other sittings* 100. *Average attendance* in morning
General Congregation 60, Sunday Scholars 40; in afternoon General
Congregation 100, Sunday Scholars 30. *Signed* Thomas East, Deputy
Registrar, Witney.
1. The parish of Ducklington also included Hardwick (*q.v.*) hamlet. The total population
of the parish was 571.

146. DUNS TEW   Population 452   HO 129/160/17
ST. MARY MAGDALENE'S PARISH CHURCH. *Erected* before
1800. *Endowed* with glebe 180 acres £250, fees £1. *Sittings* 200. *On 30
March* In morning General Congregation 70, Sunday Scholars 80; in
afternoon General Congregation 90, Sunday Scholars 80. *Signed*
Archibald Malcolm, Minister, Duns Tew.

147. DUNS TEW   HO 129/160/18
PRIMITIVE METHODIST CHAPEL. A dwelling house. *Free sittings*
53. *On 30 March* In afternoon General Congregation 53; in evening
General Congregation 65. *Average attendance* during previous 6 months,
in afternoon General Congregation 55. *Signed* John Goodwin[1], Duns
Tew.
1. Goodwin also adds the name of William Clever, Local Preacher.

148. EASINGTON   Population 18   HO 129/156/1
ST. PETER'S CHURCH. An ancient extra parochial church, and
although in the heart of the Diocese of Oxford, yet forms a portion of
the See of Lincoln. The patronage is in the Bishop of Lincoln for the time

being. Situated in a village called Easington which contains only two houses, one cottage and the Parsonage. *Erected* before 1800 as an extra parochial parish church, built when the parish was populous, anciently a handsome structure with a large Parsonage House. The population, ecclesiastical elegance, and roomy manse have all disappeared. *Endowed* with tithe commuted at £72 4s, glebe let at present for £12. *Free sittings* all the church, perhaps 100. *On 30 March* In morning General Congregation 6. *Average attendance* during previous 12 months, there is but one service alternate. Average between 7 and 10 beside minister and clerk. No children in the parish except my own. *Remarks* The entire population of my parish, exclusive of my own family has not averaged more than 14 souls for some years. There is in it no inn, no shop, no tradesman or mechanic or artizan of any kind. The extent of the parish is about 228 acres and its pursuits entirely agricultural. *Signed* Isaac Fidler, Rector.

149. ELSFIELD   Population 168   HO 129/157/18
PARISH CHURCH. *On 30 March* In morning General Congregation 60, including Sunday Scholars. *Remarks* As near as I can ascertain. *Signed* Richard Wood, Registrar.

150. EMMINGTON   Population 104   HO 129/156/25
PARISH CHURCH. *Erected* before 1800. *Endowed* with tithe of £141, glebe £9. *Free sittings* 100; *other sittings* 5. *On 30 March* In afternoon General Congregation 11, Sunday Scholars 26. *Average attendance* in afternoon Sunday Scholars 26. *Remarks* The above return of income is the net not the gross rental. *Signed* William Douglas Littlejohn, Officiating Minister.

151. ENSTONE¹   Population 1249   HO 129/162/56
PARISH CHURCH. *Erected* before 1800, parts of it being at least 700 years old. *Endowed* with land in lieu of rent charge £30, tithe rent charge £270, glebe £40, other permanent endowment £16, fees £4 10s, Easter Offerings £2. *Free sittings* 458. *On 30 March* In morning General Congregation 166, Sunday Scholars 62; in afternoon General Congregation 85, Sunday Scholars 48. *Signed* J. Jordan, Vicar.
    1. The parish of Enstone included the hamlets of Chalford, Cleveley *(q.v.)*, Gagingwell, Lidstone, and Radford *(q.v.)*.

152. ENSTONE   HO 129/162/57
WESLEYAN METHODIST CHAPEL. *Erected* 1811. A separate and entire building. Used exclusively for worship. *Free sittings* 50; *other*

sittings 90. *On 30 March* In afternoon General Congregation 100, Sunday Scholars 35; in evening General Congregation 120. *Signed* Samuel Cooke, Minister, Chipping Norton.

153. EPWELL[1]　　　Population 330　　　HO 129/163/39
ST. ANN'S CHAPEL. *Erected* before 1800. *Free sittings* 206; *other sittings* 94. *On 30 March* In morning General Congregation 32, Sunday Scholars 36. *Average attendance* during previous 12 months, in morning General Congregation 32, Sunday Scholars 36; in afternoon General Congregation 45, Sunday Scholars 36. *Remarks* The service is in the morning and afternoon alternately. *Signed* John Price, Curate.
1. A chapelry in Swalcliffe parish.

154. EPWELL　　　　　　　　HO 129/163/40
PRIMITIVE METHODIST CHAPEL. *Erected* 1830. A separate and entire building. Used exclusively for worship. *Free sittings* 110. *On 30 March* In afternoon General Congregation 129, Sunday Scholars 16; in evening General Congregation 150. *Average attendance* during previous 3 months, in afternoon General Congregation 129, Sunday Scholars 24; in evening General Congregation 150. *Signed* Samuel Turner, Minister, Crouch Street, Banbury.

155. EWELME　　　Population 673　　　HO 129/125/48
PARISH CHURCH of ST. MARY THE VIRGIN. *Consecrated* between 1450 and 1475. *Endowed* with tithe commuted at £705. *Free sittings* (including school children) 220, *other sittings* 184. 20 inches allowed to a sitting except with the school children. *On 30 March* In morning General Congregation 163, Sunday Scholars 97; in afternoon General Congregation 203, Sunday Scholars 97. Number of Sunday Scholars less than usual in consequence of the illness of the Mistress. *Average attendance* in morning General Congregation 170, Sunday Scholars 110; in afternoon General Congregation 220, Sunday Scholars 110. *Remarks* the annual outgoings are Land Tax paid to the incumbent of Elsfield, under an arrangement with the Commissioners of Queen Anne's Bounty £91 1s 8d; Poor Rates £88 18s 9d; Highway Rates £22 4s 9d; Tenths £2 3s 6d; Procurations 9s; Curate £150; School £45; Total £339 7s 8d. *Signed* William Jacobsen, Rector.

156. EWELME　　　　　　　　HO 129/125/49
WESLEYAN METHODIST CHAPEL. *Erected* 1826. A separate and entire building. Used exclusively for worship. *Free sittings* 64; *other sittings* 45. *On 30 March* In morning General Congregation 48; in

evening General Congregation 90. *Average attendance* during previous 12 months, in morning General Congregation 45; in evening General Congregation 70. *Signed* James White, Steward, Ewelme.

157. EWELME   HO 129/125/50
PRIMITIVE METHODIST CHAPEL. *Erected* 1849. A separate and entire building. Used exclusively for worship. *Free sittings* 60; *other sittings* 39. *On 30 March* In afternoon General Congregation 60; in evening General Congregation 88. *Average attendance* during previous 6 months, in afternoon General Congregation 50; in evening General Congregation 60. *Signed* G. Wallace, Minister, Primitive Methodist Chapel House, Wallingford, Berkshire.

158. EYE AND DUNSDEN[1]   Population 829   HO 129/155/22
BINFIELD HEATH CONGREGATIONAL OR INDEPENDENT CHAPEL. *Erected* 1835. A separate and entire building. Used exclusively for worship. *Free sittings* 200. *On 30 March* In afternoon General Congregation 40; in evening General Congregation 50. *Average attendance* during previous 9 months, in morning General Congregation 40; in afternoon General Congregation 50; in evening General Congregation 55. *Remarks* Having many places beside this to attend to the Chapel is supplied most sabbaths by lay preachers from Reading. *Signed* John Davies, Minister, 33 Broad Street, Reading.
1. A Liberty in the parish of Sonning, the rest of which lay in Berkshire.

159. EYNSHAM   Population 1941   HO 129/161/7
PARISH CHURCH, Acre End Street. *Erected* before 1800. *Free sittings* 300; *other sittings* 500. *On 30 March* In morning General Congregation 350, Sunday Scholars 170; in afternoon General Congregation 300, Sunday Scholars 170. *Remarks* Average about the same stated. *Signed* William Green, Parish Clerk and Registrar.

160. EYNSHAM   HO 129/161/8
PARTICULAR BAPTIST CHAPEL. *Erected* 1817. A separate and entire building. Used exclusively for worship and a day school. *Free sittings* 116; *other sittings* 95. *On 30 March* In morning General Congregation 17, Sunday Scholars 58; in afternoon General Congregation 30, Sunday Scholars 50; in evening General Congregation 48, Sunday Scholars 8. *Average attendance* during previous 12 months, in morning at meeting for prayers, General Congregation 20, Sunday Scholars 70; in afternoon General Congregation 50, Sunday Scholars 60; in evening General Congregation 70, Sunday Scholars 20. *Remarks* The

morning service is not a full service, but a meeting for prayer. There is a similar meeting before the Evening service at 5 o'clock and in the summer another at 7[?] o'clock. General sickness, and a temporary excitement in another religious denomination in the village, have produced a temporary depression in the numbers of the congregation. *Signed* Henry Matthews[1], Baptist Minister, Eynsham.

1. *Gardner* also describes Henry Matthews as a schoolmaster.

161. EYNSHAM HO 129/161/9
PRIMITIVE METHODIST CHAPEL, Mill Street. *Erected* before 1800. Not a separate and entire building. Not used exclusively for worship. *Free sittings* 66. *On 30 March* In afternoon General Congregation 82, in evening General Congregation 118. *Signed* Henry Bowerman, Steward, Mill Street, Eynsham.

162. FIFIELD Population 248 HO 129/162/23
CHURCH OF ST. JOHN THE BAPTIST.*Erected* before 1800. *Sittings* sufficient accommodation. *Signed* J. Major Talmage, Incumbent.

163. FIFIELD HO 129/162/24
CHURCH OF ST. JOHN THE BAPTIST. *Erected* before 1800. *Free sittings* 98; *other sittings* 36, gallery about 70 children. *Average attendance* in morning General Congregation 90, Sunday Scholars 60; in afternoon General Congregation 130, Sunday Scholars 70. *Signed* J. Major Talmage, Incumbent.[1]

1. This second return is dated 26 September 1851.

164. FILKINS[1] Population 606 HO 129/161/63
PRIMITIVE METHODIST CHAPEL. Not a separate and entire building. Not used exclusively for worship. *Free sittings* 50. *On 30 March* In afternoon General Congregation 45. *Average attendance* during previous 12 months, in afternoon General Congregation 40 per week. *Signed* William Puffett, Manager, Filkins.

1. A hamlet in Bradwell parish.

165. FILKINS HO 129/161/64
BAPTIST CHAPEL. *Erected* 1832. A separate and entire building. Used exclusively for worship. *Free sittings* 100. *On 30 March* In afternoon General Congregation 40. *Average attendance* 46.[1] *Signed* Andrew Walsh, Officiating Minister, Lechlade, Gloucestershire.

1. This figure written in remarks column adjacent to the heading for average attendance.

166. FINMERE   Population 399   HO 129/164/20
ST. MICHAEL'S PARISH CHURCH. *On 30 March* In morning 220; in
afternoon 220. *Average attendance* In morning 220; in afternoon 220.
Signed W.J. Palmer, Rector.

167. FINSTOCK[1]   Population 532   HO 129/162/8
HOLY TRINITY CHAPEL OF EASE. Consecrated 1840 for a
population of 600, distant 2½ miles from Parish Church. *Erected* by the
Vicar of Charlbury at a cost of £650. No endowment, the chapel served
by a curate of Vicar of Charlbury. *Free sittings* 350. *On 30 March* In
afternoon General Congregation 130, Sunday Scholars 106. *Average
attendance* during previous 12 months, in morning General
Congregation 80, Sunday Scholars 70; in afternoon General
Congregation 200, Sunday Scholars 80. *Remarks* The villages of
Finstock (Charlbury) and Ramsden (Shipton under Wychwood) form
one Cure. The Divine Service is celebrated alternately morning and
afternoon in each chapel. *Signed* W.S. Saunders, Curate of Holy Trinity,
Cornbury Park Farm, Charlbury.
1. A hamlet in Charlbury parish.

168. FINSTOCK   HO 129/162/12
WESLEYAN METHODIST CHAPEL. *Erected* 1840. A separate and
entire building. Used exclusively for worship. *Free sittings* 100; *other
sittings* 50. *On 30 March* In morning General Congregation 41; in
evening General Congregation 75. *Signed* John Shepherd[1], Chapel
Steward, Finstock.
1.*Gardner* describes John Shepherd, Finstock, as a baker.

169. FOREST HILL   Population 149   HO 129/157/12
PARISH CHURCH[1] *Average attendance* in morning General
Congregation 120.
1. See Garsington. The incumbent was Revd C.F. Wyatt. In 1854 he reported in response to
Bishop Wilberforce's visitation queries that Sunday congregations were 'seldom less than
70. Seldom more than 100 ... No meeting houses. Only one family of thorough dissenters.
No return made at the recent census'.

170. FREELAND[1]   HO 129/161/10
WESLEYAN METHODIST CHAPEL. *Erected* 1817. A separate and
entire building. Used exclusively for worship and Sunday School. *Free
sittings* 250; *other sittings* 30. *On 30 March* In morning Sunday Scholars
30; in afternoon General Congregation 80, Sunday Scholars 30; in

evening General Congregation 80. *Average attendance* as above. *Signed* John Marriott[2], Local preacher, Witney.

1. A hamlet in Eynsham parish.
2. *Gardner* describes J. Marriott, High Street, Witney as a blanket- and tilting- weaver; John Marriott, High Street, Witney is further described as an insurance agent for the London Union Company.

171. FRINGFORD   Population 357   HO 129/159/56
ST. MICHAEL'S CHURCH. An old church of the 12th and 13th century as supposed. *Free sittings* 48; *other sittings* 240. *Remarks* Not knowing the law which requires me to reply to all the above inquiries, neither the real object of them, and suspecting no good to the Church of England to be intended by them I humbly venture to decline to reply to them.[1] *Signed* H.D. Roundell, Rector.

1. Mr. Roundell's successor, the Revd H.J. De Salis, in reply to Bishop Wilberforce's visitation queries of 1854 stated that the average Sunday congregation at Fringford was 'about 150 exclusive of children, I suppose, but I have not counted them'.The Census Office apparently followed up the above incomplete return. HO 129/159/64, a supplementary inquiry form concerning Tusmore (*q.v.*), is annotated by Joseph Reynolds, Registrar on 10 March 1852 'PS The question about the parish of Fringford I am fearful I shall not be able to answer, will do my best in a few days'. The question asked has not been discovered.

172. FRINGFORD   HO 129/159/57
INDEPENDENT CHAPEL. Open for worship 1844. A separate and entire building. Used exclusively for worship. *Free sittings* 56; *other sittings* 12. *On 30 March* In afternoon General Congregation 30; in evening General Congregation 63. *Average attendance* during previous 12 months 60. *Signed* Thomas Freeman, local preacher, Launton.[1]

1. This signature seems to have been written on top of that of the person who completed the majority of the return all except the attendance figures for 30 March. Although the superseded signature is only partly legible it appears to be that of J. Elstone, London Road, Bicester.

173. FRITWELL   Population 514   HO 129/159/29
PARISH CHURCH. *Endowed* with glebe land about 22 acres, fees very trifling. *Free sittings* about 255; *other sittings* 117. *On 30 March* In morning it may be 130; in afternoon probably 200 or more. *Average attendance* in morning General Congregation 130, Sunday Scholars 90; in afternoon General Congregation 200, Sunday Scholars 90. *Signed* William Rawlings, Vicar and Officiating Minister.

174. FRITWELL   HO 129/159/30
WESLEYAN METHODIST CHAPEL. *Erected* 1827. A separate and entire building. Used exclusively for worship. *Free sittings* 70; *other sittings* 30. *On 30 March* In afternoon General congregation 68; in evening General Congregation 84. *Average attendance* during previous 12 months, in afternoon General Congregation 66; in evening General Congregation 80. *Signed* John Tebby, Steward, Carpenter, Fritwell.

175. FULBROOK   Population 406   HO 129/161/77
CHURCH an ancient (parochial) chapelry, annexed as a hamlet to Burford. *Erected* anterior to AD 1288 at which date annexed to Burford church and served from there. *Free sittings* about 155; *other sittings* about 95. *On 30 March* In afternoon General Congregation 150, Sunday Scholars attend at Burford church and school. *Remarks* Morning and evening services are performed at Burford, 1/4 mile distant. *Signed* James Gerald Joyce, Vicar, Burford Vicarage.

176. GARSINGTON   Population 635   HO 129/157/7
PARISH CHURCH.[1] *Average attendance* in morning General Congregation 200.
1. Garsington is one of a group of parishes, with Cuddesdon, Forest Hill, Horspath, and Stanton St. John, for which no principal returns have been traced for the Anglican parish churches. A supplementary return survives for each parish, giving the usual number in the General Congregation at Sunday morning service. All five of these returns are made in the same hand and signed with illegible initials, probably those of the District Registrar.
   In 1854 the Rector was the Revd Dr. John Wilson, President of Trinity College, Oxford. He was non-resident and the duty was performed by a stipendiary curate, the Revd William Charles Macfarlane, who reported in response to Bishop Wilberforce's visitation queries that his Sunday Congregations averaged 'About 250 in the afternoon about half that number in the morning. The number is increasing. ... There is no dissenting place of worhsip. There are three families of Baptists and two families of Roman Catholics in numbers about 23'.

177. GARSINGTON   HO 129/157/8
INDEPENDENT CHAPEL. A separate and entire building. *Sittings* 50. *On 30 March* In evening General Congregation 50. *Signed* Thomas Summerford.

178. GLYMPTON   Population 149   HO 129/160/23
ST. MARY'S PARISH CHURCH. *Erected* before 1800. *Endowed* with tithe £240, glebe £40, fees £1. *Free sittings* 113. *On 30 March* In morning General Congregation 33, Sunday Scholars 22; in afternoon General Congregation 26, Sunday Scholars 18. *Average attendance* in morning

General Congregation 40, Sunday Scholars 22; in afternoon General Congregation 30, Sunday Scholars 16. *Signed* T. Nucella, Minister.

179. GODDINGTON Population 87 HO 129/159/55

TRINITY CHURCH is a modern building having been erected in the year 1792. *Endowed* with land £350 p.a. *Free sittings* 86. *On 30 March* In afternoon General Congregation 50, Sunday Scholars 5. *Average attendance* in morning General Congregation 12 or 14, Sunday Scholars 8 to 10; in afternoon General Congregation 45. *Remarks* There is morning service on alternate Sundays during the summer months, but not a sermon, beside a full afternoon service. *Signed* William Perkins, Curate, Goddington.

180. GORING Population 993 HO 129/126/1

PARISH CHURCH. *Average attendance* In morning 250.

181. GORING HO 129/126/2

ST. BARTHOLOMEW'S CHAPEL. A Chaplain in holy orders having been appointed the chaple [sic] was consecrated August 24 1742 by Thomas Secker Bp of Oxford. *On 30 March* In morning General Congregation 22, Sunday Scholars 25; in afternoon General Congregation 74, Sunday Scholars 40. *Average attendance* In morning General Congregation 29, Sunday Scholars 33; in afternoon General Congregation 81, Sunday Scholars 45. *Remarks* The above named Chapel is for the use of an Alms House to which two schools, one for boys and one for girls are attached. On Sunday mornings the Almsmen and children only attend. In the afternoons it is filled by the neigbouring residents, chiefly poor persons. *Signed* R.T. Powys,[1] Chaplain, Chapel, Goring Heath.

1. A note on mourning paper appended to the return reads as follows, 'The Revd R.T. Powys sends the enclosed which he had prepared in due time, but hesitated about sending it in consequence of its being optional, and therefore fears that the information will be incorrect in very many instances. He begs to make these remarks with the greatest respect to the Registrar Gen. Goring Heath, Reading April 23 1851'

182. GORING HO 129/126/4

LADY HUNTINGDON'S CONNEXION CHAPEL. *Erected* 1793. A separate and entire building. Used exclusively for worship. *Free sittings* 150; *other sittings* 80. *On 30 March* In afternoon General Congregation 106, Sunday Scholars 20. *Average attendance* In morning General Congregation 130, Sunday Scholars 25. *Signed* Revd. James Howes, Minister, Goring.

183. GORING   HO 129/126/3
CLIFFORD'S PARTICULAR BAPTIST CHAPEL.*Erected* 1811. A
separate and entire building. Used exclusively for worship. *Free sittings*
24. *On 30 March* In morning General Congregation 60; in afternoon
General Congregation 65; in evening General Congregation 12. *Signed*
John Burgiss[1], Deacon, Goring Heath.
1. *Gardner* describes J. Burgess, Goring Heath, as a wheelwright.

184. GREAT BOURTON   HO 129/163/84
INDEPENDENT CHAPEL. *Erected* about the year 1789. A separate
and entire building. Used exclusively for worship. *Free sittings* 92; *other
sittings* 100. *On 30 March* In afternoon General Congregation 80. *Signed*
William Claridge, Manager, Great Bourton.

185. GREAT HASELEY[1]   HO 129/156/9
INDEPENDENT CHAPEL. *Erected* 1839. A separate and entire
building. Used exclusively for worship. *Free sittings* 110; *other sittings*
20. *On 30 March* In afternoon General Congregation 36. *Average
attendance* during previous 12 months, in afternoon General
Congregation 55. *Signed* Charles M. Cordy Davies, Minister, Wheatley.
1. See also Haseley.

186. GREAT MILTON   Population 754   HO 129/156/4
ST. MARY'S PARISH CHURCH. *Erected* before 1800, probably
between 1300 and 1400. *Endowed* with tithe commuted at £189 2s 6d,
other permanent endowment (from Ecclesiastical Commission) £36, fees
£5, Easter Offerings £2 10s, corn rent from rector £40. *Free sittings* 221;
other sittings 177. *On 30 March* In morning General Congregation 201,
Sunday Scholars 64; in afternoon General Congregation 231, Sunday
Scholars 61. *Remarks* NB. The above statement (of endowment) is the
gross amount. If you deduct rates and taxes etc. the net income is not
more than £220 as stated in the Clergy List — and as there is no resident
gentleman schools and other charities greatly reduce this amount. The
Great Tithes of the parish are received by the lessee of Lincoln Cathedral
and amount to £875 2s 6d out of which sum he has to pay the vicar for a
certain number of loads of hay, straw etc., which varies according to the
price of corn — and is about £40 — vide statement. *Signed* James H.
Ashurst, Vicar.

187. GREAT MILTON   HO 129/156/6
WESLEYAN METHODIST CHAPEL. *Erected* 1842. A separate and
entire building. Used exclusively for worship. *Free sittings* 80; *other*

sittings 36. *On 30 March* In afternoon General Congregation 40; in evening General Congregation 50. *Signed* Charles Surman, Society Steward, Great Milton.[1]

1. *Gardner* describes Charles Surman, Great Milton, as a farmer.

188. GREAT ROLLRIGHT   Population 445   HO 129/162/40
EPISCOPAL ESTABLISHED CHURCH. *Free sittings* 18; *other sittings* 15. *On 30 March* In morning General Congregation 97, Sunday Scholars 28; in afternoon General Congregation 117, Sunday Scholars 32. *Remarks* The Rector of this church is absent (said to be on the Continent) in consequence of pecuniary matters.[1] *Signed* Thomas Williams, Churchwarden.[2]

1. The Rector, the Revd J. Heathcote Brooks, had begun to rebuild the rectory on a grand scale, fallen into debt and disappeared during 1851.
2. *Gardner* describes Thomas Williams, Great Rollright, as a farmer.

189. GREAT ROLLRIGHT   HO 129/162/41
EBENEZER BAPTIST CHAPEL. *Erected* 1833. A separate and entire building. Used exclusively for worship. *Free sittings* All.[1] *On 30 March* In afternoon General Congregation 34, Sunday Scholars 56; in evening General Congregation 100. *Average attendance* in afternoon General Congregation 60, Sunday Scholars 59; in evening General Congregation 80. *Signed* Humphrey Webb,[2] Manager, Great Rollright.

1. HO 129/162/40A is a supplementary return, also signed by Humphrey Webb, stating that there were 90 free sittings.
2. *Gardner* describes H. Webb, Great Rollright, as a grocer and blacksmith.

190. GREAT ROLLRIGHT   HO 129/162/42
BETHEL PARTICULAR BAPTIST CHAPEL. *Erected* 1838. A separate and entire building. Used exclusively for worship. *Free sittings* 100. *On 30 March* No service. *Average attendance* in morning General Congregation 60. *Signed* John Walker, Deacon.

191. GREAT TEW[1]   Population 541   HO 129/162/61
PARISH CHURCH. *Erected* before 1800. *Endowed* with land £85, other permanent endowment £48. *Free sittings* 257; *other sittings* 314. *On 30 March* in morning General Congregation 135, Sunday Scholars 70; in afternoon General Congregation 119, Sunday Scholars 70. *Average attendance* during previous 12 months, in morning General Congregation 140, Sunday Scholars 75; in afternoon General Congregation 120, Sunday Scholars 75. *Signed* John J. Campbell, Vicar.

1. The parish of Great Tew included the chapelry of Little Tew (*q.v.*).

192. HAILEY   Population 1326   HO 129/161/44
ST. JOHN'S CHAPEL, Chapel of Ease to Witney. *Erected* before 1800. *Endowed* with land £152. *Free sittings* 300; *other sittings* 50. *On 30 March* In morning General Congregation 70, Sunday Scholars 58. *Average attendance* during previous 12 months, in afternoon General Congregation 150, Sunday Scholars 60. *Remarks* The service is usually in the afternoon. *Signed* George Crabb Rolfe, Incumbent.

193. HAILEY   HO 129/161/45
WESLEYAN METHODIST CHAPEL. *Erected* 1825. A separate and entire building. Used exclusively for worship. *Free sittings* All. *On 30 March* In morning General Congregation 30, Sunday Scholars 33; in afternoon Sunday Scholars 33; in evening General Congregation 50. *Signed* John Harris, Local Preacher, Corn Street, Witney.

194. HAILEY   HO 129/161/46
PRIMITIVE METHODIST CHAPEL, New Yatt. *Erected* 1843. A separate and entire building. Used exclusively for worship. *Sittings* free.[1] *On 30 March* In afternoon General Congregation 22. *Signed* William Collins, Member of Chaper [sic], New Yatt.
1. HO 129/161/45a is a supplementary return stating that the chapel contained 64 free sittings.

195. HAILEY   HO 129/161/47
FRIENDS' MEETING HOUSE. *Erected* before 1800. A separate and entire building. Used exclusively for worship, see remarks. *A measurement* in superficial feet floor area 544; in galleries 102. *Estimated Number of Persons capable of being seated* 180 and in gallery 40. *On 30 March* In morning 13 attendants, in afternoon 11 attendants. *Remarks* Used occasionally for meetings of the Bible and Peace Societies. *Signed* Robert Sessions,[1] Charlbury.
1. *Gardner* describes R. Sessions, Charlbury, as a draper and grocer.

196. HAMPTON GAY   Population 82   HO 129/160/40
ST. GILES' CHURCH, commonly called Hampton Gay church. The church is a distinct and separate parish. In some documents called a chapel as having been connected with the Abbey of Oseney. Date of original church unknown. Rebuilt in 1768. Most probably consecrated (but I know not of any evidence on the subject). *Endowed* with permanent endowment £20 p.a. *Free sittings* 120. *On 30 March* In morning General Congregation 21, Sunday Scholars 9; in afternoon General Congregation 33, Sunday Scholars 6. *Average attendance* during

previous 12 months, in morning General Congregation 17, Sunday
Scholars 15; in afternoon General Congregation 28, Sunday Scholars 12.
Signed John Hill, Perpetual Curate, St. Edmund Hall, Oxford.

197. HAMPTON POYLE   Population 131   HO 129/160/41
ST. MARY'S CHURCH. *Erected* before 1800. *Endowed* with tithe
about £160 p.a., glebe 25 acres. *Free sittings* 60; *other sittings* 20. *On 30
March* In morning General Congregation 30, Sunday Scholars 16; in
afternoon General Congregation 22, Sunday Scholars 18. Evening
service in summer only. *Remarks* Deduct from the above estimated value
of the living about £9 9s p.a. for rates, £10 p.a. for education of poor
and about £4 p.a. for other charges upon the living. *Signed* Joseph
Dodd, Rector, Hampton.

198. HANBOROUGH[1]   Population 1153   HO 129/161/1
PARISH CHURCH. *Endowed* with land 383 acres, rent abt £400, fees
very small amount. *Free sittings* about perhaps 100; *other sittings* about
perhaps 200 besides sittings for school children. *On 30 March* In morning
General Congregation 130, Sunday Scholars 49; in afternoon General
Congregation 230, Sunday Scholars 37. *Average attendance* not known.
Remarks Par. Church is situated at the distance of more than a mile from
3/4ths of the Parishoners' Habitations. March 30 a wet day. *Signed* P.
Wynter, Rector, St. John's College, Oxford.
1. This entry refers to Church Hanborough. The parish also included Long Hanborough.

199. HANBOROUGH   HO 129/161/2
WESLEYAN METHODIST CHAPEL. *Erected* 1827. A separate and
entire building. Used exclusively for worship. *Free sittings* 140; *other
sittings* 60. *On 30 March* In morning General Congregation 200, Sunday
Scholars 108.[1] *Signed* Thomas Weller,[2] Steward, Long Hanborough.
1. Further figures were squeezed into the section of the form concerning attendance on 30
March as follows, in morning 83, in afternoon none, in evening 219.
2. *Gardner* describes Thomas Weller, Hanborough, as a shopkeeper.

200. HANWELL   Population 301   HO 129/163/67
ST. PETER'S CHURCH. *Erected* before 1800. *Endowed* with land,
corn rent 26 acres more or less, aggregate amount £300 p.a.[1] *On 30
March* In morning General Congregation 80, Sunday Scholars 30; in
afternoon General Congregation 40, Sunday Scholars 30. *Remarks*
Fewer attendants according to weather and circumstances. *Signed*
William Pearse, Rector.
1. HO 129/163/66 is a supplementary return stating that there were free sittings 81,
appropriated sittings 160 'NB. The church is large enough for the population. Thomas
Pearse, Curate'.

201. HANWELL HO 129/163/69
WESLEYAN METHODIST CHAPEL. *Erected* before 1800. Not a separate and entire building. Not used exclusively for worship. *Free sittings* 60. *On 30 March* In evening General Congregation 47. *Signed* William Buller Junr[1], Leader, Hanwell Fields.
1. *Gardner* describes William Buller, Junr, Bilsmore Hall, Hanwell, as a farmer.

202. HARDWICK Population 66 HO 129/159/65
ST. MARY'S PARISH CHURCH. *Erected* before 1800. *Endowed* with tithes £86, permanent endowment £6 10s, fees £5. *Free sittings* 52; *other sittings* 28. *On 30 March* In afternoon General Congregation 39, Sunday Scholars 10. *Average attendance* in morning General Congregation 30, Sunday Scholars 12; in afternoon General Congregation 42, Sunday Scholars 12. *Remarks* The parishioners of the adjoining parish of Tusmore, having no church in their parish, habitually frequent the Ch in Hardwick and in returning the number of persons attending Divine Service I have included them. Several Roman Catholics in Hardwick (about 15 adults and 10 children) attend service in a chapel in the parish of Hethe. *Signed* Thomas Prater, Rector.

203. HARDWICK[1] Population 128 HO 129/161/49
CHAPEL OF EASE. Licensed only for public worship. *Erected* before 1800. *Free sittings* 56; *other sittings* 80. *Average attendance* in morning General Congregation 50; in afternoon General Congregation 90. *Signed* Thomas East, Deputy Registrar.
1. A hamlet in Ducklington parish.

204. HARPSDEN Population 215 HO 129/155/20
CHURCH. *Remarks* The Parish Clerk informs me the congregation that attends this Church is about 40. *Signed* Robert Coates, Registrar.

205. HASELEY[1] Population 750 HO 129/156/8
On 30 March in morning not known; in afternoon not known; in evening none. *Average attendance* in morning not known; in afternoon not known; in evening none. *Remarks* The clergyman of the parish, the Revd William Birkett declines giving any information.[2] *Signed* Thomas Home, Registrar of Births and Deaths.
1. Otherwise known as Great Haseley.
2. Birkett, in reply to Bishop Wilberforce's visitation queries of 1854, stated that the average congregation was about 300, 'the number much as usual for some years'.

206. HEADINGTON   Population 1653   HO 129/157/21
ST. ANDREW'S PARISH CHURCH. *Erected* before 1800. *Endowed* with land £103, other permanent endowment £15, fees £12, Easter Offerings £8. *Free sittings* 158; *other sittings* 242. *On 30 March* In morning General Congregation 176, Sunday Scholars 138; in afternoon General Congregation 259, Sunday Scholars 116. *Average attendance* in morning General Congregation 276, Sunday Scholars 120; in afternoon General Congregation 259, Sunday Scholars 112. *Remarks* The attendance on 30 March is considered an average one except in the case of the Schools. *Signed* J.C. Pring, Vicar.

207. HEADINGTON   HO 129/157/20
HOLY TRINITY CHURCH. District assigned under 16th section of Act passed in the 59th year of Geo. III AD 1818. Consecrated 22 November 1849 as an additional church. Cost of £2,209 2s 6d defrayed by private benefaction and subscription. *Endowed* with land 10 acres the rateable value of which is £9, other permanent endowment £11 19s 6d being the interest on £400 invested in Government Securities, fees about £1 10s p.a. *Free sittings* 320. *On 30 March* In morning General Congregation 82, Sunday Scholars 51; in afternoon General Congregation 77, Sunday Scholars 45. *Average attendance* during previous 12 months, in morning General Congregation about 65, Sunday Scholars about 50; in afternoon General Congregation about 80, Sunday Scholars about 50. *Signed* Thomas Masterman, Minister, Headington Quarry.

208. HEADINGTON   HO 129/157/22
WESLEYAN METHODIST CHAPEL. *Erected* 1830. A separate and entire building. Used exclusively for worship. *Free sittings* 100. *On 30 March* In morning General Congregation 4; in afternoon General Congregation 25; in evening General Congregation 42. *Average attendance* in morning General Congregation 6; in afternoon General Congregation 30; in evening General Congregation 40. *Signed* William Marcham, Local Preacher, Islip.

209. HEADINGTON   HO 129/157/23
BAPTIST CHAPEL. *Erected* 1836. A separate and entire building. Used exclusively for worship. *Free sittings* 100; *other sittings* 24. *On 30 March* In morning General Congregation 30; in evening General Congregation 60. *Average attendance* during previous 12 months, in morning General Congregation 40; in afternoon Sunday Scholars 60; in evening General Congregation 100. *Remarks* The building is used both for Public

Worship and as a Sunday School. Public Worship in the morning and evening, Sunday School in the afternoon. *Signed* Lewis North, Deacon, Headington.

210. HEMPTON[1]   HO 129/160/7
HEMPTON CHURCH. At present a barn is used for Divine Service. A church is almost completed and will probably be used in 2 months, called St. John. It may perhaps be joined to the parish of Worton but this is uncertain: if not it will be a Chapel of Ease. The barn is used with the consent of the Bishop. The barn is rented by the Revd W. Wilson and the church erected at his sole expense (of Over Worton House). Cost perhaps £400. *Free sittings* 180. The church now nearly completed. *On 30 March* In evening General Congregation 120. *Average attendance* during previous 9 months, in evening General Congregation 110. *Remarks* The circumstances will account for the indefiniteness of this return. As many Sunday Scholars as can do so attend the Parish Church morning and afternoon. Any who attend in the evening are reckoned (of necessity) with the congregation. *Signed* George Venables, Curate, Deddington.
1. A hamlet and township in the parish of Deddington. Its population in 1841 was 305.

211. HEMPTON   HO 129/160/8
INDEPENDENT OR CONGREGATIONAL CHAPEL. *Erected* in 1849 in lieu of one opened for worship in 1840. A separate and entire building. Used exclusively for worship. *Free sittings* 60; *other sittings* 90. *On 30 March* In afternoon General Congregation 60, Sunday Scholars 7. *Average attendance* during previous 15 months, in afternoon General Congregation 70. Sunday Scholars 30. *Signed* Obed Parker, Minister, Deddington.

212. HENLEY-ON-THAMES Population 3733   HO 129/155/9
ST. MARY'S PARISH CHURCH. *Erected* before 1800. *Free sittings* about 220; *other sittings* about 900, exclusive of room for children. *On 30 March* In morning General Congregation 800, Sunday Scholars 300; in afternoon General Congregation 550, Sunday Scholars 235; in evening General Congregation 450. *Average attendance* in morning General Congregation 800, Sunday Scholars 230; in afternoon General Congregation 530, Sunday Scholars 230; in evening General Congregation 350. *Remarks* I have no means of knowing the value of the living other than by report. *Signed* T.J. Burlton, Curate.

213. HENLEY-ON-THAMES HO 129/155/12
WESLEYAN METHODIST CHAPEL. A separate and entire building. Not exclusively used for worship. *Free sittings* 120. *On 30 March* In morning General Congregation 26, Sunday Scholars 19; in afternoon General Congregation 40, Sunday Scholars 19; in evening General Congregation 44. *Average attendance* during previous 12 months, in morning General Congregation 40, Sunday Scholars 19; in afternoon General Congregation 75, Sunday Scholars 19; in evening General Congregation 55. *Signed* Thomas Hodson, Minister, 31 Church Street, Reading.

214. HENLEY-ON-THAMES HO 129/155/2
FRIENDS' MEETING HOUSE. *Erected* before 1800. A separate and entire building. Used exclusively for worship. *Ad measurement* in superficial feet floor area 390; in galleries 100. *Estimated Number of Persons capable of being seated* 120 and in galleries 30. *On 30 March* In morning 7 attendants, in afternoon 6 attendants. *Signed* John Thomas Rice, Hurley Mills, near Great Marlow, Buckinghamshire.

215. HENLEY-ON-THAMES HO 129/155/13
PARTICULAR BAPTIST CHAPEL, Friday Street. *Erected* before 1800. Not a separate and entire building. Not used exclusively for worship. *Free sittings* 14. *On 30 March* In morning General Congregation 12; in afternoon General Congregation 8; in evening General Congregation 9. *Remarks* The building is also used as a dwelling house. *Signed* William Hunt, Minister, Friday Street, Henley.

216. HETHE Population 418 HO 129/159/59
PARISH CHURCH OF ST. EDMUND AND ST. GEORGE. *Erected* before 1800. *Endowed* with land £160, other permanent endowment of a close of 3½ acres, fees trifling. *Free sittings* 46, *other sittings* 84. *On 30 March* In morning General Congregation 70, Sunday Scholars 30; in afternoon General Congregation 100, Sunday Scholars 30. *Average attendance* during previous 12 months, in morning General Congregation 80, Sunday Scholars 38; in afternoon General Congregation 100, Sunday Scholars 38. *Remarks* Hethe rectory has a certain quantity of land set apart free of tithes and is let at the sum above named. *Signed* John Russell Shurlock, Rector.

217. HETHE HO 129/159/60
ROMAN CATHOLIC CHAPEL OF THE HOLY TRINITY. *Erected* since 1800. A separate and entire building. Used exclusively for worship.

Sittings 170. *Average attendance* during previous 12 months, in morning General Congregation 150. *Signed* Joseph Robson, Catholic Priest, Catholic Church, Hethe.

218. HETHE   HO 129/159/61
WESLEYAN METHODIST CHAPEL. *Erected* 1814. A separate and entire building. Used exclusively for worship. *Free sittings* 80; *other sittings* 40. *On 30 March* In morning General Congregation 30, Sunday Scholars 25; in afternoon General Congregation 60, Sunday Scholars 30; in evening General Congregation 50. *Average attendance* during previous 12 months, in morning General Congregation 30, Sunday Scholars 25; in afternoon General Congregation 60, Sunday Scholars 30; in evening General Congregation 50. *Signed* William Mansfield,[1] Steward of the Wesleyan Chapel, Hethe.

1. *Gardner* describes William Mansfield, Hethe, as a shoemaker.

219. HEYTHROP   Population 190   HO 129/162/53
PARISH CHURCH in Heythrop Park. *Erected* before 1800, supposed to be 600 or 700 years old, has undergone various repairs at different times. *Endowed* with rent charge. *Free sittings* about half, total sittings from 140-150. *On 30 March* In morning General Congregation 75, weather unfavourable. *Average attendance* in morning General Congregation from 100-120. *Remarks* We have no school. We can get no accommodation, the church and the whole parish belonging to the Earl of Shrewsbury.[1] *Signed* J. Samuel, Rector.

1. Lord Shrewsbury was a Roman Catholic.

220. HEYTHROP   HO 129/162/55
ST. MARY'S ROMAN CATHOLIC CHURCH. *Erected* before 1800. A separate and entire building. Used exclusively for worship. *Free sittings* all.[1] *On 30 March* In morning General Congregation 63; in evening General Congregation 14. *Average attendance* during previous 12 months, in morning General Congregation 100. *Signed* Patrick Hefferman, Roman Catholic Priest.

1. HO 129/162/54 is a supplementary return stating that there were 220 free sittings.

221. HOLTON   Population 289   HO 129/157/2
CHURCH. *Erected* before 1400.[1] *On 30 March* In morning General Congregation about 70, Sunday Scholars 30; in afternoon General Congregation about 90, Sunday Scholars 20. *Average attendance* during previous 12 months, in morning General Congregation 80, Sunday

Scholars 40; in afternoon General Congregation 100, Sunday Scholars 30. *Signed* Thomas George Tyndale, Rector.

1. HO 129/157/1 is a supplementary return by Tyndale, stating that there were about 100 free sittings, about 100 appropriated sittings. He estimated the population at 250.

222. HOLWELL[1]   Population 131   HO 129/161/65
HOLWELL CHURCH formerly a Chapel of Ease to Bradwell, now the church of a distinct and separate parish. Consecrated 1845 after having been rebuilt at a cost to William Hervey Esq., Bradwell Grove, of £900. *Endowed* with tithe £42, other permanent endowment £25, Easter Offerings 18s, other sources £12. *Free sittings* 80; *other sittings* 40. *On 30 March* In morning General Congregation 48, Sunday Scholars 21; in afternoon General Congregation 53, Sunday Scholars 21. *Signed* Charles T. Astley, Incumbent, Holwell.

1. Holwell continued to appear as a chapelry in Bradwell parish for civil census purposes but was recognised as a separate ecclesiastical parish as in Bishop Wilberforce's visitation returns of 1854, in which Astley reported that average attendances at Sunday Service were 'about 45 morning, 50 afternoon. It has somewhat decreased of late ... It is not so great I think as it ought to be in so small a Parish. I attribute the deficiency to too much truth from the Pulpit and too little in the Cottages'.

223. HOOK NORTON   Population 1496   HO 129/163/1
ST. PETER'S PARISH CHURCH. *Erected* before 1800 (doubtless many centuries ago). *Endowment* I decline giving an answer to this inquisitorial question. *Free sittings* 365, including 110 children's sittings in Sunday Scholars' gallery; *other sittings* 390. *On 30 March* In morning General Congregation 160, Sunday Scholars 92; in afternoon General Congregation 277, Sunday Scholars 98. *Average attendance* during previous 12 months, in morning General Congregation 200, Sunday Scholars 100; in afternoon General Congregation 300, Sunday Scholars 100. *Remarks* The number of persons who attended Divine Service on Sunday March 30, 1851, having been carefully counted, is given with considerable accuracy; but that number is doubtless below the average. In the forenoon especially, the Lord's Supper was administered, on which occasions (there being no sermon) the general congregation is almost always much less than usual. *Signed* John Richard Rushton, Perpetual Curate.

224. HOOK NORTON   HO 129/163/2
PRIMITIVE METHODIST CHAPEL, Old School Room. *Erected* 1826. A separate and entire building. Used exclusively for worship. *Free sittings* 80. *On 30 March* In morning General Congregation 60; in evening General Congregation 100. *Average attendance* in morning

General Congregation 40; in evening General Congregation 100. *Signed* Charles Walters, Minister.

225. HOOK NORTON   HO 129/163/3
WESLEYAN METHODIST CHAPEL. *Erected* 1813. A separate and entire building. Used exclusively for worship. *Free sittings* 10; *other sittings* 160. *On 30 March* In afternoon General Congregation 100, Sunday Scholars 74; in evening General Congregation 160. *Signed* Samuel Cooke, Minister, Chipping Norton.

226. HOOK NORTON   HO 129/163/4
BAPTIST MEETING HOUSE. This present building erected 1787. The former one time unknown. A separate and entire building. Used exclusively for worship. *Free sittings* 300. *On 30 March* In morning General Congregation 100, Sunday Scholars 20; in afternoon General Congregation 120, Sunday Scholars 20. *Remarks* The congregation and cause is now low owing to causes which need not be specified here, and the returns here are small compared with what they probably will be in a few months. *Signed* John Haynes,[1] Manager, Hook Norton.
1. *Gardner* describes John Frederick Haynes, Park Farm, Hook Norton and J. Haynes, sen., Lodge Farm, Hook Norton as farmers.

227. HOOK NORTON   HO 129/163/5
FRIENDS' MEETING HOUSE. *Erected* before 1800. A separate and entire building. Used exclusively for worship. *Admeasurement* in superficial feet floor area 26 by 9; in galleries 14 by 9. *Estimated Number of Persons capable of being seated* 90 and in galleries 30. *On 30 March* In morning 11 attendants. *Remarks* An evening meeting is held 6 months in the year, average attendance about 10. *Signed* William Minchin,[1] Hook Norton.
1. *Gardner* describes William Minchin, Hook Norton, as a farmer.

228. HORLEY   Population 392   HO 129/163/57
ST. ETHELDREDA'S CHURCH. *Erected* before 1800. *Endowed* with land £388, fees and dues included. *Free sittings* 55; *other sittings* 210. *On 30 March* In afternoon General Congregation 82, Sunday Scholars 48. *Average attendance* during previous 12 months, in morning General Congregation 80, Sunday Scholars 50; in afternoon Sunday Scholars 50. *Remarks* On the inclosure of the parish many years since an estate was allotted in lieu of tithes. This estate is partly in Horley and partly in the adjoining chapelry or parish of Hornton, both Co. Oxon, but profits from the estate and fees amount to £388 p.a. *Signed* W.J. Pinwell, Curate.

229. HORLEY   HO 129/163/58
WESLEYAN METHODIST CHAPEL. *Erected* before 1800. A separate
and entire building. Used exclusively for worship. *Free sittings* 84, *other
sittings* 40. *On 30 March* In morning General Congregation 75; in
evening General Congregation 90. *Signed* Richard Hirons, Steward,
Horley.

230. HORLEY   HO 129/163/59
PRIMITIVE METHODIST CHAPEL. Not a separate and entire
building. Not used exclusively for worship. *Free sittings* 50. *On 30 March*
In evening General Congregation 40. *Average attendance* in morning
General Congregation 60.*Signed* Richard Archer, Horley.

231. HORNTON   Population 591   HO 129/163/54
ST. JOHN BAPTIST CHURCH. *Erected* before 1800. *Endowed* with
land £388, rent of estate in lieu of tithes belonging to the living of Horley
cum Horton, fees and dues included. *Free sittings* 122; *other sittings* 160.
On 30 March In morning General Congregation 98, Sunday Scholars 45.
Average attendance during previous 12 months, in morning General
Congregation 80, Sunday Scholars 50; in afternoon General
Congregation 120, Sunday Scholars 50. *Remarks* The profits of the
living of Horley cum Hornton (viz) derive from an estate alloted in the
inclosure in lieu of tithes amount to £388 p.a. *Signed* W.J. Pinwell,
Curate, Horley.

232. HORTON   HO 129.163/55
PRIMITIVE METHODIST CHAPEL. *Erected* 1842. A separate and
entire building. Used exclusively for worship. *Free sittings* 72; *other
sittings* 90. *On 30 March* In morning Sunday Scholars 20; in afternoon
General Congregation 102, Sunday Scholars 20; in evening General
Congregation 140. *Average attendance* during previous 12 months, in
afternoon General Congregation 50 or 60, Sunday Scholars 20; in
evening General Congregation 120. *Remarks* The 102 as returned for the
afternoon of March 30th included the 20 scholars. *Signed* Edward Cox,
Chapel Steward, Horton.

233. HORNTON   HO 129/163/56
INDEPENDENT CHAPEL. *Erected* 1834. A separate and entire
building. Used exclusively for worship. *Free sittings* 86. *On 30 March* In
afternoon General Congregation 38. *Average attendance* during previous
12 months, in afternoon General Congregation 45. *Remarks* Not so

many as generally attend. *Signed* John Webb,[1] Manager, Hornton.
1. *Gardner* describes John Webb, Hornton, as a shoemaker.

234. HORSPATH   Population 333   HO 129/157/11
PARISH CHURCH.[1] *Average attendance* in morning General
Congregation 100.
1. See Garsington.
   In 1854 the incumbent, Revd Henry Harris, Magdalen College was non-resident, but had an assistant curate. Harris reported, in response to Bishop Wilberforce's vistation queries, average Sunday congregations of 'nearly 100, but I cannot speak with certainty. I do not preceive any change in its numbers'. There were no Dissenting meeting houses or Dissenters.

235. IBSTONE[1]   Population 148   HO 129/150/1
ST. NICHOLAS' PARISH CHURCH. *Erected* before 1800.[2] *Endowed* with land wood £4 10s, tithe rent charge £173 10s, glebe £12. *Free sittings* about 40; *other sittings* 40, gallery principally devoted to school 40, total sittings 120 or 140 including children. *On 30 March* In morning General Congregation 58, Sunday Scholars 42. *Average attendance* In morning General Congregation 50-60, Sunday Scholars 40; in afternoon General Congregation 100, Sunday Scholars 40. *Remarks* The above is the gross value of the Living of Ibstone within the limits of the Parish but I have been given to understand that there is land in the vicinity of Cuxham, another Rectory which has been hitherto held with Ibstone belonging to this Rectory and upon this point I must refer you to the Revd F. Rowden, Rector of Cuxham or to the return from that Parish in the Co. of Oxon, Thame Union. *Signed* Philip Wroughton, Churchwarden, Ibstone House.
1. Part of the parish only, the remainder being in Buckinghamshire.
2. These words in pencil and then deleted.

236. IDBURY   Population 222   HO 129/162/26
CHURCH OF ST. NICHOLAS. *Erected* before 1800. *Sittings* ample accommodation.[1] *Signed* J. Major Talmage, Incumbent, Fifield.
1. HO 129/162/25 is a supplementary inquiry form asking 'the number of free and other sittings provided at Idbury Parish Church, and the general congregation attending it.' The unsigned answer is 'Body of church 130, gallery 30, north aisle containing the school of about 70 children. Average attendance 130.'

237. IFFLEY   Population 969   HO 129/157/26
PARISH CHURCH. *On 30 March* In morning General Congregation 130, Sunday Scholars 50. *Remarks* As near as I can ascertain. *Signed* Richard Wood, Registrar.

238. IPSDEN Population 629 HO 129/155/26
ST. MARY'S an ancient Chapelry. *Endowed* with tithe about £100, glebe about £20. *Free sittings* 140; *other sittings* 40. *On 30 March* In morning General Congregation 80; in afternoon General Congregation 70. *Average attendance* in morning General Congregation 80; in afternoon General Congregation 90. *Signed* R. Twopenny, Vicar.

239. ISLIP Population 744 HO 129/159/21
PARISH CHURCH. *Erected* before 1800. *Endowed* with tithe £485, glebe £44, residence, fees about £2 10s. *Free sittings* 270; *other sittings* 120. *On 30 March* In morning General Congregation 86, Sunday Scholars 63; in afternoon General Congregation 120, Sunday Scholars 61. *Remarks* The above figures are about the average number of attendants. *Signed* William Bull, Churchwarden, Islip.[1]
1. *Gardner* includes Mr. William Bull amongst the private residents of Islip.

240. ISLIP HO 129/159/22
WESLEYAN METHODIST CHAPEL. *Erected* 1843. A separate and entire building. Used exclusively for worship. *Free sittings* 100. *On 30 March* In morning General Congregation 35; in evening General Congregation 60. *Average attendance* during previous 12 months, in morning General Congregation 30; in evening General Congregation 70. *Signed* William Birmingham, local preacher. Address by post Revd Robert Day, Wesleyan Minister, Oxford.

241. ISLIP HO 129/159/23
BAPTIST CHAPEL. Not a separate and entire building. Not used exclusively for worship. *Free sittings* 20. *On 30 March* In morning General Congregation 12; in afternoon General congregation 8. *Remarks* No preaching on this day. Met for prayer and reading the scriptures. *Signed* Robert Elliott,[1] Elder, Islip.
1. *Gardner* describes Rober Elliott, Islip, as a baker.

242. KELMSCOTT[1] Population 149 HO 129/122/27
CHAPEL OF ST. GEORGE. *Erected* before 1800. *Endowed* with land £92 9s and Easter Offerings 7s. Gross not net income £92 16s, net income about £70. *Free sittings* 50; *other sittings* 51. *On 30 March* In afternoon General Congregation 33, Sunday Scholars 21. *Average attendance* during previous 3 months, in morning General Congregation 40, Sunday Scholars 21; in afternoon General Congregation 33, Sunday Scholars 21. *Remarks* Alternate service morning and afternoon since having an asst. Curate. This Chapelry is 4 miles off, has no residence for a Clergyman

nor any fund to build one from. If a *resident* priest of ordinary diligence the congregation might be nearly doubled. *Robbed of the Gt. Tithes.* *Signed* T.W. Goodlake, Vicar and Parish Priest, Bradwell Vicarage.
1. A chapelry in Bradwell parish.

243. KENCOT   Population 206   HO 129/161/59
PARISH CHURCH. *Average attendance* General Congregation about 50.*Remarks* The best information I could get. *Signed* Thomas Cheatle,[1] Registrar.
1. Thomas Cheatle, High Street, Burford, was also a surgeon and alderman of the borough.

244. KIDDINGTON   Population 303   HO 129/160/24[1]
PARISH CHURCH. *Erected* before 1800. *Endowed* with tithe £360, glebe £100, fees £1. *Free sittings* 90; *other sittings* 46. *On 30 March* In morning General Congregation 70, Sunday Scholars 27; in afternoon General Congregation 60, Sunday Scholars 17. *Average attendance* in morning General Congregation 70, Sunday Scholars 27; in afternoon General Congregation 60, Sunday Scholars 17. *Signed* J.G. Browne, Minister, Kiddington.
1. HO 129/160/25 is a duplicate return giving exactly the same information as above.

245. KIDDINGTON   HO 129/160/26
PRIMITIVE METHODIST CHAPEL, Lower Kiddington. *Erected* before 1800. Not a separate and entire building. Not used exclusively for worship. *Free sittings* 30. *On 30 March* In evening General Congregation 74. *Signed* Absalom Wiblin, Prayer Leader, Upper Kiddington.

246. KIDLINGTON[1]   Population 1185   HO 129/160/42
PARISH CHURCH. *Erected* before 1800. *Endowed* with land in lieu of tithe £260, tithe £14, glebe house and close £30, fees about £4. *Free sittings* 480, *other sittings* 250. *On 30 March* In morning General Congregation 290, Sunday Scholars 94; in afternoon General Congregation 254, Sunday Scholars 86. *Average attendance* during previous 6 months, in morning General Congregation 325, Sunday Scholars 100; in afternoon General Congregation 345, Sunday Scholars 100. *Remarks* Below average owing to it being a wet Sunday. The nave only and one aisle of Kidlington church were used for the purposes of Divine Service until 1850 when the Sth Transept, Tower and Chancel were called into use. 150 add. sittings were thus provided. The room in

Church is now ample for the population. *Signed* Matthew Anstis, Minister, Kidlington.

1. The parish of Kidlington also included the hamlets of Gosford, Thrupp, and Water Eaton (*q.v.*). The total population of the parish was 1494.

247. KIDLINGTON   HO 129/160/43
WESLEYAN METHODIST CHAPEL. *Erected* before 1800. A separate and entire building. Used exclusively for worship. *Free sittings* 100. *On 30 March* In afternoon General Congregation 25, in evening General Congregation 40. *Signed* John Meek, Minister.

248. KIDLINGTON   HO 129/160/45
BAPTIST CHAPEL. Not a separate and entire building. Not used exclusively for worship.[1] *On 30 March* In evening General Congregation 55.[2] *Signed* James Ballard, Deacon, Kidlington.

1. HO 129/160/44 is a supplementary return made by James Ballard, Kidlington, stating that there were 30 sittings and that 'it is not a chapel it is dweling house so all they sittings is free'.
2. HO 129/160/46 is a further return for Kidlington Baptist Chapel. It also states that the place of worship was not a separate and entire building, and was not used exclusively for worship. Attendance on 30 March is given as in morning General Congregation 30, Sunday Scholars 24. This return is signed by Frederick Butler, Elder, Kidlington. *Gardner* describes Frederick Butler, Esq., Kidlington, as a surgeon.

249. KINGHAM   Population 617   HO 129/162/27
ST. ANDREW'S PARISH CHURCH. *Erected* before 1800. *Endowed* with tithe £642, glebe £230. *Free sittings* 17; *other sittings* 134, benches for school children 65. *On 30 March* In morning General Congregation 130, Sunday Scholars 72; in afternoon General Congregation 230, Sunday Scholars 43. *Average attendance* during previous 12 months, in morning General Congregation 130, Sunday Scholars 72; in afternoon General Congregation 230, Sunday Scholars 43. *Signed* John W. Lockwood, Rector.

250. KINGHAM   HO 129/162/28
BETHEL PARTICULAR BAPTIST CHAPEL. *Erected* about 1832. A separate and entire building. Used exclusively for worship. *Free sittings* 60 or 70. *Average attendance* in morning General Congregation 60 or 80. *Signed* R. Roff, Minister, Stow on the Wold, Gloucestershire.

251. KINGSEY   Population 31[1]   HO 129/156/27
PARISH CHURCH. *Erected* before 1800. *Free sittings* 100; *other sittings* 80. *On 30 March* In morning General Congregation 40, Sunday

Scholars 34; in afternoon General Congregation 90, Sunday Scholars 34. *Signed* W.N. Jackson, Minister.

1. This figure refers to part of the parish only. The remainder of the ancient parish was in Buckinghamshire. There seems to have been considerable confusion as to where the county boundary really divided the parish, consequently population figures for each part (though not for the whole) must be viewed with caution.

252. KINGSTON BLOUNT[1]   HO 129/156/20
KINGSTON INDEPENDENT CHAPEL. *Erected* 1817. A separate and entire building. Used exclusively for worship. *Free sittings* 150. *On 30 March* In morning Sunday Scholars 36; in afternoon General Congregation 96, Sunday Scholars 28; in evening General Congregation 25. *Average attendance* during previous 12 months, in morning Sunday Scholars 38; in afternoon General Congregation 10 , Sunday Scholars 30; in evening General Congregation 25. *Remarks* This Chapel is connected with the Chinnor Independent place of worship and supplied every Sunday afternoon by a Minister of that place. The congregation are *not* the same. There is also divine service on Thursday evenings at which the Minister performs. *Signed* Joseph Mason, Minister, Chinnor.

1. A township in Aston Rowant parish.

253. KIRTLINGTON   Population 716   HO 129/159/6
PARISH CHURCH. *Erected* before 1800. *On 30 March* In morning General Congregation 100, Sunday Scholars 65; in afternoon General Congregation 110, Sunday Scholars 65. *Average attendance* in morning General Congregation 100, Sunday Scholars 65; in afternoon General Congregation 110, Sunday Scholars 65. *Signed* Frederick Rogers, Clerk, Kirtlington.

254. KIRTLINGTON   HO 129/159/7
WESLEYAN METHODIST CHAPEL. *Erected* 1830. A separate and entire building. Used exclusively for worship. *Free sittings* 150. *On 30 March* In morning General Congregation 75; in evening General Congregation 102. *Average attendance* during previous 12 months, in morning General Congregation 70; in evening General Congregation 100. *Signed* William Marcham, Local Preacher, Islip.

255. LANGFORD[1]   Population 453   HO 129/122/21
PARISH CHURCH. *Erected* before 1800. *Free sittings* 247; *other sittings* 139. *On 30 March* In morning General Congregation 64, Sunday Scholars 24; in afternoon General Congregation 56, Sunday Scholars 24. *Average attendance* during previous 3 months, in morning General Congregation 80, Sunday Scholars 20; in afternoon General

Congregation 80, Sunday Scholars 20. *Remarks* The Rectorial Tithes are in the hands of the Ecclesiastical Commissioners — their value I do not know. The Vicarial emoluments arise from land commuted for Tithe, from some portion of Tithe, and from Glebe; their relative value I am not able to set down. *Signed* F.G. Lemann, Curate.

1. The parish of Langford also included Little Faringdon (*q.v.*) tithing, Grafton township and Radcot hamlet. The total population of the parish was 751.

256. LANGFORD   HO 129/122/22
PRIMITIVE METHODIST CHAPEL. *Erected* 1849. Separate and entire building. Used exclusively for worship. *Free sittings* 47; *other sittings* 73. *On 30 March* In afternoon General Congregation 60; in evening General Congregation 65. *Average attendance* during previous 12 months, in afternoon General Congregation 80; in evening General Congregation 70. *Signed* William Hemming,[1], Steward, Langford.

1. *Gardner* describes W. Hemming, Langford, as a land surveyor.

257. LANGFORD   HO 129/122/23
INDEPENDENT CHAPEL. *Erected* 1850. An old chapel built in 1842 has been closed being too small and the present erected in its stead. Separate and entire building. Used exclusively for worship. *Free sittings* 220; *other sittings* 80. *On 30 March* In morning General Congregation 140, Sunday Scholars 76; in evening General Congregation 183, Sunday Scholars 74. *Average attendance* during previous 6 months, in morning General Congregation 150, Sunday Scholars 73; in evening General Congregation 200, Sunday Scholars 40. *Signed* Mark Cunningham, Minister, Langford.

258. LAUNTON   Population 706   HO 129/159/36
ESTABLISHED CHURCH. *Free sittings* 202; *other sittings* 108. *Average attendance* in morning General congregation 80, Sunday Scholars 95; in afternoon General Congregation 150, Sunday Scholars 95; in evening General Congregation 75. *Remarks* This is as correct account as I can get as the clergyman refused to give any return.[1]

1. Unsigned but probably completed by the Registrar. See similar returns in the same hand for Stoke Lyne, Stratton Audley.

259. LAUNTON   HO 129/159/39
WESLEYAN METHODIST CHAPEL. A dwelling house. *Sittings* 50. *On 30 March* In afternoon General Congregation 16. *Remarks* The congregation has not been so large during the last twelve months as

formerly occasioned by gifts from other ministers which have more influence. *Signed* X. The mark of William Butler, Occupier, Launton, Bicester.

260. LAUNTON   HO 129/159/46
WESLEYAN METHODIST CHAPEL.[1] *Erected* 1831. Not a separate and entire building. Not used exclusively for worship. *Free sittings* 50. *On 30 March* In afternoon General Congregation 28; in evening General Congregation 16. *Remarks* Services held in a private dwelling house. *Signed* William Butler, Master of House, Launton.
1. See also HO 129/159/39. HO 129/159/47 is a third return for the 'Wesleyan Preaching House' at Launton. It includes exactly the same information as HO 129/159/46 but in a different hand, apart from the remarks which appear to have been added by the same person who completed the whole of the form HO 129/159/46.

261. LAUNTON   HO 129/159/48
BETHEL INDEPENDENT CHAPEL.*Erected* 1850. A separate and entire building. Used exclusively for worship. *Free sittings* 146; *other sittings* 54. *On 30 March* In afternoon General Congregation 120; in evening General Congregation 130. *Average attendance* during previous 6 months, in afternoon General Congregation 130; in evening General Congregation 140. *Signed* John Freeman, Deacon, Launton.

262. LEAFIELD[1]   Population 837   HO 129/162/5
CHAPEL OF EASE. *Erected* before 1800. *Endowned* with land £40, glebe £25, other permanent endowment £40, total £105 less Income Tax and rates and the rates are heavy. *Free sittings* 200; *other sittings* 200. *On 30 March* In afternoon General Congregation 400 including Sunday Scholars. *Remarks* In Leafield Chapel there is one service on the Sunday. In the morning and afternoon alternately. The Sunday Scholars are about 90. In the afternoon the chapel is not sufficiently large for the congregation. *Signed* Frederick Edwin Lott, Perpetual Curate.
1. A chapelry in Shipton under Wychwood parish.

263. LEAFIELD   HO 129/162/7
INDEPENDENT OR CONGREGATIONAL CHAPEL. *Erected* 1838. A separate and entire building. Used exclusively for worship. *Free sittings* All.[1] *On 30 March* No service. *Average attendance* during 1851 none. *Remarks* There is service performed but once a fortnight on account of the minister living at a distance. There was no service on

Sunday last but there will be next Sunday 6th April 1851 and on 21st April. *Signed* Edward Spiers, Manager, Leafield.

1. HO 129/162/6 is a supplementary return stating the number of free sittings to be 80 to 100. It also bears the following note 'Sir, I am very sorry any wrong information should have been given respecting the Chapel it is called a Congregational chapel and will seat as near as I can tell about 80 to 100 and are all free sittings. Your humble servant E. Spiers. Leafield, February 14/52'.

264. LEW[1]   Population 193   HO 129/161/20
TRINITY CHAPEL. *Erected* 1844 as an additional church for the hamlet of Lew by public subscription at a cost of about £800. *Free sittings* about 100; *other sittings* 60. *On 30 March* In morning total congregation 30. *Average attendance* during previous 12 months, in morning General Congregation 60, Sunday Scholars 20; in afternoon General Congregation 80, Sunday Scholars 20. *Remarks* The Vicars of Bampton or their Curates serve this chapel. *Signed* Dacre Adams, Vicar of 2nd Portion, Bampton.
1. A hamlet in Bampton parish.

265. LEW   HO 129/161/21
CONGREGATIONAL CHAPEL. *Erected* 1840. A separate and entire building. Used exclusively for worship. *Free sittings* 160. *On 30 March* In evening General Congregation 14. *Average attendance* during previous 12 months 33. *Signed* Robert Tozer, Minister, Witney.

266. LEWKNOR   Population 803[1]   HO 129/156/13
ST. MARGARET'S PARISH CHURCH. *Erected* before 1800. *Endowed* with land £140, tithe commuted at £190. *Free sittings* 80; *other sittings* 125. *On 30 March* In morning General Congregation 56, Sunday Scholars about 60; in afternoon General Congregation 70, Sunday Scholars about 60. *Signed* Edward B. Dean, Vicar.
1. Of that part of the parish in Oxfordshire. A further part was transferred to Buckinghamshire under the Act 7 and 8 Victoria c.61.

267. LEWKNOR   HO 129/156/14
WESLEYAN METHODIST CHAPEL. Not a separate and entire building. Not used exclusively for worship. *Free sittings* 30. *On 30 March* In evening General Congregation 25. *Average attendance* in evening 25. *Remarks* The persons who generally give instruction at the above place of worship are living at a distance that prevents the Registrar from obtaining a more correct return. *Signed* Thomas Home, Registrar.

268. LITTLE BOURTON HO 129/163/85
WESLEYAN METHODIST CHAPEL. *Erected* 1845. A separate and
entire building. Used exclusively for worship. *Free sittings* 40; *other
sittings* 44. *On 30 March* In evening General Congregation 45. *Average
attendance* during previous 12 months, in evening General Congregation
50. *Remarks* Sunday School kept in afternoons. No school in the
evenings. Any scholars present in the evening included in the number of
congregation. *Signed* J. Archer, Steward, Appletree, nr. Banbury.

269. LITTLE FARINGDON[1] Population 185 HO 129/122/24
CHAPEL. The Church of an ancient Chapelry. *Erected* before 1800.
Free sittings 70; *other sittings* 50. *On 30 March* In morning General
Congregation 22, Sunday Scholars 28; in afternoon General
Congregation 40, Sunday Scholars 35. *Average attendance* during
previous 3 months, in morning General Congregation 25, Sunday
Scholars 30; in afternoon General Congregation 38, Sunday Scholars 40.
Remarks The Vicar of Langford pays the Curate £50 p.a. The number of
occasional attendants at Church is 105. *Signed* James Cole, Minister.
1. A chapelry and tithing in Langford parish.

270. LITTLE FARINGDON HO 129/122/25
PRIMITIVE METHODIST CHAPEL. Not an entire and separate
building. Not used exclusively for worship. *Free sittings* 50. *On 30 March*
In evening General Congregation 30. *Average Attendance* during
previous 12 months, in evening General Congregation 35. *Signed* David
Lynn, Steward, Little Faringdon.

271. LITTLE MILTON Population 418 HO 129/156/5
On 30 March In morning not known; in afternoon not known; in evening
none. *Average attendance* in morning not known; in afternoon not
known, in evening none. *Remarks* The return has been made by the
Clergyman, the Revd H. Shute who declined giving any further
information.[1] *Signed* Thomas Home, Registrar of Births and Deaths, 18
October 1851.
1. Revd Hardwicke Shute, in reply to Bishop Wilberforce's visitation queries of 1854,
stated that the average Sunday congregation at Little Milton was 160 and stationary. On the
Religious Census of 1851 he further commented that, "The numbers in the census do not
fairly represent numbers of the Church and Dissenters as many who are not dissenters
occasionally attend the Meeting House in the evening. I am of the opinion that especial
pains were taken that there should be a full attendance at the Meeting House on the day
when the Census was taken."

272. LITTLE MILTON HO 129/156/7
WESLEYAN METHODIST CHAPEL. *Erected* 1831. A separate and entire building. Used exclusively for worship. *Free sittings* 90; *other sittings* 40. *On 30 March* In morning General Congregation 36, Sunday Scholars 11; in afternoon Sunday Scholars 11; in evening General Congregation 50. *Average attendance* in morning General Congregation 40, Sunday Scholars 11; in afternoon Sunday Scholars 11; in evening General Congregation 55. *Signed* Thomas Perkins, Steward, Grocer, Little Milton.

273. LITTLE ROLLRIGHT Population 30 HO 129/162/43
CHURCH. *Erected* before 1800. *Endowed* with tithe £148 9s. *Free sittings* 24; *other sittings* 9. *On 30 March* In morning General Congregation 10. *Average attendance* in morning General Congregation 20. *Signed* W.E. Stevens, Rector, Salford Rectory.

274. LITTLE TEW[1] Population 237 HO 129/162/60
ADDITIONAL CHURCH in National School House. Licensed December 1849. Cost defrayed by subscription. No endowment. *Free sittings* 80. *On 30 March* In evening General Congregation 75. *Average attendance* during previous 12 months, in morning General Congregation 40, Sunday Scholars 26; in evening General Congregation 70. *Signed* John J. Campbell, Vicar, Great Tew.
1. Although treated separately for census purposes, ecclesiastically a chapelry in Great Tew parish.

275. LITTLE TEW HO 129/162/62
BAPTIST CHAPEL. *Erected* 1829. A separate and entire building. Used exclusively for worship. *Free sittings* 40; *other sittings* 70. *On 30 March* In morning General Congregation 117. *Average attendance* in morning General Congregation 111. *Signed* Thomas Eden, Baptist Minister, Chadlington.

276. LITTLEMORE[1] Population 214 HO 129/123/39
CHURCH OF ST. MARY AND ST. NICHOLAS. Originally consecrated as a Chapel of Ease to St. Mary's Church in Oxford. Subsequently (in July 1847) a chancel and tower having been added, it was erected into a Consolidated Chapelry under the Act of 6th and 7th of Victoria, c.37. Consecrated 22 September 1836. Erected by private benefaction of £3550. *Endowed* with land £10, other permanent endowment £70 3s. 2d, fees 3. *Free sittings* 230; *other sittings* 20; includes sittings for 60 children. *On 30 March* In morning General

Congregation 100, Sunday Scholars 59; in afternoon General Congretation 93, Sunday Scholars 53. *Average attendance* in morning General Congregation 150, Sunday Scholars 59; in afternoon General Congregation 150, Sunday Scholars 53. *Remarks* The population of the Ecclesiastical District of Littlemore to which this Return refers, will not appear in as much as the Returns of the Census Officers have been made according to the Old Division of Parishes. It is about 550 souls. *Signed* Charles Walters, Perpetual Curate.

1. The whole population of Littlemore was enumerated for census purposes under the parish of St. Mary the Virgin, Oxford, 1801 — 31. Thereafter it appears in two parts: that in Bullingdon Hundred had an enumerated population in 1851 of 214, that still appearing under the parish of St. Mary the Virgin 733. The latter had risen from 353 in 1841, a spectacular growth accounted for by the erection of the Oxfordshire and Berkshire Pauper Lunatic Asylum in 1846, and its extension in 1847.

277. LITTLEMORE   HO 129/157/27
BAPTIST CHAPEL. *Erected* about 1809. A separate and entire building. Used exclusively for worship. *Free sittings* 150. *On 30 March* In evening General Congregation 30. *Average* attendance during previous 9 months, in evening General Congregation 40. *Remarks* This chapel was closed for about two years — but was reopened July 1850. *Signed* Charles Underhill, Minister, 11 Beaumont Street, Oxford.

278. LITTLEMORE   HO 129/123/38
PRIVATE CHAPEL of the Oxfordshire and Berkshire Pauper Lunatic Asylum.[1] The Chapel is not consecrated but the Chaplain is licensed to it by the Bishop of the Diocese, under the 8th and 9th Victoria, c.126. *On 30 March* In morning General Congregation 214; in afternoon General Congregation 221. *Average attendance* during previous 12 months, in morning General Congregation 190; in afternoon General Congregation 196. *Remarks* There are two services every Sunday, Christmas Day and Good Friday and prayers every morning at $\frac{1}{2}$ past 8. *Signed* Edwin Pulling, Chaplain, Littlemore Asylum.

1. On 31 December 1851 the asylum contained 347 patients.

279. LONG COMBE   Population 655   HO 129/160/30
PARISH CHURCH. *Erected* before 1800. Permanent endowment £90. *Free sittings* 200;*other sittings* 60. *On 30 March* In morning General Congregation 120, Sunday Scholars 30; in afternoon General Congregation 200, Sunday Scholars 40. *Average attendance* in morning General Congregation 120, Sunday Scholars 30; in afternoon General Congregation 200, Sunday Scholars 40. *Signed* William Barrett, Chaplain.

280. LONG COMBE HO 129/160/31
WESLEYAN METHODIST CHAPEL. *Erected* 1835. A separate and entire building. Used exclusively for worship. *Free sittings* 112; *other sittings* 56. *On 30 March* In afternoon General Congregation 60, Sunday Scholars 20; in evening General Congregation 120, Sunday Scholars 20. *Signed* Robert Cross,[1] Chapel Steward, Combe.
1. *Gardner* describes Robert Cross, Long Combe, as a farmer.

281. LOWER ASSENDEN HO 129/155/1
MR. BIRCH'S[1] CHAPEL. Church of England, situated at Lower Assenden in Henley Parish. *On 30 March* about 30 persons including about 10 of the children that are scholars that are educated at school held in this chapel. *Remarks* This information is given by one of the congregation. There is service on Wednesdays in the morning only but not during the Hay and Grain harvest as at such time few persons would attend. *Signed* Robert Coates, Registrar.
1. J.W.N. Birch, Esq., of Henley Park.

282. LOWER HEYFORD Population 605 HO 129/159/3
PARISH CHURCH. *Erected* before 1800. *Average attendance* during previous 6 months, in morning General Congregation 200, Sunday Scholars 50; in afternoon General Congregation 200, Sunday Scholars 50. *Remarks* The space available for about 300 persons mostly free sittings and pews for about 100 and about the usual average attendance on March 30th 1851. *Signed* George Cooper, Overseer and Enumerator, Lower Heyford.

283. LOWER HEYFORD HO 129/159/7a
WESLEYAN METHODIST CHAPEL.[1] A separate and entire building. Used exclusively for worship. *Average attendance* in morning General Congregation 50. *Remarks* A return for this has been made for by the Superintendent of the Circuit in the Brackley District. *Signed* George Cooper, Overseer, Lower Heyford.[2]
1. HO 129/159/8 is a supplementary return for the Wesleyan Methodist Chapel, here described as being situated in Caulcott hamlet (*q.v.*)in the parish of Lower Heyford, stating that it contains free sittings 46, appropriated sittings 12.
2. Cooper, also appears as signatory on the return for Lower Heyford Parish Church. Judging by the uniformity of handwriting on these returns, and in all or part of other returns for this district it appears that Cooper may well have done more than merely deliver blank forms to clergy or leading Dissenters.

284. MAPLEDURHAM   Population 509   HO 129/126/13
PARISH CHURCH. *Erected* before 1800. *Endowed* with tithe £828, glebe £50, fees 10s, Easter offerings 15s. *Total sittings* 200. *On 30 March* In morning General Congregation 120, Sunday Scholars 33; in afternoon General Congregation 45, Sunday Scholars 24. *Signed* George Hutchins, Minister.

285. MAPLEDURHAM   HO 129/126/14
CHAISE HEATH INDEPENDENT CHAPEL. Began to be used for public worship about 1800. A room hired in a cottage. *Free sittings* 35. *On 30 March* In evening General Congregation 27. *Average attendance* during previous 12 months, in evening General Congregation 26. *Signed* William Legg, BA, Superintendent, 85 Castle Street, Reading, Berks.

286. MARSH BALDON   Population 351   HO 129/123/43
PARISH CHURCH. *Erected* before 1800. *Free sittings* 120; *other sittings* 45. *On 30 March* In morning General Congregation 84, Sunday Scholars 44. *Average attendance* I cannot tell but there is little or no variation during the year. *Remarks* As I am only the Curate of this Parish, and the Rector is abroad and engaged in a law-suit with the Patron about the Tithes, it is impossible for me to say anything about the amount of the endowment. *Signed* Frederick Reynoux, Curate, Toot Baldon.

287. MARSTON   Population 471   HO 129/157/19
PARISH CHURCH. *On 30 March* In morning General Congregation 75, Sunday Scholars 60 with the above. *Remarks* As near as I could ascertain. *Signed* Richard Wood, Registrar.

288. MERTON   Population 200   HO 129/159/44
ST. SWITHIN'S PARISH CHURCH. *Erected* before 1800. *Endowed* with land about £70. *Free sittings* 120; *other sittings 60. On 30 March* In morning General Congregation 45, Sunday Scholars 28; in afternoon General Congregation 100, Sunday Scholars 28. *Signed* Charles Ross de Havilland, Minister.

289. MERTON   HO 129/159/45
PROTESTANT DISSENTER[1] INDEPENDENT CHAPEL. Opened for worship about 2 years. An inhabited cottage. Not used exclusively for worship. *Free sittings* 35. *On 30 March* In evening General Congregation 32. *Average attendance* during previous 12 months, in evening General

Congregation 30. *Signed* John Elstone, Deacon and Local Preacher, London Road, Bicester.

1. The words 'Protestant Dissenter' are crossed through, probably by a census official.

290. MIDDLE BARTON[1]   HO 129/160/9
WESLEYAN METHODIST CHAPEL. *Erected* about 1831. A separate and entire building. Used exclusively for worship. *Free sittings* 130; *other sittings* 120. *On 30 March* In morning General Congregation 181, Sunday Scholars 45; in afternoon Sunday Scholars 40; in evening General Congregation 188. *Average attendance* during previous 6 months, in morning General Congregation 180, Sunday Scholars 40; in afternoon Sunday Scholars 42; in evening General Congregation 200. *Remarks* Morning sermon. School afternoon. Evening sermon. *Signed* Simon Huggins[2], Steward, Wescott Barton.

1. A hamlet and township in Steeple Barton parish.
2. *Gardner* describes Simon Huggins, Manor House, Westcott Barton, as a farmer and corn merchant.

291. MIDDLETON STONEY Population 307   HO 129/159/4
PARISH CHURCH. *Erected* before 1800. *Free sittings* 125; *other sittings* 128. *On 30 March* In morning General Congregation 85, Sunday Scholars 40; in afternoon General Congregation 85, Sunday Scholars 40. *Average attendance* in morning General Congregation 85, Sunday Scholars 40; in afternoon General Congregation 85, Sunday Scholars 40.

292. MILCOMBE[1]   Population 241   HO 129/163/13
MILCOMBE CHAPEL. *Erected* before 1800. *Endowed* with land about 65 acres under Enclosure of 1794. *Free sittings* 90; *other sittings* 48. *On 30 March* In afternoon General Congregation 48, Sunday Scholars 28. *Remarks* A separate endowment of about 45 acres annexed to the Rectory of Wigginton, Oxon, by Eton College, for one fourth of the monthly Sunday duties. *Signed* E.N. Maddock, Officiating Minister. George Bell, Vicar of Bloxham cum Milcombe Chapelry.

1. A chapelry in Bloxham parish.

293. MILCOMBE   HO 129/163/14
BAPTIST CHAPEL. *Erected* 1824. A separate and entire building. Used exclusively for worship. *Free sittings* 80. *On 30 March* In morning General Congregation 51. *Average attendance* during previous 45 months, in morning General Congregation 51. *Signed* David Nunnick, Minister, Bloxham.

294. MILTON UNDER WYCHWOOD[1]

Population 799   HO 129/162/2

PRIMITIVE METHODIST CHAPEL. *Erected* 1834. A separate and entire building. Used exclusively for worship. *Free sittings* 80; *other sittings* 45. *On 30 March* In afternoon General Congregation 101; in evening General Congregation 96. *Average attendance* in morning General Congregation 110. *Signed* William Coulling, Trustee and Class Leader, Milton.

1. A township in Shipton under Wychwood parish.

295. MILTON UNDER WYCHWOOD   HO 129/162/3

BAPTIST CHAPEL, Upper Chapel. *Erected* 1840. A separate and entire building. Used exclusively for worship. *Free sittings* 180; *other sittings* 56. *On 30 March* In morning General Congregation 120, Sunday Scholars 80; in evening General Congregation 200. *Signed* William Cherry, Minister, Milton.

296. MILTON UNDER WYCHWOOD   HO 129/162/4

ZOAR PARTICULAR BAPTIST CHAPEL. *Erected* 1846. A separate and entire building. Used exclusively for worship. *Free sittings* 190. *On 30 March* In afternoon General Congregation 161. *Average attendance* during previous 6 months, in afternoon General Congregation 140. *Signed* William Gibson, Manager, Milton.

297. MILTON[1]   Population 164   HO 129/163/20

PRIMITIVE METHODIST CHAPEL. *Erected* before 1800. A separate and entire building. Used exclusively for worship. *Free sittings* 200. *On 30 March* In afternoon General Congregation 35, Sunday Scholars 25; in evening General Congregation 27. *Average attendance* in morning General Congregation 35, Sunday Scholars 28. *Signed* Thomas Tarver,[2] Steward, Bodicote.

1. A hamlet in Adderbury parish.
2. *Gardner* describes T. Tarver, Bodicote, as a tailor and tea-dealer.

298. MINSTER LOVELL   Population 450   HO 129/161/57

ST. KENELM'S CHURCH. *On 30 March* In morning Sunday Scholars 60; in afternoon Sunday Scholars 60. *Average attendance* in morning General Congregation 30, Sunday Scholars 60; in afternoon General Congregation 120, Sunday Scholars 66.[1] *Signed* W.R. Powell, Curate.

1. HO 129/161/56 is a supplementary return stating there to be free sittings 19 x 5 = 95, appropriated sittings 10 x 5 = 50. 'The free sittings are capable on an average of holding about five persons.'

299. MIXBURY   Population 402   HO 129/164/19
ALL SAINTS' PARISH CHURCH. *Remarks* The Statutes 13 and 14
Vict. c 53[1] do not appear to relate to the subject of this form or schedule
in the particulars stated. *Signed* W.J. Palmer, Rector.
1. The returns were headed 'Census of Great Britain 1851 (13 and 14 Victoriae, cap. 53)'.

300. MOLLINGTON[1]   Population 241   HO 129/163/81
CHURCH. *On 30 March* In morning General Congregation 100.
Remarks Revd Mr. Sheldon, Curate refused to make any return. *Signed*
Thomas Pearce, Registrar, Bourton, nr. Banbury.
1. A chapelry lying partly in Cropredy parish and partly in Kington Hundred,
Warwickshire.

301. MOLLINGTON   HO 129/163/82
PRIMITIVE METHODIST CHAPEL. *Erected* 1845. A separate and
entire building. Used exclusively for worship. *Free sittings* 60; *other
sittings* 60. *On 30 March* In morning Sunday Scholars 16; in afternoon
General Congregation 60, Sunday Scholars 16; in evening General
Congregation 86. *Average attendance* during previous 12 months, in
evening General Congregation 100. *Signed* John Frost, Manager, Shoe
Maker, Mollington.

302. MONGEWELL   Population 197   HO 129/125/54
ST. JOHN THE BAPTIST PARISH CHURCH. *Erected* before 1800.
Free sittings 88; *other sittings* 14. *On 30 March* In morning General
Congregation 43, Sunday Scholars 17; in afternoon General
Congregation 28, Sunday Scholars 12. *Remarks* Many of the inhabitants
of this Parish are at a great distance from their Church. *Signed* Glyd
White, Curate.

303. MORTON[1]   HO 129/156/36
BETHEL PRIMITIVE METHODIST CHAPEL. *Erected* 1839. A
separate and entire building. Used exclusively for worship. *Free sittings*
200. *On 30 March* In morning Sunday Scholars 40; in afternoon General
Congregation 40, Sunday Scholars 30; in evening General Congregation
45. *Average attendance* in morning Sunday Scholars 50; in afternoon
General Congregation 50, Sunday Scholars 45; in evening General
Congregation 60. *Remarks* Only school on Sunday mornings. *Sittings* all
free. *Signed* Isaac Mott, Manager, Morton, Thame.[2]
1. A hamlet in Thame parish. Population not separately enumerated but *Gardner* describes
it as containing about 30 houses including several labourers' cottages.
2. *Gardner* describes Isaac Mott, Morton, as a chair maker.

304. MURCOTT[1]   HO 129/159/10
PRIMITIVE METHODIST CHAPEL. *Erected* 1843. A separate and
entire building. Used exclusively for worship. *Free sittings* 60. *On 30
March* In morning General Congregation 40, Sunday Scholars 25. *Signed*
William Badger, Superintendent, Murcott.
1. Murcott was a hamlet in Charlton on Otmoor parish. With the nearby hamlet of Fencot
it had a population of 289.

305. NEITHROP[1]   Population 4180   HO 129/163/110
CHRIST CHURCH CHAPEL OR PRESBYTERIAN CHAPEL.
Unitarian. Built in the year of 1849 and 1850 opened and set apart for
religious worship August 1850. Consists of a nave and chancel, south
aisle and vestry with open roof, clustered pillars and pointed arches. Old
English gothic and apart from all other building. Used exclusively for
worship. *Free sittings* when wanted room to provide apart 85; *other
sittings* 240. *On 30 March* In morning General Congregation 124,
Sunday Scholars boys 32, girls 47; in evening General Congregation 214.
Average attendance during previous 7 months, in morning General
Congregation about 120, Sunday Scholars 92; in evening General
Congregation about 140. *Remarks* The scholars attend Divine Service as
schools only in the morning; in the afternoon join a short religious
service during the time they are assembled in the school; some of the
elder scholars sing with the evening congregation. Our former school
called 'The Old or great meeting house' was used by the congregation for
about 300 years. The new one was erected on the adjoining ground:
though part is in Banbury and the part on which the new chapel is built in
Neithrop. *Signed* Henry Hunt Piper, Minister, Banbury.
1. A township in Banbury parish.

306. NEITHROP   HO 129/163/111
BAPTIST CHAPEL, South Bar. *Erected* 1834. A separate and entire
building. Used exclusively for worship. *Free sittings* 50; *other sittings*
120. *On 30 March* In morning General Congregation 70, Sunday
Scholars 39; in afternoon Sunday Scholars 37; in evening General
Congregation 77. *Signed* David Lodge, Minister, South Bar, Banbury.

307. NETHER WORTON   Population 85   HO 129/160/10
ST. JAMES' PARISH CHURCH. *Erected* before 1800. *Endowed* with
land £30, other permanent endowment, Queen Anne's Bounty £21, fees
very small. *Free sittings* 30; *other sittings* 120. *On 30 March* In morning
General Congregation 76, Sunday Scholars 23. *Average attendance*
during previous 12 months, in morning General Congregation 75,

Sunday Scholars 20. *Remarks* A very small parish joining another small parish 'Upper Worton'. The service is by mutual consent of ministers in the morning at Nether Worton and in the afternoon at Upper Worton. *Signed* George Venables, Curate, Deddington.

308. NETTLEBED   Population 754   HO 129/155/29
ST. BARTHOLOMEW'S PARISH CHURCH. Recently rebuilt upon a larger scale. Consecrated after rebuilding 3 December 1846 in lieu of the old Church. Erected at a cost of about £2,600 by subscription etc from parishioners and others and grant of £300 from Incorporated Society. *Endowed* by annual payment by Lord Camoys owner of rent charge £35 and augmented by Queen Anne's Bounty. *Free sittings* 210; *other sittings* 110. *On 30 March* In morning General Congregation 165, Sunday Scholars 64. *Average attendance* during previous 12 months, in morning General Congregation 160, Sunday Scholars 60; in afternoon General Congregation 200, Sunday Scholars 50. *Remarks* Nettlebed as a Benefice is united with Pishill and a sum of £35 is the original endowment of both churches. The income of the incumbent of both parishes with the Bounty Office augemented is about £130. *Signed* James Hazel, Incumbent.

309. NETTLEBED   HO 129/155/30
CONGREGATIONAL CHAPEL. Erected 1838. Separate and entire building. Used exclusively for worship. *Free sittings* 100. *On 30 March* in afternoon General Congregation 53; in evening General Congregation 50. *Average attendance* in morning General Congregation 60. *Remarks* In connection with Henley Home Missionary. Mr. Becker Preacher. *Signed* Thomas Fox, Manager, Nettlebed.[1]
1. *Gardner* describes Thomas Fox, Nettlebed, as a blacksmith.

310. NEWINGTON   Population 454   HO 129/125/41
ST. GILES' CHURCH. Consecrated before legal memory. *Free sittings* 129; *other sittings* 40. *On 30 March* In morning General Congregation 61, Sunday Scholars 53; in afternoon General Congregation 42, Sunday Scholars 26. *Average attendance* estimated at about 120 with the children. *Remarks* I have no means of making the correct estimate of the number of average attendance for any past period. *Signed* Septimus Cotes, Rector.

311. NEWNHAM MURREN Population 237   HO 129/125/52
ST. MARY'S PARISH CHURCH. *Erected* before 1800. *Free sittings* 90; *other sittings* 10. *Average attendance* during previous 6 months, in morning General Congregation 60, Sunday Scholars 27. *Remarks* This

Church just restored by voluntary contributions is with the exception of the Chancel fitted throughout with free sittings. *Signed* Frederick Carroll, Curate, The Retreat, Wallingford, Berkshire.

312. NEWNHAM MURREN   HO 129/125/53
ST. MARY'S PARISH CHURCH. *Erected* before 1800. *Endowed* with tithe £550. *Free sittings* 70; *other sittings* 15. *On 30 March* in morning General Congregation 45, Sunday Scholars 20. *Signed* Charles Fuller, Church Warden, Newnham Farm, near Wallingford.

313. NEWTON PURCELL WITH SHELSWELL[1]
                           Population 117 and 43 HO 129/159/58
PARISH CHURCH. *Endowed* with tithe rent charge upon 13,000 [sic] acres of land, glebe 27 acres. *Free sittings* 65; *other sittings* 55. *On 30 March* In morning General Congregation 45, Sunday Scholars 20; in afternoon General Congregation 44, Sunday Scholars 16. *Average attendance* in morning General Congregation 50, Sunday Scholars 25; in afternoon General Congregation 50, Sunday Scholars 25. *Remarks* Many of the boys usually attending the Sunday School were about in the fields bird-keeping on Sunday March 30th. *Signed* John Meade, Rector, Newton Purcell.

1. Shelswell had no church, the living being a curacy annexed to the rectory of Newton Purcell.

314. NOKE   Population 140   HO 129/159/20
PARISH CHURCH. *Erected* before 1800. *Endowed* with tithe commuted at £72, glebe let at £56, house and gardens, fees and dues little more than nominal and seldom accepted, the inhabitants being generally poor. *Free sittings* 66, small gallery for singers only. *On 30 March* In morning, prayers only, General Congregation 31; in afternoon General Congregation 51. *Average attendance* in afternoon General Congregation about 60. *Remarks* The Sunday scholars are not taken to church under control nor necessarily present at Divine Service being many of them engaged in bird-keeping etc. etc. Those present are included in the general congregation. *Signed* J. Carlyle, Rector.

315. NORTH ASTON   Population 308   HO 129/160/19
ST. MARY'S PARISH CHURCH. *Erected* before 1800. *Endowed* with tithe £188, glebe £10, fees £1. *Free sittings* 80; *other sittings* 70. *On 30 March* In morning General Congregation 60, Sunday Scholars 14; in afternoon General Congregation 70, Sunday Scholars 14. *Signed* C. Rede Clifton, Vicar, North Aston.

316. NORTH LEIGH Population 725 HO 129/161/3
ST. MARY'S PARISH CHURCH. *Erected* before 1800. *Free sittings*
120; *other sittings* 130. *On 30 March* In morning General Congregation
70, Sunday Scholars 30; in afternoon General Congregation 120, Sunday
Scholars 30. *Average* attendance in morning General Congregation 70,
Sunday Scholars 30; in afternoon General Congregation 120; Sunday
Scholars 30. *Signed* Isaac Gillam, Vicar.

317. NORTH LEIGH HO 129/161/4
WESLEYAN METHODIST CHAPEL. *Erected* before 1800. A separate
and entire building. Used exclusively for worship. *Free sittings* 90; *other
sittings* 35. *On 30 March* In morning General Congregation 50, Sunday
Scholars 36; in afternoon Sunday Scholars 39; in evening General
Congregation 70. *Signed* Joseph Sheppard[1], Steward, Baker, North
Leigh.
1. *Gardner* describes Joseph Sheppard, North Leigh, as a farmer and miller.

318. NORTH NEWINGTON[1] Population 436 HO 129/163/30
INDEPENDENT CHAPEL. *Erected* 1837. A separate and entire
building. Used exclusively for worship. *Free sittings* all.[2] *On 30 March* In
afternoon General Congregation 80; in evening General Congregation
62, Sunday Scholars 31. *Signed* John George Walford, Superintendent,
Silversmith, Banbury.
1. A hamlet in Broughton parish.
2. HO 129/163/29a is a supplementary return stating the number of free sittings to be 110.

319. NORTH STOKE Population 160 HO 129/125/55
PARISH CHURCH. Consecrated by Thomas a Becket before the year
1170. *Endowed* with small tithe £35 3s 4d., glebe sold out for £220 13s.
Free sittings 30; *other sittings* 80. *On 30 March* In afternoon General
Congregation 96.[1] *Average attendance* during previous 12 months, in
afternoon General Congregation 70.[1] *Signed* Thomas White, Gentleman,
Prospect House, North Stoke.
1. Further figures of 28 are entered in the totals section of the evening attendance columns
for both 30 March and the average. These may be intended to refer to Sunday Scholars.

320. NORTHMOOR Population 375 HO 129/161/12
ST. DENIS' PARISH CHURCH. *Erected* before 1800. *Endowed* with
land £52,other permanent endowment £70, fees say £1 10s. *Sittings* about
200. *On 30 March* in morning General Congregation 45, Sunday
Scholars 33; in afternoon General Congregation 55, Sunday Scholars 30.
Average attendance during previous 12 months, in morning General
Congregation 50, Sunday Scholars 40; in afternoon General

Congregation 60; Sunday Scholars 35. *Remarks* The above numbers are somewhat below the usual average wh. as far as I can judge is as stated in the other column. *Signed* Henry Heming, Officiating Minister.

321. NORTHMOOR   HO 129/161/13
PRIMITIVE METHODIST CHAPEL. *Erected* 1842. A separate and entire building. Used exclusively for worship. *Free sittings* 140. *On 30 March* In morning Sunday Scholars 19; in afternoon General Congregation 90; in evening General Congregation 150. *Signed* John Moss, Steward, Northmoor.

322. NUFFIELD   Population 251   HO 129/155/28
HOLY TRINITY PARISH CHURCH. *Erected* before 1800. *Free sittings* 160; *other sittings* 44. *On 30 March* In morning General Congregation 102, Sunday Scholars 56; in afternoon General Congregation 105, Sunday Scholars 47. *Signed* W. T. Hopkins, Minister.

323. NUNEHAM COURTENAY Population 358   HO 129/123/4
EPISCOPAL CHURCH. *On 30 March* In morning General Congregation 120, Sunday Scholars 50. *Signed* John Polley, District Registrar.

324. ODDINGTON   Population 126   HO 129/159/19
ST. ANDREW'S PARISH CHURCH. *Erected* before 1800. *Endowed* with tithe about £200, glebe £65. No other sources of emolument. *Free sittings* 45; *other sittings* 70. *Remarks* I cannot give an exact account of the attendance on Divine Service. I may state generally that the whole population, with the exception of a very few dissenters are very constant in attending the services of the church. *Signed* P. Serle,   Rector.

325. OXFORD ALL SAINTS Population 559   HO 129/159/7
CHURCH OF ALL SAINTS. The cure and chaplaincy attached to Lincoln College, Oxford. *Erected* before 1800. *Endowed* with land £18, other permanent endowment £12, fees £10, Easter Offerings £18, other sources £45. *Sittings* 350. *On 30 March* In morning General Congregation 210; in evening General Congregation 152. *Average attendance* during previous 3 months, in morning General Congregation 200; in evening General Congregation 190. *Signed* Thomas Espinell Espin, Chaplain, Lincoln College.

326. OXFORD HOLY TRINITY HO 129/158/10
DISTRICT CHURCH.[1] Consecrated October 14 1845 as a separate parish church for ecclesiastical purposes. *Erected* by Underwood, Architects, and Gardiners, Builders, at a cost of £3,700, defrayed by the Ecclesiastical Commissioners £300, and by subscription £3,400. *Endowed* by the Ecclesiastical Commissioners with permanent endowment £150, fees about £7, Easter Offerings £2 6s. *Free sittings* 500; *other sittings* 200. *On 30 March* in morning General Congregation 400, Sunday Scholars 35; in afternoon General Congregation 350, Sunday Scholars 35. *Average attendance* in morning General Congregation 450, Sunday Scholars 40; in afternoon General Congregation 550, Sunday Scholars 40. *Signed* Joseph West, Minister, 17 St. John's Street.
1. Holy Trinity Church lay in Blackfriars Road in the ancient parish of St. Ebbe.

327. OXFORD ST. ALDATE[1] Population 1481 HO 129/158/9
PARISH CHURCH. *Erected* before 1800. *Endowed* with land £12, in lieu of tithes £109 14s. Parsonage House £30, fees £25, Easter Offerings £15. *Free sittings* 66; *other sittings* 370, children 100. *On 30 March* In morning General Congregation 320, Sunday Scholars 80; in afternoon General Congregation 350. *Signed* Henry Swabey, Rector.
1. Another part of the parish of St. Aldate, i.e. Grandpont tithing, lay in Berkshire.

328. OXFORD ST. CLEMENT Population 2139 HO 129/157/16
PARISH CHURCH. *Erected* before 1800, instead of an old church, subsequently taken down. Cost of £6530 and land for site defrayed by subscription. *Endowed* with tithe £79, glebe £5, other permanent endowment £50, fees £7 4s, other sources £2 10s. *Free sittings* 702; *other sittings* 361 allowing 20 inches for each sitting. *On 30 March* In morning General Congregation 260, Sunday Scholars 90; in afternoon General Congregation 160, Sunday Scholars 104. *Remarks* Having only been in residence for 2 months I have ascertained from the Archdeacon the amount of gross receipts for the last year, with the exception of fees; these last I have calculated for the year by multiplying the amount received during the last 2 months by 6. *Signed* William Strong Hore, Rector.

329. OXFORD ST. CLEMENT HO 129/157/29
PRIMITIVE METHODIST CHAPEL. *Erected* 1839. A separate and entire building. Used exclusively for worship. *Free sittings* 40; *other sittings* 60. *On 30 March* In afternoon General Congregation 50; in evening General Congregation 120. *Average attendance* during previous 3 months, in afternoon General Congregation 50; in evening General

Congregation 120. *Remarks* The primitive methodists rent this chapel and have occupied it for the past 3 months only. *Signed* Samuel West, Minister, 29 Observatory Street, St. Giles, Oxford.

330. OXFORD ST. CLEMENT   HO 129/157/33
NEW JERUSALEM CHURCH. A room for divine worship at Mr. Debens, High Street. Used exclusively for worship. *Free sittings* 50. *On 30 March* In evening General Congregation 40. *Remarks* Meet for the purpose of worshipping Jehovah Jesus Christ. 'In whom dwells *all* the fullness of the Godhead bodily'. Coll 2 - 9. *Signed* William Ray, Leader, Rose Hill, Oxford.

331. OXFORD ST. CLEMENT   HO 129/157/32
ROMAN CATHOLIC CHAPEL OF ST. IGNATIUS.[1] *Erected* before 1800. A separate and entire building. Used exclusively for worship. *Signed* Henry Brigham.

1. HO 129/157/31 is a supplementary return asking Richard Wood, Registrar 'the number of free and other sittings provided in St. Ignatius Roman Catholic Chapel, St. Clements, Headington also the general congregation attending it'. Wood answered that 'I called on the Priest of the Chapel yesterday who declined giving any Information. Indeed he said should not except he was compelled. Having a friend of that religion who regular [sic] attends chapel who gave me the under information as near as he could inform me which I believe is nearly correct. Vizt. Number of sittings about 70-80, about half free, others about half. The General Congregation attending about fifty. This is the best information I am able to give'.

332. OXFORD ST. CROSS OR HOLYWELL
                       Population 901   HO 129/158/4
PARISH CHURCH.*Erected* before 1800, anciently a chapel of ease to St. Peters in the East. *Endowed* with land £14 11s 3d, other permanent endowment £21 7s 2d, Easter offerings at the outside £39, other sources £10. *Free sittings* 50; *other sittings* 400. *On 30 March* In morning General Congregation 266, Sunday Scholars 40; in afternoon General Congregation 181, Sunday Scholars 40. *Average attendance* in morning General Congregation 266, Sunday Scholars 40; in afternoon General Congregation 200, Sunday Scholars 40. *Remarks* I think it possible that some of the children were twice counted in the afternoon of the 30th. A violent storm thinned the congregation below the usual number. *Signed* John Llewellyn Roberts, Fellow of Queens College and Curate.

333. OXFORD ST. EBBE   Population 4656   HO 129/158/11
PARISH CHURCH. *Erected* before 1800. *Endowed* with land £87, other permanent endowment £18 1s 10d, fees £20, Easter Offerings £6.

Free sittings 400; *other sittings* 350. *On 30 March* in morning General Congregation 266, Sunday Scholars 165; in evening General Congregation 615, Sunday Scholars 100. *Average attendance* in morning General Congregation 270, Sunday Scholars 170; in evening General Congregation 500, Sunday Scholars 100. *Remarks* By free sittings are understood to mean those for school children and open sittings for adults, by other sittings pews appropriated. *Signed* George Thomas Cameron, Curate.

334. OXFORD ST. EBBE   HO 129/158/12
ADULLAM PARTICULAR BAPTIST CHAPEL. *Erected* 1832. A separate and entire building. Used exclusively for worship. *Free sittings* 800. *On 30 March* In morning General Congregation 500, Sunday Scholars 43; in afternoon Sunday Scholars 43; in evening General Congregation 600. *Average attendance* in morning General Congregation 500, Sunday Scholars 50; in afternoon Sunday Scholars 50; in evening General Congregation 600. *Signed* Willoughby Willey, Minister, Henley House, Summertown, Oxford.

335. OXFORD ST. EBBE   HO 129/158/13
PRIMITIVE METHODIST CHAPEL. *Erected* 1843. A separate and entire building. Used exclusively for worship. *Free sittings* 50; *other sittings* 96. *On 30 March* In morning General Congregation 60; in evening General Congregation 70.[1] *Average attendance* during previous 12 months, in morning General Congregation 100, Sunday Scholars 62. *Signed* Samuel West, Minister, 29 Observatory Street, Oxford.
1. The same figures as those given for average attendance were originally entered for 30 March, then struck through and these figures squeezed in at the top of the form.

336. OXFORD ST EBBE   HO 129/158/14
JEWISH SYNAGOGUE. Held for about 3 years. Not a separate and entire building. Used exclusively for worship. *Free sittings* 24; *other sittings* 6. *Remarks* Saturday March 29th 1851. 10 in attendance in the morning only. *Signed* Nathan Jacobs, Reader, Little Clarendon Street, Oxford.

337. OXFORD ST. GILES   Population 4882   HO 129/157/34
ST. GILES' CHURCH. *Erected* before 1800. *Free sittings* 100; *other sittings* 400,school children's seats 180. *On 30 March* In morning General Congregation 300, Sunday Scholars 110; in afternoon General Congregation 220, Sunday Scholars 100. *Remarks* There are only 2 Faculty Pews. But the greater part of the sittings are appropriated to

parishioners who attend the church. I have no account of the endowments of the living. The vicar will return them. *Signed* Frederick J. Morrell, Churchwarden.

338. OXFORD ST. GILES   HO 129/158/24
QUAKER MEETING HOUSE, St. Giles.[1] *Erected* 1670. A separate and entire building. Used exclusively for worship. *Free sittings* 300; *other sittings* 250. *Average attendance* in morning General Congregation 100.
1. This return is made on the standard form for non-Anglican places of worship, and not on the separate form provided for the Society of Friends. This, together with the fact that the form is unsigned and refers to Quakers rather than the Society of Friends, suggests that it was not completed by a member of the meeting but probably by the Registrar.

339. OXFORD ST. MARTIN   Population 449   HO 129/158/8
ST. MARTIN'S CHURCH, CARFAX. Time of consecration unknown but the church, excepting the tower rebuilt 1822. Rebuilt under a Committee of Citizens and Parishioners with the exception of the tower which remains. Cost defrayed by Subscription of the Corporation £600, by parish trust money transferred £520, by parochial rates mortgaged and raised [?] on parish property £1150, and by private benefaction and subscription £1500. Probable Total Cost £3370. *Endowed* with land deducting land tax £28, other permanent endowment £7 10s, £10 10s from Queen Anne's Bounty, and a bequest, fees for burial, marriage etc. £6, trust monies held by parish for [?] £1 12s, Easter Offerings about £11. *Free Sittings* about 30; *other sittings* about 700. Population last census 490, vide remarks. *On 30 March* In morning General Congregation 235, Sunday Scholars 110; in evening General Congregation 400, Sunday Scholars 110. *Average attendance* is the same as given above. *Remarks* About 40 and 70 sittings are appropriated by voluntary agreement to the use of Alderman Nickson's foundation school and the City Blue Coat School, and about 40 to the use of the Mayor, Alderman, and Council of the City, having about (730 — 150) = 500 [sic] sittings to a population of 490 only. *Signed* William Hayward Cox, Rector, 15 Beaumont Street, Oxford.

340. OXFORD ST. MARY MAGDALEN   HO 129/158/21
PARISH CHURCH, Magdalen Street. *Erected* before 1800. *Endowed* with land £50, other permanent endowment £80 added £1850 for a provision for St. George the Martyr, Chapel of Ease, fees £30, Easter and Mich[aelmas] offerings £75, other sources £22 13s. *Free sittings* 150, school children 125; *other sittings* 525. Add from St. George etc. 450. *On 30 March* Rough estimate in morning General Congregation 355, Sunday

Scholars Girl's School 45; in afternoon General Congregation 205, Sunday Scholars 45 Girls' School, 50 Boys' School. *Remarks* I have. made a return, acting on my personal desire to promote the Census, but rather against my sense of the public good; for this sort of voluntary inquisition will some day be found to have been the too ready test of arbitary wills. *Signed* Jacob Ley, Vicar, Christ Church, Oxford.

341. OXFORD ST. MARY MAGDALEN   · HO 129/158/22
ST. GEORGE THE MARTYR'S CHAPEL OF EASE, George Street. Consecrated Feast of St. Andrew 1850. An additional church. *Erected* by private subscription at a cost of about £5,000, not yet settled. *Endowment* The Vicar of St. Mary Magdalen is responsible for its service. *Free sittings* 370, school children 80. *On 30 March* Estimate in morning General Congregation 125, Sunday Scholars 50; in evening General Congregation 275. *Remarks* I have made a return, acting upon my personal desire to promote the Census, but rather against my sense of the public good; for this sort of voluntary inquisition will some day be found a too ready tool of arbitary wills. *Signed* Jacob Ley, Vicar, St. Mary Magdalen, Christ Church, Oxford.

342. OXFORD ST. MARY MAGDALEN   HO 129/158/23
INDEPENDENT OR CONGREGATIONAL CHAPEL, George Street. *Erected* 1832. A separate and entire building. Used exclusively for worship. *Free sittings* 314; *other sittings* 430. *On 30 March* In morning General Congregation 253, Sunday Scholars 98; in evening General Congregation 264. *Signed* John Tyndale, Minister, 5 Plantation Road, Oxford.

343. OXFORD ST. MARY THE VIRGIN
                          Population 391   HO 129/158/5
PARISH CHURCH OF ST. MARY THE VIRGIN (used also as the University Church). *Endowed* with land £8, other permanent endowment stipend from Oriel Coll. £40, fees £3 ? [sic], Easter Offerings £13 10s, other sources, university dues allowed by Rectors (Oriel Coll.) to Vicar £35 ? [sic]. *Free sittings* about 200, gallery 600; *other sittings* 200. *Remarks* the church is capable of containing more than twice the population of the parish but is filled occasionally as at Assize Sermons and other public occasions. *Signed* Charles Marriott, Vicar, Oriel College.

344. OXFORD ST. MICHAEL   HO 129/158/20
PARISH CHURCH, Cornmarket Street. *Endowed* with land £25, other permanent endowment £1 12s 8d, pew rents 15s, fees £16, Easter Offerings £22, other sources £10. *Sittings* 400. *On 30 March* In morning General Congregation 213, Sunday Scholars 24; in afternoon General Congregation 90, Sunday Scholars 23. *Average attendance* during previous 6 months, in morning General Congregation 240, Sunday Scholars 30; in afternoon General Congregation 120, Sunday Scholars 30. *Signed* Frederick Metcalfe, Minister, Lincoln College, Oxford.

345. OXFORD ST. PAUL   HO 129/157/28
ST. PAUL'S CHURCH Clarendon Street. *On 30 March* In morning General Congregation 760 including Sunday Scholars. *Remarks* As near as I could ascertain. *Signed* Richard Wood, Registrar.

346. OXFORD ST. PAUL   HO 129/158/3
PARTICULAR BAPTIST. William Higgon's Room, Clarendon Place. *Erected* 1843. A separate and entire building. Used exclusively for worship. *Average attendance* during previous 12 months, in morning General Congregation 60. *Signed* William Higgons, Deacon, Grocer, Oxford.

347. OXFORD ST. PETER IN THE EAST
                    Population 1144   HO 129/158/1
PARISH CHURCH. *On 30 March* In morning General Congregation 4 to 500, Sunday Scholars 32; in afternoon General Congregation 80 to 100, Sunday Scholars 32; in evening General Congregation 4 to 500, Sunday Scholars 25.

348. OXFORD ST. PETER LE BAILEY   HO 129/158/6
WESLEYAN METHODIST CHAPEL. *Erected* 1817. A separate and entire building. Used exclusively for worship. *Free sittings* 186; *other sittings* 516. *On 30 March* In morning General Congregation 350, Sunday Scholars 98; in afternoon General Congregation 500; in evening General Congregation 400. *Average attendance* during previous 6 months, in morning General Conregation 380, Sunday Scholars 120; in afternoon General Congregation 120; in evening General Congregation 600. *Remarks* A special service was held in the afternoon, consequently the congregation was much larger, and the attendance at the evening service much smaller than usual. *Signed* John E. Cooke[1], Minister, Oxford.

1. *Gardner* describes the Revd J. Cooke as one of the ministers of the Wesleyan chapel, New Inn Hall Street.

349. OXFORD ST. PETER LE BAILEY
Population 1315   HO 129/158/16
PARISH CHURCH. *Erected* before 1800. *Endowment* Total income is I believe under £100. *Free sittings* upwards of 500. *On 30 March* In morning General Congregation 180, Sunday Scholars 56; in evening General Congregation 450, Sunday Scholars 56. *Average attendance* in morning General Congregation 160, Sunday Scholars 60; in evening General Congregation 500, Sunday Scholars 60. *Remarks* In consequence of much sickness amongst children the number of scholars of Sunday School is small. During summer months it has averaged above 100. *Signed* Richard William Hales, Curate.

350. OXFORD ST. PETER LE BAILEY   HO 129/158/17
NEW ROAD BAPTIST CHAPEL. *Erected* before 1800. A separate and entire building. Used exclusively for worship. *Free sittings* 200; *other sittings* 450. *Average attendance* during previous 6 months, in morning General Congregation 350, Sunday Scholars 100; in evening General Congregation 470. *Remarks* As I was absent from Oxford on Sunday 30th March I have not reported the numbers attending on that day but have filled up the form below it 'to the best of my belief' Edward Bryan, Folkestone, Kent. *Signed* Edward Bryan, Minister, Oxford.

351. OXFORD ST. PETER LE BAILEY   HO 129/158/18
NEW ROAD BAPTIST CHAPEL. *Erected* before 1800. A separate and entire building. Used exclusively for worship. *Free sittings* 200; *other sittings* 600. *On 30 March* In morning General Congregation 319, Sunday Scholars 70; in evening General Congregation 600. *Average attendance* during previous 12 months, in morning General Congregation 400, Sunday Scholars 70; in evening General Congregation 400. *Signed* John Alden, Deacon, 13, Walton Place, Oxford.

352. OXFORD ST PETER LE BAILEY   HO 129/158/19
WESLEYAN (REFORMED) SOCIETY AND PREACHING HOUSE, New Inn Hall Street. A separate and entire building. Used exclusively for worship. *Free sittings* 95. *On 30 March* In morning General Congregation 86; in evening General Congregation 71. *Average attendance* during previous 2 months, in morning General Congregation 83; in evening General Congregation 105. *Remarks* No. 4 ['when erected'] the house is *hired* for the purpose of holding religious services. *Signed* Silas Butler, Steward, 39 Cornmarket Street, Oxford.

353. OXFORD   ST. THOMAS THE MARTYR
Population 4205   HO 129/158/2
PARISH CHURCH. An old church, enlarged by addition of an aisle in 1847. Cost of enlargement defrayed by private benefaction and subscription £1,200. *Endowed* with total of £140. *Free sittings* 500; *other sittings* 200, children 200. *Average attendance* during previous 5 months, in morning General Congregation 500; in evening General Congregation 750. *Remarks* More than half is now taken off by the District Church of St. Paul's, but the parish is not divided. There is also the Chapel for Boatmen and persons working at the Wharf. The parish includes the poorest and worst part of the city. *Signed* J. Chamberlain, Perpetual Curate.

354. OXFORD   ST. THOMAS   HO 129/158/15
WARD'S BOATMEN'S CHAPEL. Licensed AD 1839 as an additional chapel for boatmen, men employed in the wharf and residents on the banks of the canal near the chapel. *Erected* by Mr. Henry Ward of Oxford as a private benefaction. *Free sittings* 120. *On 30 March* In afternoon General Congregation 35, Sunday Scholars 25. *Average attendance* during previous 12 months, in afternoon General Congregation 55, Sunday Scholars 25. *Remarks* There is service also on Wednesday evenings. *Signed* Edward Miller, Chaplain, New College, Oxford.

355. PIDDINGTON   Population 420   HO 129/159/34
ST. NICHOLAS' PARISH CHURCH. The church of an ancient Chapelry, but now a distinct and separate parish. *Erected* before 1 January 1800. *Endowed* with tithe rent charge £300, dues say £1 10s. *Free sittings* 154, space for 30 more if fitted up; *other sittings* 53, total sittings 207 besides seats for children. *On 30 March* In morning General Congregation 82, Sunday Scholars 39; in afternoon General Congregation 55, Sunday Scholars 41. *Remarks* I do not consider the above an average number of attendants by at least 20 at each service. It should likewise be observed that there are two farm houses and four cottages with a population of 33 situate on the confines of the Parish whose occupants as being more convenient attend public worship at the adjoining parishes either of Brill or Boarstall. *Signed* J. Cleoburey, Incumbent.

356. PIDDINGTON   HO 129/159/35
INDEPENDENT CHAPEL. *Erected* 1848. A separate and entire building. Used exclusively for worship. *Free sittings* all. *On 30 March* In

afternoon General Congregation 60; in evening General Congregation 60. *Signed* Robert Ann, Minister, Marsh Gibbon, Bucks.

357. PISHILL Population 192 HO 129/155/32
PARISH CHURCH. *Erected* before 1800. *Endowment* see return for Nettlebed. *Free sittings* about 90, *other sittings* about 20. *On 30 March* In afternoon General Congregation 86, Sunday Scholars 7. *Average attendance* during previous 12 months, in morning General Congregation 75, Sunday Scholars 10; in afternoon General Congregation 85, Sunday Scholars 10. *Signed* James Hazel, Incumbent.

358. PISHILL HO 129/155/33
RUSSELL WATER WESLEYAN METHODIST CHAPEL. *Erected* 1836. A separate and entire building. Used exclusively for worship. *Free sittings* 40; *other sittings* 14. *On 30 March* In afternoon General Congregation 20, Sunday Scholars 7; in evening General Congregation 23, Sunday Scholars 11. *Signed* Silas Lovegrove, Trustee, Russell Water.

359. PYRTON Population 692 HO 129/155/42
EPISCOPAL CHURCH. *On 30 March* In morning General Congregation 40, Sunday Scholars 30; in afternoon General Congregation 49, Sunday Scholars 30. *Remarks* Information given by the Parish Clerk, Pyrton.

360. PYRTON HO 129/155/39
ROMAN CATHOLIC CHURCH.[1] *Average attendance* in morning General Congregation 120, Sunday Scholars 50. *Remarks* From a person who attends choise [?] services regularly. Information given by the Schoolmistress.
1. This return may refer to the Roman Catholic chapel at Stonor Park, which lay in Pyrton parish and for which no other return appears.

361. PYRTON HO 129.155/47
PRIMITIVE METHODIST CHAPEL. *Free sittings* 40. *On 30 March* In evening General Congregation 30. *Signed* H.J. Allen, Primitive Methodist Minister, Chapel House, Chinnor.

362. RADFORD[1] HO 129/162/58
ROMAN CATHOLIC CHURCH OF THE HOLY TRINITY. *Erected* 1841. A separate and entire building. Used exclusively for worship. *Other sittings* 120. *On 30 March* In morning General Congregation 53, Sunday Scholars 15; in afternoon General Congregation 34; Sunday

Scholars 15. *Signed* Edward Walter Winter, Roman Catholic Priest, Radford.
1. A hamlet in Enstone parish.

363. RAMSDEN[1]   Population 403   HO 129/161/54
ST. JAMES'S CHAPEL OF EASE. *Erected* in 1840 by the Vicar of Shipton under Wychwood at a cost of £550. A population of 400, more than 5 miles distant from the parish church. *Free sittings* 242; *other sittings* 58. *On 30 March* In morning General Congregation 59, Sunday Scholars 65; in evening* General Congregation 85, Sunday Scholars 65. *Average attendance* during previous 12 months, in morning General Congregation 50, Sunday Scholars 55; in afternoon General Congregation 100, Sunday Scholars 65. *Remarks* The Curate of Finstock, Charlbury, serves this chapel. There is a service once a day, but during Lent evening prayers and Catechising. Hence the return marked *. Curacy of Finstock and Ramsden £100. *Signed* W.S. Saunders, Curate, Cornbury Park Farm, Charlbury.
1. A chapelry and hamlet in Shipton under Wychwood parish.

364. RAMSDEN   HO 129/161/55
WESLEYAN METHODIST CHAPEL. *Erected* 1832. A separate and entire building. Used exclusively for worship. *On 30 March* General Congregation about 50. *Signed* Richard Bosley, Chapel Steward, Ramsden.

365. ROKE[1]   HO 129/125/46
ROKE BAPTIST CHAPEL. *Erected* before 1800. A separate and entire building. Used exclusively for worship. *Free sittings* 100. *On 30 March* In evening General Congregation 84. *Signed* P.G. Scorey, Occasional Preacher, Wallingford, Berkshire.
1. A hamlet in Benson parish.

366. ROSE HILL[1]   HO 129/157/25
WESLEYAN METHODIST CHAPEL. *Erected* 1835. A separate and entire building. Used exclusively for worship. *Free sittings* 110; *other sittings* 50. *On 30 March* In morning General Congregation 31; in afternoon General Congregation 24. *Signed* Benjamin Leonard, Manager, Rose Hill.
1. A hamlet in Cowley parish.

367.   ROTHERFIELD GREYS Population 1518   HO 129/155/14
HOLY TRINITY CHURCH. Consecrated 4 August 1848 as an additional church (or district church) for the part of Grey's [sic] parish adjoining the town of Henley. *Erected* by general subscription assisted by grants from the Incorporated and Diocesan Church Building Societies at a total cost of about £3,000, of which £2,400 was raised by subscription and £650 by grants from the societies. *Endowed* with tithe £18, glebe 2½ acres, other permanent endowment from money invested in land and stock £1,000, pew rents £9, fees £5, by payment from the Rector of Greys £20. *Free sittings* 475; *other sittings* 25. *On 30 March* In morning General Congregation 120, Sunday Scholars 24; in afternoon General Congregation 170, Sunday Scholars 20. *Remarks* I have no means of judging with any degree of accuracy as to the numbers present at Divine Service yesterday. The numbers given are the rough estimate of another and I cannot speak to the correctness of them. *Signed* W.P. Pinckney, Incumbent or Perpetual Curate.

368.   ROTHERFIELD GREYS   HO 129/155/15
PARISH CHURCH, Mortuary Chapel and Vestry. The Church was built in the reign of King John and Henry III by Walter de Grey, Archbishop of York, Lord of the Manor. *Free sittings* all; *other sitting* 1 Faculty pew.[1] *On 30 March* In morning General Congregation 80, Sunday Scholars 36; in afternoon General Congregation 50, Sunday Scholars 36. *Average attendance* in morning General Congregation 100-200, Sunday Scholars 36-38; in afternoon General Congregation 10 [sic] to 200, Sunday Scholars 36-38. *Remarks* The Rector has been too ill to state any information with respect to Church or Schools and these statements are the best that I can give. *Signed* James C.L. Court, Curate of Rotherfield Greys, Greys Green, Henley-upon-Thames.
1. HO 129/155/14A is a supplementary return made in response to further inquiries concerning sittings. '*Free sittings* in the Church 50, large gallery 50, and chancel rough pews, these are all free, more than required. *Appropriated* about 200. Total 300, beside aisles and chancel. *Remarks* The greater part of the poor inhabitants live in distant [sic] 3 and 4 miles from Church, which prevents ill and old from attending it. Those within reach come to Church. *Signed* J. Smith, Rector.'

369.   ROTHERFIELD GREYS   HO 129/155/16
INDEPENDENT OR CONGREGATIONAL CHAPEL. *Erected* 1719, enlarged 1829. A separate and entire building. Used exclusively for worship. *Free sittings* 200; *other sittings* 500. *On 30 March* in morning General Congregation 329, Sunday Scholars 120; in afternoon Sunday Scholars 170; in evening General Congregation 343. *Average attendance* in morning General Congregation 400, Sunday Scholars 150; in

afternoon Sunday Scholars 180; in evening General Congregation 500. *Signed* James Rowland, Minister, Henley-on-Thames.

370. ROTHERFIELD PEPPARD   Population 406   HO 129/155/17
PARISH CHURCH. *Endowed* with tithe rent charge £540 10s, glebe £60. *Free sittings* 40; *other sittings* 104. *On 30 March* in morning General Congregation 53, Sunday Scholars 17; in afternoon General Congregation 65, Sunday Scholars 17. *Signed* Henry Reynolds, Rector.

371. ROTHERFIELD PEPPARD   HO 129/155/18
PROVIDENCE INDEPENDENT   OR   CONGREGATIONAL CHAPEL. *Erected* about 1796. A separate and entire building. Used for a chapel and Sunday School only. *Free sittings* 280; *other sittings* 20. *On 30 March* In morning General Congregation 88, Sunday Scholars 65; in afternoon General Congregation 103, Sunday Scholars 47. *Average attendance* during previous 6 months, in morning General Congregation 70, Sunday Scholars 65; in afternoon General Congregation 108, Sunday Scholars 50. *Signed* Isaac Caterer, Minister, Peppard.

372. ROUSHAM   Population 134   HO 129/160/20
ST.MARY'S PARISH CHURCH. *Endowed* with glebe £210, fees 7s 6d. *Free sittings* 90; *other sittings* 70. *On 30 March* In morning General Congregation 57, Sunday Scholars 13; in afternoon General Congregation 60, Sunday Scholars 13. *Remarks* The afternoon attendance on the above day was about 10 under the average. *Signed* George Dandridge, Rector.

373. SALFORD   Population 372   HO 129/162/44
ST. MARY'S CHURCH. *Erected* before 1800. *Endowed* with glebe £300. *Free sittings* 94; *other sittings* 73. *On 30 March* In morning General Congregation 28, Sunday Scholars 20; in afternoon General Congregation 53, Sunday Scholars 19. *Average attendance* during previous 12 months, in morning General Congregation 20, Sunday Scholars 27; in afternoon General Congregation 73, Sunday Scholars 30. *Signed* W.E. Stevens, Rector.

374. SALFORD   HO 129/162/45
WESLEYAN METHODIST CHAPEL. *Erected* 1847. A separate and entire building. Used exclusively for worship. *Free sittings* 90. *On 30 March* In afternoon General Congregation 40; in evening General

Congregation 61.[1] *Signed* Charles Simms, Steward, Salford.
1. These figures have been written just above the line dividing the space intended for the number of Sunday Scholars and that intended for overall totals. Since no other figures appear it has been assumed that the numbers given refer to overall attendance.

375. SANDFORD ON THAMES Population 273 HO 129/123/40
ST. ANDREW'S PARISH CHURCH, Wet Sandford. *Free sittings* 120.
On 30 March In morning General Congregation 32, Sunday Scholars 37; in afternoon General Congregation 53, Sunday Scholars 37. *Remarks* The living of Sandford is a donation. *Signed* Richard Allen, Churchwarden.[1]
1. *Gardner* describes Richard Allen, Sandford, as a farmer.

376. SANDFORD ST. MARTIN Population 526 HO 129/160/12
ST. MARTIN'S PARISH CHURCH. *Erected* before 1800. *Endowed* with land £155, tithe £50, fees £2. *Free sittings* 139; *other sittings* 137. *On 30 March* In morning General Congregation 140, Sunday Scholars 70; in afternoon General Congregation 160, Sunday Scholars 60. *Average attendance* the same. *Remarks* The tithe commuted to a rent charge. *Signed* Thomas Curme, Minister, Sandford.

377. SARSDEN Population 188 HO 129/162/30
PARISH CHURCH. *Erected* before 1800. *Endowed* with land commutation at time of enclosure £252, other permanent endowment charged on Merriscourt estate £50. *Free sittings* 150. *On 30 March* In morning General Congregation 60. *Average attendance* in morning General Congregation 100. *Remarks* This parish adjoining Churchill and being now practically as it is about to be legally united with it, schools common to both parishes are held at Churchill and the scholars frequent Churchill church, ten singing boys attending at Sarsden. *Signed* Charles Barter, Rector, Sarsden Rectory.

378. SHENINGTON Population 437 HO 129/163/44
HOLY TRINITY PARISH CHURCH. *Erected* before 1800. *Endowed* with land 192 acres, glebe about 18 acres, other permanent endowment value about £7 p.a. *Free sittings* 123; *other sittings* 125, sittings for children 65. *On 30 March* in morning General Congregation about 100, Sunday Scholars 60; In afternoon General Congregation about 90, Sunday Scholars 60. *Signed* Robert E. Hughes, Rector.

379. SHENINGTON HO 129/163/45
INDEPENDENT CHAPEL. *Erected* 1817. A separate and entire building. Used exclusively for worship. *Free sittings* 100. *Average attendance* during previous 12 months, in morning General Congregation 30, Sunday Scholars 20; in evening General Congregation 55. *Remarks* Given up in the morning to another denomination. *Signed* John Bligh, Minister, Wroxton.

380. SHENINGTON HO 129/163/46
PRIMITIVE METHODIST CHAPEL. *Erected* about 1817. A separate and entire building. Used exclusively for worship. *Free sittings* 60; *other sittings* 40. *On 30 March* In afternoon General Congregation 80. *Average attendance* during previous 12 months, in morning General Congregation 90. *Signed* Joseph Cox, Steward, Shenington.

381. SHIFFORD[1] Population 44 HO 161/17
DISTRICT CHURCH. *Erected* before 1800. *Sittings* 100. *On 30 March* In morning General Congregation 52, Sunday Scholars 11. *Average attendance* during previous 12 months, in morning General Congregation 50, Sunday Scholars 12; in afternoon General Congregation 50, Sunday Scholars 12. *Remarks* This church is served by the Vicars of Bampton and has no separate endowment. *Signed* Dacre Adams, Vicar of 2nd Portion, Bampton.
1. A chapelry in Bampton parish.

382. SHILTON[1] Population 319 HO 129/161/60
PARISH CHURCH. *Average attendance* General Congregation from 60 to 80. *Remarks* The best information to be had. *Signed* Thomas Cheatle, Registrar.
1. A part of Shilton parish was a detached portion of Berkshire.

383. SHILTON HO 129/161/61
BAPTIST CHAPEL. *Erected* 1826. Not a separate and entire building. Not used exclusively for worship. *Free sittings* 60. *On 30 March* In evening General Congregation 48. *Average attendance* 48. *Remarks* This chapel is used as a dwelling house but the congregation assemble when they think proper. William Maisey. Ono Allen[1], Filkins.
1. *Gardner* describes Onah Allen, Filkins, as a tailor.

384. SHIPLAKE Population 569 HO 129/155/19
CHURCH. *Endowed* with tithe £140, glebe 3 acres, other permanent endowment £20, other sources £10. *Free sittings* 210, benches for children 40. *On 30 March* In morning General Congregation 110, Sunday

Scholars 40. *Remarks* By free sittings I intend all the fixed seats in the Church, pews as well as open seats. *Signed* Drummond Rawnsley, Vicar.

385. SHIPTON ON CHERWELL Population 135   HO 129/160/39
ST. JEROME'S CHURCH, a new church built in 1831 on the site of the old one and not reconsecrated. *Endowed* with glebe £250. *Free sittings* 60; *other sittings* 30. *On 30 March* In morning General Congregation 38, Sunday Scholars 21. *Average attendance* during previous 12 months, in morning General Congregation 28, Sunday Scholars 20; in evening General Congregation 28, Sunday Scholars 20. *Remarks* The church has been entirely rebuilt and at the entire cost of the present Patron and Incumbent which was nearly eleven hundred pounds and it was built in the year 1831. *Signed* H.J. Passand, Rector.

386. SHIPTON UNDER WYCHWOOD[1]
Population 616   HO 129/162/1
ESTABLISHED CHURCH. *Erected* before 1800. *Free sittings* 200 and upwards; *other sittings* 250 or thereabouts. *Average attendance* in morning General Congregation 400, Sunday Scholars 230; in afternoon General Congregation 450. *Signed* Robert Phillimore, Vicar.
1. The parish included Langley and Lyneham hamlets, Leafield (*q.v.*) and Ramsden (*q.v.*) chapelries, and Milton under Wychwood (*q.v.*) township. The total population of Shipton parish was 2968.

387. SHIRBURN Population 250   HO 129/156/12
PARISH CHURCH. *Erected* before 1800. *Endowed* with land £48, tithe commuted to £80, gross amount. *Total sittings* 250. *On 30 March* In morning General Congregation 70, Sunday Scholars 19. *Average attendance* during previous 12 months, in morning General Congregation 80, Sunday Schools 20; in afternoon General Congregation 130, Sunday Scholars 20. *Signed* James Beauchamp, Vicar.

388. SHORTHAMPTON[1] Population 309   HO 129/162/13
CHURCH OF AN ANCIENT CHAPELRY. *Erected* before 1800. *Sittings* 150. *On 30 March* In afternoon General Congregation 100, Sunday Scholars 20. *Remarks* The sittings are all free, but many of the pews are appropriated by the Churchwardens. *Signed* Thomas Andrew Walker, Curate.
1. A chapelry in Charlbury parish.

389. SHUTFORD[1]   Population 416   HO 129/163/41
ST. MARTIN'S CHAPEL. *Erected* before 1800. *Free sittings* 197; *other sittings* 66. *On 30 March* In afternoon General Congregation 45, Sunday Scholars 26. *Average attendance* during previous 12 months, in morning General Congregation 35, Sunday Scholars 29; in afternoon General Congregation 50, Sunday Scholars 30. *Remarks* The service is in the morning and afternoon alternately, *Signed* John Price, Curate.
1. A chapelry in Swalcliffe Parish. The chapelry consisted of East Shutford (population 24) and West Shutford (population 392).

390. SIBFORD GOWER[1]   Population 549   HO 129/163/35
HOLY TRINITY CHURCH, new church built under provisions of 1 and 2 Vict. cap. 38. Consecrated 1840. Built by subscription at a cost of £1,850. *Signed* So far as it [the return] is made[2] William S. Miller, Perpetual Curate.
1. A township in Swalcliffe parish.
2. HO 129/163/34 is a supplementary return stating that there were free sittings 360, appropriated sittings 140. Average congregation including Sunday Scholars, in morning 320, in afternoon 400. 'The above is the estimated number of sittings as the church will usually accommodate a larger number. William S. Miller'.

391. SIBFORD GOWER   HO 129/163/36
FRIENDS' MEETING HOUSE.[1] *Erected* before 1800. A separate and entire building. Used exclusively for worship and for Society Discipline. *Sittings* all free. *On 30 March* In morning General Congregation 107, Sunday Scholars 5. *Signed* Richard Routh, Clerk of the Preparative Meeting, Sibford School.
1. This return made on general non-Anglican form rather than on the special form intended for the Society of Friends. See also HO 129/163/38.

392. SIBFORD GOWER   HO 129/163/38
FRIENDS' MEETING HOUSE.[1] *Erected* before 1800. A separate and entire building. Used exclusively for worship. *Admeasurement* in superficial feet floor area 720; in galleries 216. *Estimated Number of Persons capable of being seated* about 200. *On 30 March* In morning 112 attendants. *Remarks* The meeting is held in the afternoons 6 months a year and the average attendance about 100. *Signed* Richard Routh, Sibford School.
1. This return made on the special form intended for the Society of Friends, unlike HO 129/163/36 above.

393. SIBFORD   HO 129/163/37
WESLEYAN METHODIST CHAPEL. *Erected* 1827. A separate and
entire building. Used exclusively for worship. *Free sittings* 60; *other
sittings* 60. *On 30 March* In afternoon General Congregation 100,
Sunday Scholars 30; in evening General Congregation 90. *Signed* Samuel
Cooke, Minister, Chipping Norton.

394. SOMERTON   Population 342   HO 129/159/28
ST. JAMES' PARISH CHURCH. Date unknown, but more than 300
years ago as there are monuments of that date. *Endowed* with fixed
payment in lieu of tithe £150, glebe £105 12s, other permanent
endowment £18 15s, fees £1 10s. *Free sittings* 250. *On 30 March* In
morning General Congregation 83, Sunday Scholars 34; in afternoon
General Congregation 115, Sunday Scholars 36. *Remarks* All the sittings
are free, i.e. without payment, but eleven pews are appropriated to the
principal inhabitants who occupy them. These would contain about 50.
Many of the seats are open benches and the number 250 includes all. If
repaired the church might be made to accommodate many more. *Signed*
R.C. Clifton, Rector.

395. SOULDERN   Population 619   HO 129/159/31
ST. MARY'S PARISH CHURCH. *Endowed* with land £206 5s, tithe
commuted at £431 10s 10d, subject to rates about £60, land tax £26 9s 5d,
£345 1s 7d, glebe £20, a cottage £3, fees about 15s, Easter offerings about
£1 10s. *Free sittings* 101; *other sittings* 118, singers' gallery 15. *On 30
March* In morning General Congregation 118, Sunday Scholars 36; in
afternoon General Congregation 112, Sunday Scholars 37. *Average
attendance* during previous 12 months, in morning General
Congregation 148, Sunday Scholars 36; in afternoon General
Congregation 142, Sunday Scholars 37. *Remarks* The congregations in
the church were fewer than usual. *Signed* L. Stephenson, Rector.

396. SOULDERN   HO 129/159/11
WESLEYAN METHODIST PREACHING ROOM. *Erected* 1850. Not
a separate and entire building. Not used exclusively for worship. *Free
sittings* 5; *other sittings* 57. *On 30 March* In morning Sunday Scholars
50; in evening General Congregation 108. *Average attendance* during
previous 6 months, in morning Sunday Scholars 35; in evening General
Congregation 70. *Remarks* Established Xmas 1850. *Signed* William
Smith, Steward, Souldern.

397. SOUTH LEIGH[1]   HO 129/161/5
CHAPEL OF EASE to church of Stanton Harcourt. *Endowed* with land
£24, tithe £13, fees £1, Easter Offerings £1. *Free sittings* 200; *other
sittings* 50. *On 30 March* In afternoon General Congregation 150,
Sunday Scholars 39. *Signed* W.P. Walsh, Minister, Stanton Harcourt.
1. A chapelry in the parish of Stanton Harcourt.

398. SOUTH LEIGH   HO 129/161/6
WESLEYAN METHODIST MEETING HOUSE, cottage inhabited by
William Widdows. A private dwelling. *Sittings* 180. *Average attendance*
during previous 12 months, in evening General Congregation 100. *Signed*
Peter C. Horton, Minister, Mount House, Witney.

399. SOUTH NEWINGTON Population 419   HO 129/163/8
ST. PETER'S PARISH CHURCH. *Erected* before 1800. *Endowed* with
land £66 10s, other permanent endowment £74 11s. 8d, fees 10s, Easter
Offerings 16s, other sources £86. *Free sittings* 240; *other sittings* 180. *On
30 March* In morning General Congregation 77, Sunday Scholars 50; in
afternoon General Congregation 116, Sunday Scholars 50. *Remarks* The
above numbers are somewhat smaller than they were five years ago as
regards attendance at church in consequence of 72 persons having
emigrated to America. *Signed* Henry Duke Harrington, Vicar.

400. SOUTH NEWINGTON   HO 129/163/11
WESLEYAN METHODIST CHAPEL. *Erected* 1692[1]. A separate and
entire building. Used exclusively for worship. *Sittings* Free.[2] *On 30
March* In evening General Congregation 110. *Average attendance* during
previous 6 months, in evening General Congregation 90. *Signed* Thomas
Page, Steward, Carrier, South Newington.
1. Originally a Quaker meeting house. In 1851 leased by the Methodists.
2. HO 129/163/10 is a supplementary return stating that all sittings were free and totalled
150. HO 129/163/9 is a covering note reading 'Sir, the chapel at Southnewington will
accommodate one hundred and fifty with seats if filled. I am Sir you obdt servant Thomas
Page'.

401. SOUTH STOKE[1] Population 856   HO 129/125/56
ST. ANDREW'S PARISH CHURCH. *Endowed* with land £75, tithe
£41, other permanent endowment from Dean and Chapter of Christ
Church, Oxford £30, fees £2 2s., other sources 10 10s. *Free sittings* 250;
other sittings 20. *On 30 March* In morning General Congregation 26 and
25 children; in afternoon General Congregation 50 and 25 children.
Average attendance in morning General Congregation 30, Sunday
Scholars 25; in afternoon General Congregation 35, Sunday Scholars 25.

Remarks I enclose some remarks relating to the number of attendants at Church.[2] *Signed* Henry Robinson Wad[more?], Curate.
1. The parish of South Stoke included the Chapelry of Woodcote (*q.v.*).
2. These do not survive with the main return.

402. SOUTH STOKE   HO 129/125/58
INDEPENDENT CHAPEL. *Average attendance* in morning General Congregation 35.

403. SOUTH WESTON   Population 98   HO 129/156/11
WESLEYAN METHODIST CHAPEL. *Erected* 1823. A separate and entire building. Used exclusively for worship. *Free sittings* 40; *other sittings* 18. *On 30 March* In afternoon General Congregation 23; in evening General Congregation 30. *Average attendance* in afternoon General Congregation 30; in evening General Congregation 30. *Signed* Joseph Ravering, Chapel Steward, South Weston.

404. SPELSBURY[1]   Population 578   HO 129/162/18
ALL SAINTS' PARISH CHURCH. *Erected* before 1800. *Sittings* 300. *Remarks* There is another chapel belonging to the Church of England at which some of the more distant inhabitants attend. *Signed* Charles Carey, Curate.
1. The parish of Spelsbury included Dean, Fulwell, and Taston (*q.v.*) hamlets.

405. SPELSBURY   HO 129/162/19
PRIVATE CHAPEL of Viscount Dillon, Ditchley House. Consecrated before 1800. *Erected* by the Earl of Litchfield [sic] 1722. *Sittings* about 150. *On 30 March* In afternoon General Congregation 80, weather unfavourable. *Average attendance* in afternoon General Congregation 100 to 120, every seat full. *Remarks* Divine Service has been regularly performed in the above chapel for several years. *Signed* J. Samuel, Domestic Chaplain.

406. STADHAMPTON   Population 401   HO 129/123/46
ST. JOHN THE BAPTIST EPISCOPAL CHURCH. *Free sittings* 130. *On 30 March* In morning General Congregation 150, Sunday Scholars 50. *Signed* John Polley, District Registrar.

407. STADHAMPTON   HO 129/123/48
PARTICULAR BAPTIST CHAPEL. *Erected* 1837. Separate and entire building. Used exclusively for worship. *Sittings* all free. *Average attendance* during previous 12 months, in morning General

Congregation 80, Sunday Scholars none; in afternoon General Congregation 80, Sunday Scholars none. *Signed* William Doe, Minister, South Moreton, Berkshire.

408. STANDLAKE Population 810 HO 129/161/14
ST. GILES' PARISH CHURCH. *Erected* before 1800. *Endowed* with land a beneficial lease granted to increase the Revenue of Living by Magd. College Oxford £70, tithe £466 11s. 9d, glebe £50, fees say £5, Easter Offerings say £3. *Sittings* 700. *On 30 March* In morning General Congregation 176, Sunday Scholars 77; in afternoon General Congregation 109, Sunday Scholars 77. *Average attendance* in morning General Congregation 230, Sunday Scholars 70; in afternoon General Congregation 230, Sunday Scholars 90. *Signed* Frank Burges, Officiating Minister.

409. STANDLAKE HO 129/161/15
BAPTIST CHAPEL. *Erected* 1832. A separate and entire building. Used exclusively for worship. *Free sittings* 180. *On 30 March* In evening General Congregation 106. *Average attendance* during previous 12 months, in evening General Congregation 160-180. *Remarks* NB. This chapel is one of four others in connection with the Baptist Congregation at Coate, and was erected by that congregation in the year specified. It is used as a Sunday School morning and afternoon, and the evening worship is conducted by the Minister of Coate chapel and the other members of that congregation. *Signed* John Jackson, Minister, Aston House, nr Bampton.

410. STANTON HARCOURT[1] Population 699 HO 129/161/11
PARISH CHURCH. *Endowed* with land £81 9s 6d, other permanent endowment £20, fees £3, Easter Offerings £2, other sources £13 6s 6d. *Free sittings* 250; *other sittings* 100. *On 30 March* In morning General Congregation 284. *Signed* W.P. Walsh, Vicar.
1. The parish of Stanton Harcourt also included the chapelry of South Leigh (*q.v.*).

411. STANTON ST. JOHN Population 555 HO 129/157/13
PARISH CHURCH[1]. *Average attendance* in morning General Congregation 160.
1. See Garsington.

Revd Henry Stonhouse had been incumbent since 1835. In 1854, in response to Bishop Wilberforce's visitation queries, he reported that he did not know the size of the average Sunday congregation. There was one small chapel but he did not know the number of Dissenters. As to the accuracy of the 1851 religious census return he wrote 'Have not got, or seen it'.

412. STANTON ST. JOHN HO 129/157/10
PRIMITIVE METHODIST CHAPEL. Opened 10 November 1844. A
separate and entire building. Used exclusively for worship. *All sittings*
free.[1] *On 30 March* In afternoon General Congregation 49; in evening
General Congregation 48. *Average attendance* during previous 12
months, in afternoon General Congregation 50; in evening General
Congregation 80. *Signed* James Rogers, Local Preacher, Stanton St.
John.

1. HO/129/157/9 is a supplementary entry, also signed by James Rogers, stating the
number of free sittings to be 70.

413. STEEPLE ASTON[1] Population 601 HO 129/160/1
ST. PETER'S CHURCH. Parish comprises the two townships of Steeple
Aston proper and Middle Aston. *Erected* before 1228. Rebuilt in 1842 at
a cost of £1,014 5s, defrayed by private benefaction. *Endowed* with
land* £580. *Free sittings* 350 besides forms for children. *On 30 March* In
afternoon General Congregation 160, Sunday Scholars 40. *Average
Attendance* in morning General Congregation 140, Sunday Scholars 40;
in afternoon General Congregation 160, Sunday Scholars 40. *Remarks*
The Rector declines to make a return. My figures are vague as I am
churchwarden at another church where I *counted* the congregation on
March 30 but I was at the church in question at the afternoon service of
that day. *Signed* William Wing, Enumerator, Steeple Aston. *433 a. Or.
36 p.

1. The total population, including Middle Aston township, was 702.

414. STEEPLE BARTON[1] Population 757 HO 129/160/16
ST MARY'S PARISH CHURCH. *Erected* before 1800. *Endowed* with
land £60 less land tax etc., tithe £45 about, fees not paid except for
marriages. *Sittings* now under repair. *On 30 March* In morning General
Congregation 94; in evening General Congregation 136. *Average
attendance* in morning General Congregation 90; in evening General
Congregation 150. *Remarks* The Parish Ch. being under repair, no part
being fit for service except the chancel, a morning service is held there,
while an evening one is provided for the Steeple Barton people in the
church of Westcott, the adjoining parish. The vicar of Steeple Barton of
course officiates at this service. The chancel contains about 90 persons.
Signed Arthur Pakenham, Vicar.

1. The parish of Steeple Barton included the hamlets of Seswells Barton and Middle Barton
(*q.v.*).

415. STOKE LYNE   Population 631   HO 129/158/37

ESTABLISHED CHURCH. *Sittings* 150. *On 30 March* In afternoon General Congregation 30. *Remarks* This account is as correct as I possibly can get as the clergyman will not give any return.[1]

1. Unsigned but probably completed by the Registrar. See similar returns in the same hand for Launton, Stratton Audley.

416. STOKE LYNE   HO 129/159/66

WESLEYAN METHODIST CHAPEL. *Erected* 1838. Not used exclusively for worship. *Free sittings* 85. *On 30 March* In afternoon General Congregation 68. *Average attendance* in morning General Congregation 50. *Remarks* This being a dwelling house occupied by a labourer there are no seats or sittings other than what are provided for use of the family. *Signed* James Phillips, occupier, Stoke Lyne.

417. STOKENCHURCH   Population 1492   HO 129/150/2

PARISH CHURCH. *Erected* before 1800. *Endowed* with tithe £130, fees £8. *Free sittings* 500. *On 30 March* In morning General Congregation 100, Sunday Scholars 120; in afternoon   General Congregation 180, Sunday Scholars 120. *Average attendance* during previous 12 months, in morning General Congregation 120, Sunday Scholars 120; in afternoon General Congregation 250, Sunday Scholars 120. *Remarks* The afternoon of Sunday the 30 March being very stormy our attendance was not so large as usual. The rates and taxes amount to upwards of £43 annually leave £95 for the Minister. *Signed* J. Mayo, Perpetual Curate.

418. STOKENCHURCH   HO 129/150/14

INDEPENDENT CHAPEL. *Erected* 1820. A separate and entire building. Used exclusively for worship and Sunday School. *Free sittings* 80; *other sittings* 130. *On 30 March* In morning General Congregation 120; in evening General Congregation 150. *Average attendance* Sab. eg. General Congregation 200, Sunday Scholars 80[1]. *Signed* Charles Hyatt, Minister, Stokenchurch.

1. These figures written across morning and afternoon columns.

419. STOKENCHURCH   HO 129/150/13

PRIMITIVE METHODIST CHAPEL. *Erected* about 1847. A separate and entire building. Used exclusively for worship. *Free sittings* 12; *other sittings* 10. *On 30 March* In afternoon 80, in evening 95. *Signed* Joseph Stockwell, Local Preacher, Grocer and Baker.

420. STOKE ROW[1] HO 129/155/11
ST. JOHN THE EVANGELIST'S CONSOLIDATED DISTRICT
CHURCH. *Consecrated* about 18 or 20 October 1846 as an additional
church at a cost of £1100 raised by public subscription and a grant from
the Bounty Office. Permanent *endowment* £85. *Free sittings* about 190.
On 30 March In morning General Congregation 35; in afternoon General
Congregation 73. *Signed* J. Arrowsmith, Perpetual   Curate.
1. Hamlet in Ipsden parish.

421. STOKE ROW HO 129/155/27
INDEPENDENT CHAPEL. *Erected* 1816. A separate and entire
building. Used exclusively for worship. *Free sittings* 110; *other sittings*
30. *On 30 March* In morning General Congregation 77, Sunday Scholars
25; in evening General Congregation 125. *Average attendance* during
previous 12 months, in morning General Congregation 77, Sunday
Scholars 25; in evening General Congregation 125. *Signed* Richard
Marks, Deacon and Manager, Stoke Row.[1]
1. *Gardner* describes Richard Marks, Stoke Row, as a shoemaker.

422. STOKE TALMAGE Population 106 HO 129/156/10
PARISH CHURCH. *Erected* before 1800. *Endowed* with land £20, glebe
£35, other permanent endowment about £200. *Free sittings* about 45;
other sittings about 37. *On 30 March* In morning General Congregation
48, Sunday Scholars 14; in afternoon General Congregation 16, Sunday
Scholars 18. *Remarks* There is scarcely any variation in the number of
the congregation. Some parishioners reside nearer to other Parish
Churches and presently attend them. *Signed* T.B. Fookes, Curate.

423. STONESFIELD Population 630 HO 129/160/29
ST. JAMES' CHURCH. *Erected* before 1800. *Endowed* with land £120,
fees £1, Easter Offerings 15s. *Free sittings* 157, children 60; *other sittings*
78. *On 30 March* In morning General Congregation 90, Sunday Scholars
80; in afternoon General Congregation 130, Sunday Scholars 80.
Average attendance The attendance on the 30th as near the average as
possible. *Remarks* The Endowment consists of land in lieu of tithes,
there has been a great reduction in its amount within the last two years.
Signed Francis Robinson, Rector.

424. STRATTON AUDLEY Population 305 HO 129/159/38
ESTABLISHED CHURCH. *Free sittings* 140, *other sittings* 160. *On 30
March* In morning General Congregation 40; in afternoon General

Congregation 40. *Remarks* This account is as correct as I possibly can get as the clergyman will not give any return.[1]

1. Unsigned but probably completed by the Registrar. See similar returns in the same hand for Launton and Stoke Lyne.

425. STUDLEY[1]   HO   129/157/15

STUDLEY CHAPEL. *Erected* by Sir George Croke, Knt probably about 1600 or a little later. *Endowed* with rent charge on an estate in Bucks £20. *Sittings* about 150. *On 30 March* In morning General Congregation, including Sunday Scholars 130; in afternoon General Congregation including Sunday Scholars 113. *Average attendance* during previous 6 months, in morning General Congregation including Sunday Scholars 120; in afternoon General Congregation including Sunday Scholars 110. *Signed* Philip Bliss[2], Minister of or Preacher at the above named Chapel, Studley Priory.

1. In the parish of Beckley. The census gives separate population figures for Horton-cum-Studley hamlet (351) and Studley hamlet (75).*Gardner* states that Studley church had fallen into decay 'many years since'. The lady of the manor, Lady Croke, allowed the chapel of her mansion, Studley Priory, to be used for divine service.
2. Bliss was Principal of St. Mary Hall, Oxford.

426. SUMMERTOWN   HO   129/157/35

ST. JOHN THE BAPTIST'S CHURCH. In the district-parish of Summertown, built AD 1831/2 and consecrated in 1832. An additional church to the parish of St. Giles out of which the district was subsequently taken. Cost defrayed by College and other private subscriptions, aided by a grant from the Church Building Society. *Endowed* with a grant from St. John's College £21, from Queen Anne's Bounty £19, pew rents £16. *Free sittings* 300; *other sittings* 100. *On 30 March* In morning General Congregation 200; in afternoon General Congregation 150. *Average attendance* in morning General Congregation 250; in afternoon General Congregation 250. *Signed* John Sansom, Perpetual Curate, 4 New College Lane, Oxford.

427. SUMMERTOWN   HO   129/157/36

CONGREGATIONAL CHAPEL. *Erected* 1844. A separate and entire building with a room for day and Sabbath School. Used exclusively for worship. *Free sittings* 80; *other sittings* 120. *On 30 March* In morning General Congregation 185, Sunday Scholars 70; in afternoon Sunday Scholars 70; in evening General Congregation 180. *Average attendance* during previous 12 months, in morning General Congregation 160, Sunday Scholars 80; in afternoon Sunday Scholars 85; in evening General Congregation 190. *Remarks* NB The official char[acter][1]

signature applies to the year 1850 and only occasionally to 1851. *Signed* Josiah M. Crapper,[2] Preacher of the Gospel, 47 St. John Street, Oxford.
1. ie. 'Preacher of the Gospel'.
2. *Gardner* describes J.M. Crapper, 47 St. John St., as running an academy taking boarders.

428. SWALCLIFFE[1]   Population 367   HO 129/163/33
CHURCH OF ST. PETER AND ST. PAUL. *Erected* before 1800. *Endowed* with land 179 acres, other permanent endowment £9, fees £5. *On 30 March* In morning General Congregation 130, Sunday Scholars 42; in afternoon General Congregation 132, Sunday Scholars 44. *Remarks* There is nearly double the amount of free sittings and other sittings, that is requisite in consequence of two thirds of the original population having been assigned to a district church in the year 1840.[2] *Signed* Edward Payne, Vicar.
1. The parish of Swalcliffe also included the chapelries of Epwell (*q.v.*) and Shutford East, and the townships of Shutford West (*q.v.*), Sibford Ferris (*q.v.*) and Sibford Gower (*q.v.*). The total population of the parish was 2012.
2. HO 129/163/32 is a supplementary return stating the total sittings to be 340. 'I am unable to give the actual number of the appropriated or the free sittings: but there are only three pews for which a Faculty is claimed: no pews are let: and there is a free sitting for every man, woman, and child in the parish, were they all in Church at the same time. Edward Payne, Vicar of Swalcliffe.'

429. SWERFORD   Population 440   HO 129/162/63
PARISH CHURCH. *Erected* before 1800. *Endowed* with land £300, tithe rent charge £110. *Free sittings* about 150; *other sittings* 30, besides seats for school. *On 30 March* In morning General Congregation 70, Sunday Scholars 64; in afternoon General Congregation 100, Sunday Scholars 65. *Signed* T. Harris, Rector.

430. SWINBROOK   Population 195   HO 129/161/79
PARISH CHURCH belonging to a distinct and separate parish. *Erected* before 1800. *Endowed* with land* £35 18s 1d, glebe # house and garden £25, stipend £15 10s 8d, surplice fees 16s 8d, dividends and interest from Governors of Queen Anne's Bounty £9 17s 2d. *Free sittings* 30; *other sittings* 120. *On 30 March* In afternoon General Congregation 70, Sunday Scholars 50. *Average attendance* in morning General Congregation 60, Sunday Scholars 50; in afternoon General Congregation 70, Sunday Scholars 50. *Remarks* *Land purchased by Governors of Queen Anne's Bounty from funds in their hands. # House and garden assessed at £25, liable to Parish rates and window tax not deducted in above statement. Divine Service is performed once every Sunday alternately morning and afternoon. The Sunday Scholars

belonging to Swinbrook and Widford attend at both churches (in number about 50) but meet for school instruction at Swinbrook. *Signed* William Raine, Perpetual Curate.

431. SWYNCOMBE   Population 428   HO 129/155/34
ST. BOTOLPH'S PARISH CHURCH. *Free sittings* children 48, adults 91; *other sittings* adults 77. *On 30 March* In morning General Congregation 160. *Signed* Henry Alfred Napier, Rector.

432. SYDENHAM   Population 394   HO 129/156/21
ST. MARY'S PARISH CHURCH. *Erected* before 1800. *Endowed* with land £95, glebe £2, fees £2. *Free sittings* 130; *other sittings* 35. *On 30 March* In morning General Congregation 56, Sunday Scholars 60; in afternoon General Congregation 102, Sunday Scholars 57. *Remarks* In the afternoon several boys have to tend to their plough horses, and six or seven are bird minding. *Signed* W. Douglas Littlejohn, Vicar.

433. SYDENHAM   HO 129/156/22
OLD BAPTIST CHAPEL. *Erected* 1823. Building with a cottage attached. Used exclusively for worship. *Free sittings* 150. *Remarks* Three services. Congregation very fluctuating, no Sunday School. *Signed* William Allnutt, Minister, Henton, Chinnor.

434. SYDENHAM   HO 129/156/24
NEW BAPTIST CHAPEL. *Erected* 1844. A separate and entire building. Used exclusively for worship. *Free sittings* all.[1] *On 30 March* In morning General Congregation 20, Sunday Scholars 30; in afternoon General Congregation 80, Sunday Scholars 34; in evening General Congregation 20. *Signed* Thomas Juggins, Minister, Thame.
1. HO 129/156/23 is a supplementary return giving the number of free sittings as 100.

435. TACKLEY   Population 558   HO 129/160/21
PARISH CHURCH (supposed St. Nicholas). *Erected* before 1800. *Endowed* with tithe liable to rates £750, glebe £50. *Free sittings* 70; *other sittings* 180, Sunday School 80. *On 30 March* In morning General Congregation 52, Sunday Scholars 65; in afternoon General Congregation 56, Sunday Scholars 48. *Average attendance* in morning General Congregation 65, Sunday Scholars 70; in afternoon General Congregation 70, Sunday Scholars 50. *Remarks* The church is large enough for the population but not conveniently situated for the infirm and the idle. *Signed* L.A. Sharpe, Rector.

436. TACKLEY   HO 129/160/22

WESLEYAN METHODIST CHAPEL. *Erected* before 1820. A separate and entire building. Used exclusively for worship. *Other sittings* 150. *On 30 March* In morning General Congregation 72; in evening General Congregation 112. *Average attendance* during previous 12 months, in morning General Congregation 90. *Signed* Thomas Chilton,[1] Manager, Tackley.

1. *Gardner* describes Thomas Chilton, Tackley, as a farmer.

437. TADMARTON   Population 450   HO 129/163/31

ST. NICHOLAS' CHURCH. *Erected* before 1800. *Endowed* with land 358 acres, fees 10s. *Free sittings* 140; *other sittings* 120. *On 30 March* In morning General Congregation 80, Sunday Scholars 40; in afternoon General Congregation 156, Sunday Scholars 47. *Remarks* I have set down the amount of acres of land from which the yearly income of the living is derived. I hold a large portion of this in my own hands. What ought to be set down as the income of the whole exactly I cannot in these times pretend to say. *Signed* Thomas Lea, Rector.

438. TASTON[1]   HO 129/162/20

PRIMITIVE METHODIST CHAPEL. *Erected* in 1848. Not a separate and entire building. *Free sittings* 90. *On 30 March* In evening General Congregation 78. *Signed* William Watts, Primitive Methodist Minister, Fulwell.

1. A hamlet in Spelsbury parish.

439. TAYNTON   Population 379   HO 129/161/76

PARISH CHURCH. *Erected* before 1800. *Free sittings* 180; *other sittings* 66. *Signed* Thos. Lewes,[1] Vicar.

1. He replied to Bishop Wilberforce's 1854 visitation enquiries that the average Sunday congregation was '120, and increasing ... no dissenting places of worship, and we have no dissenters except Wesleyans who attend the Church'.

440. TETSWORTH   Population 512   HO 129/156/15

PARISH CHURCH. *Erected* before 1800. *Endowed* with tithe £95, fees £3 10s, other sources £1 6s. *Free sittings* 68; *other sittings* 73. *On 30 March* In morning General Congregation 84, Sunday Scholars 102; in afternoon General Congregation 112, Sunday Scholars 95. *Average attendance* in morning General Congregation 80, Sunday Scholars 95; in afternoon General Congregation 126, Sunday Scholars 102. *Signed* John Witherington Peers, Minister.

441. TETSWORTH   HO 129/156/16
INDEPENDENT CHAPEL. *Erected* 1823. A separate and entire building. Used exclusively for worship. *Free sittings* 35; *other sittings* 75. *On 30 March* In morning General Congregation 30; in evening General Congregation 35. *Signed* James Young, Minister.

442. THAME[1]   Population 3259   HO 129/156/30
ST. MARY'S. *Erected* before 1800. *Endowed* with land £160, tithe £21, dues £23 12s. *Free sittings* 400; *other sittings* 590. *On 30 March* In morning General Congregation 510, Sunday Scholars 140; in afternoon Sunday Scholars did not attend as a school; in evening General Congregation 404. *Average attendance* in morning General Congregation 550, Sunday Scholars 140; in evening General Congregation 500. *Remarks* I have much pleasure in giving you the above information, as I shall have in replying to any further inquiries. *Signed* James Prosser, Vicar.
1. The parish included the hamlet of Morton (*q.v.*).

443. THAME   HO 129/156/31
BARONESS WENMAN'S PRIVATE CHAPEL. *Erected* supposed 2 to 3 hundred years. Built by private benefaction. Cannot get at the total cost. £1000 has recently been expended in decoration. *Free sittings* nil; *other sittings* 12. *On 30 March* In morning General Congregation 20. *Average attendance* in morning General Congregation 20. *Remarks* Revd Amos Hayton refuses to give any information. *Signed* T.H. Simmons, Registrar.

444. THAME   HO 129/156/32
INDEPENDENT OR CONGREGATIONAL CHAPEL. *Erected* 1827. A separate and entire building. Used exclusively for worship. *Free sittings* 169; *other sittings* 131. *On 30 March* In morning General Congregation 107, Sunday Scholars 123; in afternoon General Congregation 30, Sunday Scholars 141; in evening General Congregation 166. *Remarks* I may remark the number of Sunday Scholars present yesterday morning is considerably less than the average attendance usually present. I may also remark we have an Adult Female Bible Class for communicating religious instruction to domestic servants, who meet on Sunday afternoons in my house. The estimated number of persons present on Sunday 30 March was 10. *Signed* John Elrick, Independent Minister,   Thame.

445. THAME HO 129/156/33
NEW JERUSALEM PRIMITIVE METHODIST CHAPEL. Opened 1849. Room, not a separate and entire building. Set apart for worship. *Free sittings* 150. *On 30 March* In morning General Congregation 30; in afternoon General Congregation 60; in evening General Congregation 100. *Average attendance* in morning General Congregation 25; in afternoon General Congregation 100; in evening General Congregation 150. *Remarks* Entirely poor people that attend. It is in the lowest part of the town. Not room sufficant for a school but it as been a blessing to neighbourhood. Less fiting and quarling since the room has beign opened. *Signed* James Phillip, Leader and Steward, Grocer, Thame.

446. THAME HO 129/156/34
BAPTIST CHAPEL. A separate and entire building. Not used exclusively for worship. *Sittings* 35 all free. *On 30 March* In morning General Congregation 20; in evening General Congregation 25. *Signed* Thomas Juggins, Minister, Thame.

447. THAME HO 129/156/35
PARTICULAR BAPTIST CHAPEL. *Erected* 1825. A separate and entire building. Used exclusively for worship. *Sittings* all free. *On 30 March* In morning General Congregation 37, Sunday Scholars 45; in afternoon General Congregation 103, Sunday Scholars 47, in evening General Congregation 34. *Remarks* The return made is the average number in the last 12 months except the evening congregation which was fewer in number than usual. *Signed* Steven Walker, Minister, High Street, Thame.

448. TOOT BALDON Population 290 HO 129/123/44
PARISH CHURCH. *Erected* before 1800. *Permanent endowment* £30 7s. *Free sittings* 115; *other sittings* 36. *On 30 March* in afternoon General Congregation 72, Sunday Scholars 36. *Average attendance* It is impossible for the clergyman to state the average number of attendants during the 12 months preceeding as he has never kept any accounts but he can state that there is little or no variation in attendance during the year. *Signed* Frederick Reynoux, Minister.

449. TOOT BALDON HO 129/123/45
PRIMITIVE METHODIST CHAPEL. *Erected* 1839. Not a separate and entire building. Used exclusively for worship. *Free sittings* 12; *other sittings* 60. *On 30 March* In afternoon General Congregation 12; in evening General Congregation 15. *Average attendance* during previous

12 months, in morning General Congregation 13. *Signed* Thomas Weston, Attendant, Marsh Baldon.

450. TOWERSEY[1]   Population 448   HO 129/156/26
ST. CATHERINE'S CHURCH *Endowed* with glebe £75, other permanent endowment Queen Anne's Bounty £6, fees £1. *Free sittings* 140; *other sittings* 80. *On 30 March* no service. *Average attendance* during previous 12 months, in morning General Congregation 30, Sunday Scholars 50; in afternoon General Congregation 140, Sunday Scholars 50. *Remarks* Divine Service has been performed during the time that the church is under repair in a Schoolroom licenced [sic] by the Bishop. *Signed* S.W. Barnett, Vicar.
1. Included as part of pre-1974 Oxfordshire although not transferred from Buckinghamshire until 1939.

451. TOWERSEY   HO 129/156/28
PRIMITIVE METHODIST CHAPEL. *Erected* Nine years. Separate and entire building. Used exclusively for worship. *Free sittings* 60. *On 30 March* In afternoon General Congregation 50; in evening General Congregation 50. *Average attendance* in afternoon General Congregation 170; in evening General Congregation 170. *Remarks* Minister from home. Best information I could get. *Signed* T.H. Simmons. Registrar, Thame.

452. TOWERSEY   HO 129/156/29
BAPTIST CHAPEL. *Erected* about 1827. Separate and entire building. Used exclusively for worship. *Free sittings* 120; *other sittings* 27. *On 30 March* In morning General Congregation 100, Sunday Scholars 50; in afternoon General Congregation 80; in evening General Congregation 120. *Remarks* Including scholars. Cannot say about the congregation in March it is so long ago and what I have stated is as near as I can tell. *Signed* William Ellson, Deacon, Towersey. 30 October 1851.

453. TUSMORE[1]   Population 52   HO 129/159/64
A supplementary inquiry form from the Census Office asked, '1st whether the parish of Tusmore has a separate church or not. 2nd if it has the number of free and other sittings provided therein and also the general congregation attending it'. The Registrar, Joseph Reynolds replied 10 March 1852 that "no church at Tusmore. They attend Hardwick only a short mile distant. PS The question about the parish of Fringford I am fearful I shall not be able to answer, will do my best in a few days.
1. A hamlet in Hardwick parish.

454. UPPER HEYFORD   Population 399   HO 129/159/25
PARISH CHURCH. *Endowed* with tithe, glebe, fees unknown. *Free sittings* 25; *other sittings* 8. *On 30 March* In morning General Congregation 92. *Signed* William Baker, Rector.

455. UPPER HEYFORD   HO 129/159/26
WESLEYAN METHODIST CHAPEL. *Erected* before 1800. A separate and entire building. Used exclusively for worship. *Free sittings* 37; *other sittings* 90. *On 30 March* In morning General Congregation 22; in afternoon General Congregation 92; in evening General Congregation 101. *Signed* William Austin, Chapel Steward, Upper Heyford.[1]
1. *Gardner* describes William Austin, Upper Heyford, as a farmer.

456. UPPER HEYFORD   HO 129/159/27
PRIMITIVE METHODIST MEETING HOUSE, William Hudson's cottage. *Erected* 1848. A separate and entire building. Dwelling House. *Free sittings* 50. *Average attendance* during previous 3 months, in morning General Congregation 40. *Signed* John Edmunds, Leader. Henry Hays, Superintendant[1].
1. This second name is added in the same hand.

457. UPPER WORTON   Population 85   HO 129/160/11
HOLY TRINITY PARISH CHURCH. *Erected* before 1800. *On 30 March* In afternoon General Congregation 50, Sunday Scholars 12. *Remarks* The two parishes of Upper and Nether Worton being very small and close to each other, Divine Service is performed once on each Sunday in either church.[1]
1. The return is unsigned but in the same hand as that for Nether Worton, which was signed by George Venables, Curate, Deddington.

458. WARBOROUGH   Population 729   HO 129/125/37
PARISH CHURCH. *Endowed* with tithe £668 1s, glebe £38 9s 9d. *Free sittings* 243; *other sittings* 243. *On 30 March* In morning General Congregation 169, Sunday Scholars 52; in evening General Congregation 138, Sunday Scholars 40. *Signed* Herbert White, Perpetual Curate.

459. WARBOROUGH   HO 129/125/38
BAPTIST MEETING HOUSE. A separate and entire building. Used exclusively for worship. *Free sittings* 80. *On 30 March* In evening General Congregation 56. *Signed* Thomas Carey Venimore, Occasional Preacher, High Street, Wallingford, Berkshire.

460. WARBOROUGH   HO 129/125/39

WESLEYAN METHODIST CHAPEL. A separate and entire building. Used exclusively for worship. *Free sittings* 50. *On 30 March* In afternoon General Congregation 30. *Signed* Benjamin Saunders, Local Preacher, Warborough.

461. WARBOROUGH   HO 129/125/40

FRIENDS' MEETING HOUSE. *Erected* before 1800. A separate and entire building. Not used exclusively for worship; occasionally for Discipline. *Admeasurement* in superficial feet floor area 560; no gallery. *Estimated Number of Persons capable of being seated,* 150. *On 30 March* in morning 12 attendants. *Signed* Alfred Pearman, Wallingford, Berkshire.

462. WARDINGTON[1]   Population 861   HO 129/163/112

CHURCH. *Free sittings* 12; *other sittings* 70. *On 30 March* In morning General Congregation 70, Sunday Scholars 40; in afternoon General Congregation 100, Sunday Scholars 40. *Signed* Johm Simco[2], Wardington, Churchwarden.

1. A chapelry in Cropredy parish.
2. *Gardner* describes John Simco, Wardington, as a farmer.

463. WARDINGTON   HO 129/163/95

WESLEYAN METHODIST CHAPEL. *Erected* 1826. A separate and entire building. Used exclusively for worship. *Free sittings* 127; *other sittings* 50. *On 30 March* In morning Sunday Scholars 73; in afternoon General Congregation 126, Sunday Scholars 75; in evening General Congregation 127. *Average attendance* during previous 6 months, in morning Sunday Scholars 75; in afternoon General Congregation 120, Sunday Scholars 75; in evening General Congregation 120. *Remarks* Many of the Sunday School Scholars attend the evening worship which are not here reckoned so the number who attend is more than is stated. The same must apply to the account of the average for the last six months. *Signed* G. Watson,[1] Local Preacher, Wardington.

1. *Gardner* describes George Watson, Wardington, as a farmer.

464. WATER EATON[1]   Population 119   HO 129/160/47

WATER EATON CHAPEL. It is the private chapel of the old manor house, the property of C. Sawyer, Esq. and is used once a Sunday alternately in the morning and evening for the benefit of the inhabitants of Water Eaton by permission of the proprietor. *Erected* before 1800. No endowment. *Free sittings* about 55; *other sittings* 25. Sittings only used as free or otherwise by custom. *On 30 March* In morning General Congregation 41, Sunday Scholars 11. *Average attendance* during previous 12 months, in morning General Congregation 36, Sunday Scholars 10; in afternoon General Congregation 40, Sunday Scholars 10. *Remarks* The population is much scattered and many live at long distances from the chapel. The hamlet is connected with Kidlington for all ecclesiastical purposes. *Signed* Thomas Whitehead, Curate.

1. A hamlet in Kidlington parish.

465 WATERPERRY   Population 258   HO 129/156/60[1]
ST. MARY THE VIRGIN PARISH CHURCH. *Erected* AD1200. *Endowed* with fees 10s, all sources £60. *Free sittings* 20; *other sittings* 80. *On 30 March* in morning General Congregation 64, Sunday Scholars 24; in afternoon General Congregation 50, Sunday Scholars 24. *Average attendance* in morning General Congregation 80, Sunday Scholars 30; in afternoon General Congregation 70, Sunday Scholars 25. *Remarks* Church is of mixed style. Chancel Arch with Nave which is early English Decorated AD1300. Arches have no mouldings to soffits. Font plain. Stem 1300 rectangular basin Perpendicular. Pulpit Charles 2nd, Reading Pew 1632. Centre of north wall exquisite sculpture by Sir F. Chantrey. Under Perpendicular canopy Lord's aisle knight in plate armour of 1420. Name in Domesday Book Peryn land of Robert de Oily. Knight was probably John Fitz Elys, friend of Chapen the poet a hero of Agincourt. *Signed* Thomas Pearce, Curate with sole charge.

1. HO 129/156/61 is a duplicate return.

466. WATERSTOCK   Population 141   HO 129/156/59
PARISH CHURCH. *Erected* before 1800. *Endowed* with land £25, tithe £208, glebe house, Easter Offerings 1s. *Free sittings* 80; *other sittings* 40. *On 30 March* In morning General Congregation 58, Sunday Scholars 34; in afternoon General Congregation 62, Sunday Scholars 34. *Signed* Gibbes Walker Jordan, Rector.

467. WATLINGTON   Population 1884   HO 129/155/41
ST. MARY'S PARISH CHURCH. *Erected* before 1800. *Endowed* with land £100, with tithe £100, glebe £10, fees £10. *Free sittings* 100; *other sittings* 200. *On 30 March* in morning General Congregation 350; in afternoon General Congregation 400. *Average attendance* in morning General Congregation 300; in afternoon General Congregation 350. *Signed* William Langford, Vicar.

468. WATLINGTON   HO 129/155/42
WESLEYAN METHODIST CHAPEL. *Erected* 1812. A separate and
entire building. Used exclusively for worship. *Free sittings* 141; *other
sittings* 187. *On 30 March* In morning General Congregation 125,
Sunday Scholars 82; in evening General Congregation 220. *Average
attendance* during previous 12 months, in morning General
Congregation 150, Sunday Scholars 80; in evening General Congregation
280. *Signed* Edmund Lockyer, Wesleyan Minister, Watlington.

469. WATLINGTON   HO 129/155/44
INDEPENDENT CHAPEL, commonly called the Lower Chapel.
Erected 1815. A separate and entire building. Used exclusively for
worship. *Free sittings* 36; *other sittings* 64. *On 30 March* in afternoon
General Congregation 20. *Average attendance* during previous 12
months in afternoon General Congregation 25. *Remarks* It is not known
when the building was erected but converted into a Chapel in the year
1815 being previously a house. *Signed* James Young, Minister.

470. WATLINGTON   HO 129/155/45
PRIMITIVE METHODIST CHAPEL, Church Street. It is a Rented
Room attached to a house, opened 1849. Not a separate and entire
building. A day school is taught in it. *Sittings* 100 all free. *On 30 March*
in afternoon General Congregation 24; in evening General Congregation
43. *Average attendance* during previous 12 months, in afternoon General
Congregation 20; in evening General Congregation 30. *Signed* Henry
James Allen, Primitive Methodist Minister, Chapel House, Chinnor.

471. WEALD[1]   Population 833   HO 129/161/24
WESLEYAN METHODIST CHAPEL. Not known when erected.
Formally a cottage for poor persons. A separate and entire building.
Used exclusively for worship. *Free sittings* 60. *On 30 March* In morning
General Congregation about 20; in evening General Congregation about
25. *Average attendance* about the same as above stated, no school.
Signed Richard Haynes, Bampton.
1. A hamlet in Bampton parish.

472. WENDLEBURY   Population 242   HO 129/159/1
PARISH CHURCH. *Endowed* with glebe £180, other permanent
endowment £27 10s, fees 10s. *Free sittings* 7; *other sittings* 56. *On 30
March* In morning General Congregation 45, Sunday Scholars 47; in
afternoon General Congregation 70, Sunday Scholars 47. *Signed* Walter
L. Brown, Rector.

473. WESTCOTT BARTON Population 279   HO 129/160/13
PARISH CHURCH was I believe dedicated to St. Edward. It is a neat
little edifice of various dates of construction. The most modern is
Elizabethan. Some Norman remains are visible in the interior. It is
miserably deficient in fitting up but might at a considerable outlay be
made comfortable and pretty. *Erected* before 1800. *Endowed* with land
about £180, fees about £5. *Sittings* The open sittings are mostly claimed
by long occupation by the inhabitants in number to accommodate about
80 persons; *other sittings* pews to contain about 100 persons. Benches are
consequently placed down the aisle of the church and in the chancel for
the school children 40. *On 30 March* In morning General Congregation
80, Sunday Scholars 47; in afternoon General Congregation 110, Sunday
Scholars 40. *Average attendance* during previous 12 months, in morning
General Congregation 80, Sunday Scholars 47; in afternoon General
Congregation 120, Sunday Scholars 47. *Remarks* Appended in adjoining
paper.[1] *Signed* Samuel Young Seagrave, Rector, Westcott Barton.

1. HO 129/160/12a and b. It is almost impossible to make a return of the average number
of attendants on public worship in this parish during the present year such as will be
satisfactory. The parish church of the adjoining parish of Steeple Barton having been
pronounced unsafe from its dilapidated state I consented at the request of the Vicar of
Steeple Barton to allow the congregation of that parish to attend my church and join my
congregation in the morning until their chancel which was being rebuilt should be in a
proper state to accommodate them. This continued for many weeks. Their chancel has been
completed in the meantime and the S B parishioners attend morning service there now as
far as room will furnish them. Many still attend Westcott Barton church in the evenings
where a service solely for their accommodation is performed by their vicar at five o'clock
our own services being regularly performed at 10½ am and 2½ pm for our own parishioners.
This state of things will go on until such time as the Steeple Barton church shall be rebuilt
and arrangements are in progress for that purpose. I would also draw the attention of Her
Majesty's Secretary of State to a circumstance respecting the population return which may
lead to error in taking the census. These parishes of Steeple Barton and Westcott Barton —
there are several cottages containing inhabitants which have hitherto been considered to
belong to Westcott Barton parish. But upon examination of the award of the parishes taken
at the time of the enclosure these cottages appear to me to have been erected on lands
belonging to Steeple Barton parish and consequently that the inmates should be returned as
belonging to that parish. This is a matter of *amicable* dispute between the two parishes as
between their several incumbents. At present the poor people in these cottages have the
ministries of both the clergy, but as matters may not always go on so smoothly it strikes me
that now may be the fittest time   finally to adjust the matter in dispute. If I in have
troubling you thus transgressed the bounds of propriety I beg most humbly to apologize,
anxious to maintain the peace and goodwill which now prevails between our several flocks.
I have the honour to remain.
          Your obt humble servt
          S.Y. Seagrave
               Rector of Westcott Barton
March 31st 1851

474. WESCOTT BARTON   HO 129/160/14
PRIMITIVE METHODIST CHAPEL. A separate and entire building.
Used exclusively for worship. *Free sittings* 115. *On 30 March* In
afternoon General Congregation 130; in evening General Congregation
136. *Average attendance* during previous 6 months, in afternoon General
Congregation 100, in evening General Congregation 100. *Remarks* For
want of room we have upwards of 40 out side. *Signed* Henry Brooks,
Steward, Middle Barton, Oxfordshire.

475. WESTON ON THE GREEN   Population 517   HO 129/159/2
PARISH CHURCH. *Erected* before 1800. *On 30 March* In morning
General Congregation 130; in afternoon General Congregation 110.
Average attendance in morning General congregation 140; in afternoon
General Congregation 100. *Signed* A.H. Matthews, Vicar.

476. WESTON ON THE GREEN   HO 129/159/16
WESLEYAN METHODIST CHAPEL. *Erected* 1839. A separate and
entire building. Used exclusively for worship. *Free sittings* 32; *other
sittings* 50. *On 30 March* In afternoon General Congregation 80; in
evening General Congregation 82. *Signed* Robert East, Manager,
Weston on the Green.

477. WEST SHUTFORD   HO 129/163/42
WESLEYAN METHODIST CHAPEL. *Erected* 1837. A separate and
entire building. Used exclusively for worship. *Free sittings* 80; *other
sittings* 32. *On 30 March* In afternoon General Congregation 80, Sunday
Scholars 15; in evening General Congregation 100, Sunday Scholars 12.
Signed Thomas Perkins[1], Steward, Shutford West.
1. *Gardner* describes Thomas Perkins, Shutford, as a baker.

478. WESTWELL   Population 186   HO 129/161/67
PARISH CHURCH. *Erected* 1200. *Endowed* with land, a farm let at
£206. *Free sittings* enough for about fifty or sixty persons; *other sittings*
about forty. *On 30 March* in morning General Congregation 40, Sunday
Scholars 23; in afternoon General Congregation 40. *Remarks* The
congregation was smaller in the afternoon if not in the morning, than
usual, and as I keep no account I can supply no average. In making this
return I think it is right to add that any calculation as to the proportion
of dissent and church principles in this place founded on it, and taking
into account the evening congregation at the meetinghouse *must* be
fallacious, as it is attended in the evenings by many Church-People.
Signed John Ernest Bode, Rector.

479. WESTWELL   HO 129/161/68
PROTESTANT NONCONFORMIST, 'The Room'[1]. *Erected* before
1800. A separate private chapel. Used exclusively for worship. *Free
sittings* 60. *On 30 March* In morning General Congregation 13; in
evening General Congregation 14. *Average attendance* during previous
12 months from 12 to 20. *Remarks* 'The Room' referred to is situate on
my own premises, licensed as a Place of Religious Worship and has been
so listed upwards of 11 years. *Signed* Richard Pinnell,[2] Usual Minister or
Manager, Westwell.
1. The Revd J.E. Bode, Rector of Westwell, in response to Bishop Wilberforce's visitation
inquiries of 1854, reported that 'there is a room licensed for worship attached to a farmer's
residence, who himself preaches. It was licensed for Plymouth Bretheren, but I should say
that the attendance did not belong to any denomination. Another house is licensed for
Particular Baptists but very rarely used. I think the number of regular dissenters (adults) is
15 at the most. I have reason to know that the children of one of the farmers (a P. Baptist)
are favourably disposed to the Church'.
2. *Gardner* Lists Mr. Richard Pinnell amongst the private residents of Westwell. John
Pinnell, Esq., was lord of the manor.

480. WHEATLEY[1]   Population 1037   HO 129/157/4
DISTRICT CHURCH. *Erected* before 1800. *Endowed* with land £60,
glebe about £22, other permanent endowment £31, fees about £5. *Free
sittings* 250; *other sittings* 350. *On 30 March* In morning General
Congregation 153, Sunday Scholars 96; in afternoon General
Congregation 226, Sunday Scholars 90. *Remarks* I cannot discover to
what saint the church was dedicated at its consecration. *Signed* Arthur
Dendy, Officiating Minister. 3 April 1851.
1. A chapelry in Cuddesdon parish.

481. WHEATLEY   HO 129/157/6
WYCLIFFE INDEPENDENT CHAPEL. *Erected* 1842. A separate and
entire building. Used exclusively for worship. *Free sittings* 150; *other
sittings* 100. *On 30 March* In morning General Congregation 58, Sunday
Scholars 61; in afternoon Sunday Scholars 61; in evening General
Congregation 135. *Signed* Charles M. Cordy Davies, Minister,
Wheatley.

482. WHITCHURCH[1]   Population 893   HO 129/126/11
PARISH CHURCH. By Bacon's Liber Regis the Parish Church of
Whitchurch, Oxon was dedicated to St. Mary. It is an ancient Parish
Church. *Erected* before 1800 but when unknown. *Endowed* with land
rent of £360, tithe rent charge in lieu of the [?] years average £96, corn
rents this year £16, glebe £8. *Free sittings* 170; *other sittings* 230. *On 30*

March In morning General Congregation 200, Sunday Scholars 62; in afternoon total 173. *Signed* E. Hoare, Rector.

1. Part of the parish lay in Berkshire but was not distinguished for census purposes until 1861.

483. WHITCHURCH   HO 129/126/12
WESLEYAN METHODIST CHAPEL. *Erected* 1849. A separate and entire building. Used exclusively for worship. *Free sittings* about 80; *other sittings* about 20. *On 30 March* In morning General Congregation 40; in afternoon General Congregation 50. *Signed* R.N. Fewster.[1]

1. *Gardner* describes Richard N. Fewster as farmer, Copyhold Farm.

484. WIDFORD   Population 43   HO 129/161/78
PARISH CHURCH belonging to a distinct and separate parish. *Erected* before 1800. *Endowed* with land * £10 13s., tithe # rent charge in lieu of tithes £82 10s 11d, surplus fees 2s, interest from Governors of Queen Anne's Bounty 12s 8d. *Free sittings* 20; *other sittings* 30 and benches for Sunday School children. *On 30 March* In morning General Congregation 10, Sunday Scholars 50. *Average attendance* in morning General Congregation 10, Sunday Scholars 50; in afternoon General Congregation 15, Sunday Scholars 50. *Remarks** Land purchased by Governors of Queen Anne's Bounty from funds in their hands. #The rent-charge is liable to parish rates, which are not deducted in the above statement. The service is performed twice on every Sunday alternately morning and afternoon. The Sunday Scholars belonging to Widford and Swinbrook attend at both churches (about 50) but meet for school instruction at Swinbrook. *Signed* William Raine, Rector, Swinbrook.

485. WIGGINTON   Population 314   HO 129/163/6
PARISH CHURCH. *Endowed* with land £300, other permanent endowment £100. *Free sittings* 99; *other sittings* 119. *On 30 March* In morning General Congregation, including Sunday Scholars 109; in afternoon General Congregation including Sunday Scholars 117. *Remarks* Many of Sunday Scholars mixed with the rest of the Congregation, and several in afternoon not at Church. *Signed* John Williams, Rector.

486. WIGGINTON   HO 129/163/7
PARTICULAR BAPTIST CHAPEL. *Erected* 1835. A separate and entire building. Used. exclusively for worship. *Free sittings* 100. *On 30 March* In evening General Congregation 35. *Average attendance* in

evening General Congregation 50. *Signed* Daniel[?] Warmington[1], Manager, Hook Norton.

1. *Gardner* describes Daniel Warmington, Hook Norton, as grocer, draper, tea dealer, and tailor, auctioneer and appraiser, agent to the Dissenters and General Fire and Life Office, and sub-postmaster.

487. WILCOTE[1]   Population 10   HO 129/161/53
PARISH CHURCH . *Erected* before 1800. *Sittings* 120. *Remarks* There being only two houses in the parish it is vain to send a return of the attendance. The congregation being made up from the neighbouring parishes varying according to weather.[1] *Signed* Charles Carey, Curate, Spelsbury.

1. The words 'Imperfect. Another written for' are written across the return.

488. WITNEY[1]   Population 3099   HO 129/161/34
BAPTIST CHAPEL, Witney Street. *Erected* before 1800. A separate and entire building. Used exclusively for worship. *Free sittings* 100; *other sittings* 72. *On 30 March* In morning General Congregation 40, Sunday Scholars 30; in afternoon General Congregation 40, Sunday Scholars 30; in evening Sunday Scholars 30. *Signed* William Cherry, Minister, Milton, nr. Chipping Norton.

1. The parish of Witney included the hamlets of Crawley (*q.v.*) and Curbridge (*q.v.*), together with Hailey (*q.v.*) chapelry. The total population of the parish was 5,437.

489. WITNEY   HO 129/161/35
ABRAHAMITE PRIMITIVE METHODIST CHAPEL, Corn Street. *Erected* 1824. A separate and entire building. Used exclusively for worship. *Free sittings* 6. *On 30 March* None. *Signed* Thomas Fox, layman, Witney.

490. WITNEY   HO 129/161/36
PRIMITIVE METHODIST CHAPEL, Corn Street. *Erected* in 1845. A separate and entire building. Used exclusively for worship. *Free sittings* 176; *other sittings* 40. *On 30 March* In afternoon general Congregation 110; in evening General Congregation 100. *Signed* Henry Hays, Minister, Corn Street, Witney, and John Clack, Trustee.

491. WITNEY   HO 129/161/37
CONGREGATIONAL CHAPEL, High Street. *Erected* 1828. A separate and entire building. Used exclusively for worship. *Free sittings* 172, *other sittings* 230. *On 30 March* In morning General Congregation 117, Sunday Scholars 106; in afternoon General Congregation 53,

Sunday Scholars 54; in evening General Congregation 192. *Signed* Robert Tozer, Minister, Witney.

492. WITNEY   HO 129/161/38
WESLEYAN METHODIST CHAPEL. *Erected* in 1850 on site of one existing before that year. A separate and entire building. Used exclusively for worship. *Free sittings* 378; *other sittings* 376. *On 30 March* In morning General Congregation 332, Sunday Scholars 202; in evening General Congregation 600. *Average attendance* during previous 12 months, the above is about the average. *Signed* Peter C. Horton, Superintendent Minister, Mount House, Witney.

493. WITNEY   HO 129/161/39
FRIENDS' MEETING HOUSE, Wood Green.[1] *Erected* before 1800. A separate and entire building. Used exclusively for worship. *Free sittings* 200. *On 30 March* In morning General Congregation 13; in afternoon General Congregation 11. *Average attendance* during previous 12 months, in morning General Congregation 156; in afternoon General Congregation 132, *Signed* Hannah Smith,[2] Overseer, Bridge Street Witney.
1. This return was made on a standard non-Anglican return and not on the separate form intended for the Society of Friends.
2. *Gardner* describes Hannah Smith, Bridge Street, Witney, as a linen draper.

494. WITNEY[1]   HO 129/161/43
HOLY TRINITY CHURCH, Woodgreen, Hailey. *Consecrated* in the year 1849 as an additional church. *Erected* by Parliamentary Grant £250 and public subscription £1150. *Free sittings* 2; *other sittings* 497. *Average attendance* in morning General Congregation 300, Sunday Scholars 60; in evening General Congregation 600. *Remarks* The grant of £250 was made on conditions that the seats for 497 persons should be set apart and declared to be free for ever. *Signed* Thomas East, Deputy Registrar.
1. Holy Trinity Church was in that part of the town of Witney which lay in the hamlet and chapelry of Hailey.

495. WOODCOTE[1]   HO 129/125/57
ST. LEONARD'S CHAPEL. Chapel of Ease to the Liberty of Woodcote, parish of South Stoke. Rebuilt 1845-6, consecrated 23 April 1846 by Bishop of Oxford. Building cost £1350, £100 of which was raised by parochial rate and £1250 by subscription of the neighbourhood and by private benefaction. *Endowment* These questions are answered by Mr. Wad[more?] Curate of South Stoke in his return for the parish. *Free*

sittings 165; *other sittings* 80. *On 30 March* In morning General Congregation from 180 to 200; in afternoon General Congregation from 180 to 200. *Average attendance* in morning General Congregation 150 to 180, Sunday Scholars 30; in afternoon General Congregation 180 to 200, Sunday Scholars 20. *Remarks* The inhabitants of Woodcote are for the most part attendants at church and usually regular in their attendance. *Signed* Philip Henry Nind, Vicar, Woodcote.
1. Chapelry in South Stoke parish.

496. WOODCOTE   HO 129/125/59
PRIMITIVE METHODIST PREACHING HOUSE. Not a separate and entire building. Not used exclusively for worship. *Free sittings* 50. *On 30 March* in afternoon General Congregation 40; in evening General Congregation 40. *Average attendance* during previous 9 months, in afternoon General Congregation 40; in evening General Congregation 40. *Signed* Joseph Coling[1], Local Preacher, Woodcoat.
1. *Gardner* describes Joseph Coling, Woodcote, as a shoemaker.

497. WOODEATON   Population 168   HO 129/157/18
PARISH CHURCH. *On 30 March* In morning General Congregation 60, including Sunday Scholars. *Remarks* As near as I can ascertain. *Signed* Richard Wood, Registrar.

498. WOODSTOCK   Population 1262   HO 129/160/33
ST. MARY'S CHAPEL, Ancient Chantry.[1] *Erected* before 1800.[2] *On 30 March* In morning General Congregation 284, Sunday Scholars 74; in afternoon General Congregation 344, Sunday Scholars 74. *Average attendance* in morning General Congregation 284, in afternoon General Congregation 344. *Remarks* There is no endowment for Woodstock Chapel. *Signed* G.W. St. John, Rector of Bladon cum Woodstock.
1. Ecclesiastically Woodstock remained a chapelry of Bladon parish.
2. HO 129/160/32 is a supplementary return giving free sittings about 520, appropriated sittings 500, none let. It is signed by G.W. St. John.

499. WOODSTOCK   HO 129/160/34
BAPTIST CHAPEL, Park Street. *Erected* 1825. A separate and entire building. Used exclusively for worship.*Free sittings* 160; *other sittings* 140. *On 30 March* in morning General Congregation 71, Sunday Scholars 51; in afternoon Sunday Scholars 66; in evening General Congregation 99. *Average attendance* during previous 12 months, in morning General Congregation 80, Sunday Scholars 50; in afternoon Sunday Scholars 66; in evening General Congregation 120. *Signed* John Freer, Minister, Mount Pleasant, Woodstock.

500. WOODSTOCK   HO 129/160/35
WESLEYAN METHODIST CHAPEL, New Woodstock. *Erected* 1825.
A separate and entire building. Used exclusively for worship and Sunday
School. *Free sittings* 60; *other sittings* 90. *On 30 March* In morning
General Congregation 60; in evening General Congregation 130. *Average
attendance* during previous 12 months, in morning General
Congregation 50, Sunday Scholars 30; in afternoon Sunday Scholars 30;
in evening General Congregation 120. *Signed* Thomas Meek[1], Trustee
and Steward, Woodstock.
1. *Gardner* describes Thomas Meek, Woodstock, as a glover.

501. WOOTTON[1]   Population 1250   HO 129/160/27
PARISH CHURCH. *Erected* before 1800, before the Reformation.
Endowed with land £500, tithe and glebe £200, heavy deductions have to
be made from these sums, in consequence of agricultural distress. *Free
sittings* 170; *other sittings* 230. *On 30 March* In morning General
Congregation 157, Sunday Scholars 75; in afternoon General
Congregation 162, Sunday Scholars 65. *Average attendance* during
previous 3 months, in morning General Congregation 155, Sunday
Scholars 60; in afternoon General Congregation 155, Sunday Scholars
55. *Remarks* We were about 15 short, on account of the Rector's absence
from home with his family, and the Squire's daughter having died on the
day before. *Signed* John A. Clarke, Officiating Curate.
1. Wootton parish extended as far as the river Glyme and included the hamlet of Old
Woodstock.

502. WOOTTON   HO 129/160/28
WESLEYAN METHODIST CHAPEL. *Erected* 1840. A separate and
entire building. Used exclusively for worship. *Free sittings* 60; *other
sittings* 40. *On 30 March* In morning General Congregation 50, Sunday
Scholars 40; in afternoon Sunday Scholars 45; in evening General
Congregation 55. *Average attendance* in morning General Congregation
60, Sunday Scholars 65. *Signed* John Barratt, Trustee, Wootton.

503. WROXTON[1]   Population 789   HO 129/163/60
ALL SAINTS PARISH CHURCH. *Erected* before 1800. *Free sittings*
164; *other sittings* 183. *On 30 March* In morning General Congregation
134, Sunday Scholars 49. *Signed* Michael Harrison, Curate.
1. The parish of Wroxton included the chapelry of Balscott (*q.v.*).

RELIGIOUS CENSUS 1851 117

504. WROXTON HO 129/163/62
WESLEYAN METHODIST CHAPEL. *Erected* about 1820. A separate
and entire building. Used exclusively for worship. *Free sittings* 60; *other
sittings* 30. *On 30 March* In afternoon General Congregation 78; in
evening General Congregation 43. *Signed* William Gardner[1], Chapel
Steward, Wroxton.

1. *Gardner* describes William Gardner, Wroxton, as a farmer.

505. WROXTON HO 129/163/63
INDEPENDENT CHAPEL. *Erected* 1826. A separate and entire
building. Used exclusively for worship. *Free sittings* 60; *other sittings* 60.
On 30 March In evening General Congregation 50-60. *Average
attendance* during previous 12 months, in morning General
Congregation 50-60; in evening General Congregation 60-70. *Signed*
John Bligh, Minister, Wroxton.

506. YARNTON Population 317 HO 129/160/48
PARISH CHURCH of remote antiquity consecrated before AD1235.
Endowed with land a garden of 32 perch [sic], tithe commuted as
returned to Bishop Jan. 1 £253 2s 4½d, other permanent endowment as
ancient rent charge £3 p.a., fees about 10s p.a. *Free sittings* 97; *other
sittings* 67 with 24 for school children. *On 30 March* In morning General
Congregation 63, Sunday Scholars 24; in afternoon General
Congregation 44, Sunday Scholars 13. *Average attendance* the foregoing
maybe taken as the general average. *Remarks* The church stood in the
midst of the dwelling-houses of the parish, till the dispersion of the
parish property and the destruction of the park and mansion in 1714.
Since that time tenements have been erected dispersedly and at a distance
from the church having wet or dirty roads to pass. *Signed* Vaughan
Thomas, Vicar of the Parish.

507. YELFORD Population 17 HO 129/161/16
PARISH CHURCH. *Erected* before 1800. *Endowed* with tithe about
£120, fees say 6d. *Sittings* say 45. *On 30 March* In afternoon General
Congregation 16. *Signed* Frank Burges, Officiating Minister.

INDEX OF PERSONS

Roman numerals refer to the page nos. of the intro., Arabic to entry nos. in the text.

INDEX OF PLACES

A place name is indexed only where it occurs outside its main entry. Roman numerals refer to the page nos. of the intro., Arabic to entry nos. in the text.